G000270621

ISBN 978 0 904491 84 5

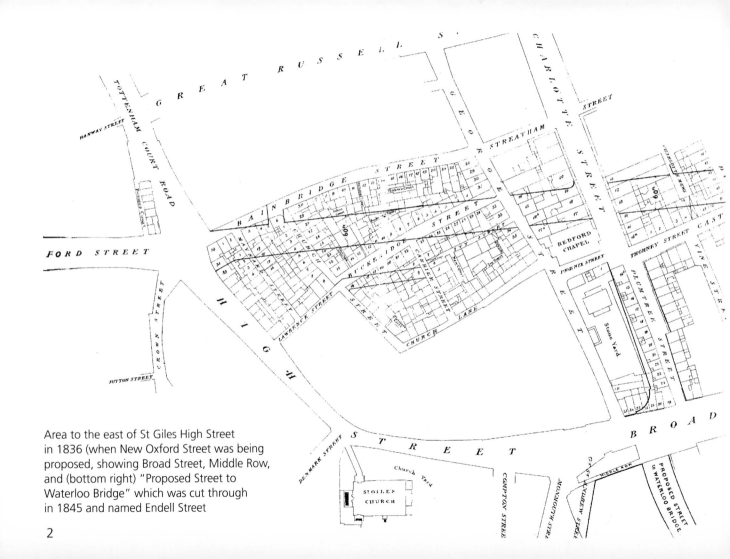

Area to the east of St Giles High Street in 1836 (when New Oxford Street was being proposed, showing Broad Street, Middle Row, and (bottom right) "Proposed Street to Waterloo Bridge" which was cut through in 1845 and named Endell Street

Streets of St Giles

A survey of streets, buildings and former residents in a part of Camden

Compiled by the Camden History Society

Edited by Steve Denford and David Hayes

General editor of Camden History Society Publications F Peter Woodford

Designed by Ivor Kamlish

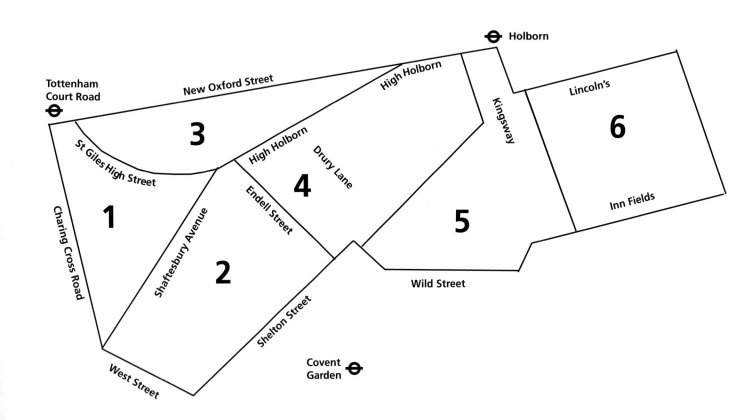

Tottenham Court Road

Holborn

New Oxford Street

High Holborn

St Giles High Street

High Holborn

Drury Lane

Kingsway

Lincoln's

3

1

Endell Street

4

Shaftesbury Avenue

2

5

6

Inn Fields

Charing Cross Road

Wild Street

Shelton Street

West Street

Covent Garden

Contents

Diagram of the walks   4

**Present street names
and their origins**   6

List of illustrations   7

Historical overview   8

Route 1
The domain of the Leper Hospital
Circular walk from St Giles Circus   13

Route 2
Seven Dials and Endell Street
Circular walk from St Giles Circus   29

Route 3
London's spinal cord
*Linear walk from St Giles High Street
to Kingsway*   56

Route 4
Tributaries of Drury Lane
Circular walk from Holborn Station   74

Route 5
Kingsway and Great Queen Street
Circular walk from Holborn Station   89

Route 6
Lincoln's Inn Fields
Circular walk from Holborn station   106

Sources   126

Index   128

Present street names and their origins

Betterton Thomas, actor (c.1635-1710)

Bucknall Ralph, C17 brewer and vestryman

Cambridge George, Duke of, opened Charing Cross Road in 1887

Charing Cross Located near south end of road

Compton Henry, Bishop of London, founded neighbouring parish of St Anne Soho, 1676

Denmark Prince George of, eventual consort of Queen Anne

Drury Sir William, C16 resident of Drury House at south end of Lane

Dyott Married name of daughter of the street's C17 developer, Henry Bainbridge; also C17 vestryman

Earlham Once Earl Street, honouring no particular earl

Earnshaw Thomas (1749-1829), celebrated chronometer maker of High Holborn

Endell James Endell Tyler, C19 rector of St Giles

Flitcroft Henry, architect of the present St Giles Church (1733)

Grape Successor to Vine Street, on probable site of a vineyard

Holborn 'Holeburne' (stream in the hollow), otherwise the Fleet River, on the borough's eastern boundary

Keeley Robert, actor, born Carey Street 1793

Kemble Notable C18 & C19 theatrical family

King Edward VII opened Kingsway in 1905

Macklin Charles, Irish actor (c.1699-1797)

Mercer The Mercers' Company, local landlords

Monmouth James, Duke of, illegitimate son of Charles II

Neal Thomas Neale, C17 developer of Seven Dials

Newton William, speculative builder (fl.1635)

Nottingham Daniel Finch, 2nd Earl of (1647–1730), local resident

Parker Philip, local resident, c.1620

Phoenix Former tavern in Stacey Street

Queen Anne of Denmark, wife of James I

Remnant Lord Remnant was MP for Holborn 1900–28

St Giles Graeco-Provençal hermit (d.c.710), patron saint of outcasts

Sardinia The Sardinian Embassy and Chapel stood nearby

Shaftesbury Anthony Ashley Cooper, 7th Earl of, factory reformer and philanthropist

Shelton William, C17 vestryman and charity school founder

Short William, C17 vestryman and gardener

Smart Family of house-builders (early C18)

Stacey James, C16 local landowner

Stukeley Rev. William, C18 antiquarian and rector of St George the Martyr

Tower Erstwhile local public house

Twyford Location of the Remnants' country seat, in Berkshire

West The street lies on St Giles' western boundary

West Central The GPO's adjacent *WC* sorting office

Wild Corruption of *Weld*: the Weld family occupied C17 Weld House

Illustrations

Map, east of St Giles High Street
in 1836   2

Diagram of the walks   4

Historical Overview
1 Seal of St Giles Hospital   8
2 Parish of St Giles
and adjacent parishes   10

Route 1
3 St Giles Circus in 1950   14
4 Interior of blacksmith's, Denmark Place   16
5 Dudley Street (Gustave Doré, 1872)   24
6 Nos.114-116 Charing Cross Road
in 1904   27

Route 2
7 Neal's Yard in 1962   31
8 Seven Dials, c. 1780   33
9 'The Morning Toilet, Seven Dials'   35
10 'Low lodging house, St Giles'   37
11 'Queen Anne's Bath', 1840s   49
12 Christ Church, Endell Street   52

Route 3
13 A cellar in the Rookery   58
14 Escape route from the Rookery   60
15 Middle Row, Bloomsbury   64
16 Tallis view (1838) of Bowl Yard,
Broad Street, etc.   66
17 Holborn Restaurant   73

Route 4
18 James Wyld's map of 1828   75
19 New Middlesex Theatre of
Varieties, 1911   78
20 Brownlow House   80
21 Sudbury Dairy, Drury Lane 1906   82

Route 5
22 Little Queen Street Chapel, 1832   89
23 John Opie, self-portrait   93
24 The 1774 Freemasons' Hall   95
25 Great Queen Street, 1850   98
26 Benjamin Franklin, 1780s   102

Route 6
27 Lincoln's Inn Fields before 1735   107
28 Lincoln's Inn Fields from
north-west corner, 1810   111
29 Nell Gwyn and her two sons   117
30 Triple archway under Nos. 53-54
Lincoln's Inn Fields   119
31 Earl of Mansfield, c.1775   121

Historical Overview

A mile or so west of the ancient City of London lies the parish of St Giles-in-the-Fields, within whose historical boundaries the whole of this book is set.

The countryside here was once very marshy. It was probably to avoid boggy ground that the Roman road striking westward from Londinium forsook the usual straight line of Roman roads to sweep southward in an arc along the line of St Giles High Street, as modern westbound traffic still does.

To the west of the Roman city, 7th-century Saxon invaders established a trading settlement, described by Bede as a 'mart of many peoples coming by land and sea'. This thrived until 9th-century Viking raids forced the inhabitants to move inside the old city walls for protection. Archaeological finds since 1986 have located the Saxon town of *Lundenwic* (or 'London-port') in the Strand–Covent Garden area; the land which became St Giles would have been on its northern fringes. *Aldwych*

(or 'old-port'), the name now borne by the Edwardian crescent off the Strand, once identified places in St Giles: the whole length of Drury Lane was once Aldewychstrate; a field on which Great Queen Street lies was known as 'Aldwych Close'; and an 'Aldwych Cross' once stood in the parish, probably at the junction of Drury Lane and High Holborn.

The medieval settlement of St Giles began c.1117-18, when a leper hospital was founded there, near where the Roman road met a track running north from Westminster. It was built for Queen Matilda (or Maud), the wife of Henry I, daughter of Malcolm III of Scotland, and granddaughter of Duncan. She earmarked the 60 shillings of income from a property at Queenhithe (City) to support fourteen lepers, under the wardenship of two City of London appointees. The 'hospital' and its chapel [1] were dedicated to Athens-born St Giles, who lived as a hermit in a forest in Provence, and died c.710 to become the patron saint of cripples, lepers and all outcasts. One

A full size drawing of a metal plate on the North side of the North boundary wall of Lincolns Inn (facing the rear of 291-293 High Holborn) showing the seal of the Hospital of Saint Giles.

of only three such institutions in England, St Giles Hospital merged in 1299 with that of Burton Lazars in Leicestershire, becoming a cell of the order of St Lazarus of Jerusalem.

The Hospital oratory stood on the site of the present parish church; to its west was the Master's House; to the east were the four Spittle (i.e. hospital) Houses. The walled precincts covered an area corresponding to that surrounded by modern Charing Cross Road, Shaftesbury Avenue and St Giles High Street. The chapel also served as a place of public worship. The parish of St Giles has existed since at least 1222, the suffix *in campis* being added to its name to distinguish it from other namesakes, particularly St Giles Cripplegate.

In the 13th century St Giles was a prosperous village, noted for its inns and houses of entertainment; the surrounding marshland had been partly drained and turned over to pasture. The manor in the northern half of the parish was acquired by William Blemonde, which as Blemundsbury evolved into modern Bloomsbury; while the more southerly manor of St Giles was the property of

the Hospital. At the Reformation, in 1536–37, Henry VIII struck a deal with the Master of Burton Lazars whereby the latter's land in St Giles was exchanged for Crown property in Leicestershire. In 1539, therefore, the Hospital closed; parishioners continued to use its chapel, and a new church was built on its site in 1624.

The king granted the western part of the manor to Sir John Dudley (Lord Lisle). Land on the eastern side was inherited in 1545 by a 5-year-old Katherine Legh, daughter of Sir Thomas Legh, formerly Henry's 'visitor of the monasteries'; she later married Lord Mountjoy. Lord Lisle built a manor-house for himself, and by the early 17th century five large houses stood to the west of the church. St Giles, however, was still very much a village, linked to London by the old Roman road, and separated from it by acres of pastureland. Land ownership in the parish had by now become very fragmented; we shall encounter the names of some of the owners on our walks.

Urbanisation of the parish really began in the east, where (Great) Queen Street was developed during the first three decades of the 17th century, and completed at about

the same time as the Earl of Bedford's nearby Covent Garden Piazza. The street was initially colonised by the nobility, for whom life in the City was no longer attractive, and by foreign ambassadors. Large aristocratic houses also then lined the southern end of Drury Lane, an ancient route bisecting our area. In time the upper classes migrated still further west, and (Great) Queen Street became middle-class. The Lane, wholly built up by mid-century, sank considerably lower in the social scale. Further west, and north of the church, a field named Pitaunce Croft was developed c.1650 by Henry Bainbridge. 'Pretty good houses' sums up Strype's opinion of this development 70 years later.

Meanwhile, in 1665, St Giles was the parish where the Great Plague first erupted, and one of the areas worst affected by it.

Yet to be developed was the Marshland, a field in the parish's south-west corner, then still an open space. Known also as St Giles Fields or Cock & Pye Fields, it was crossed diagonally by footpaths corresponding to the main axes of the star-shaped street pattern of Seven Dials, a planned housing development

2 The boundaries of
St Giles-in-the-Fields
with neighbouring parishes in 1899.

(**W** indicates territory ceded to the City of
Westminster in 1900, and thus excluded from the
Borough of Holborn and from modern Camden)

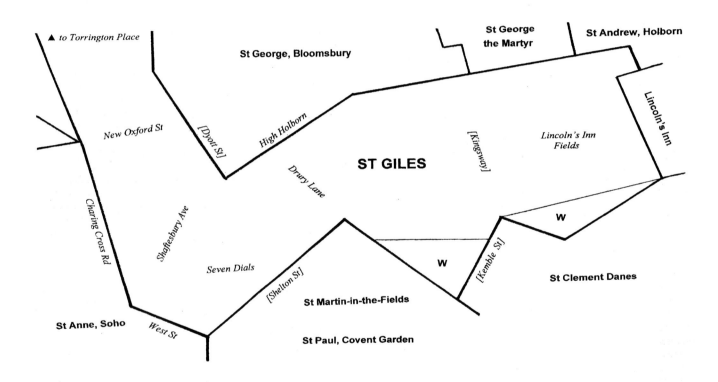

begun in 1693 by Thomas Neale.

At the eastern edge of the parish were the fields together known as Lincoln's Inn Fields, long jealously guarded from development by the benchers of Lincoln's Inn but beginning to be bordered by grand houses from 1635 onwards. The Fields were the setting for the activities of footpads and duellists, right up to the end of the 18th century, and for three other major violent events: the execution there in 1683 of Lord William Russell for his part in the Rye House Plot, and the sackings of the nearby Catholic chapel in 1688 after James II's flight abroad and again in 1780 during the Gordon Riots. The Rye House Plot was a failed conspiracy to assassinate Charles II and his brother James at Rye House in Hertfordshire, in the hope of securing the succession of the Protestant Duke of Monmouth. In 1694 William III raised Russell's father the Earl of Bedford to a dukedom in recognition of his son's sacrifice to the Protestant cause. These events, except for the Rye House Plot and the subsequent execution, are related in more detail in Route 6.

1733 saw the consecration of the third, and present, parish church of St Giles-in-the-Fields (p 19). Two years earlier, the new parish of St George's Bloomsbury had been created (see diagram, Fig 2), carved out of St Giles' north-east corner; the two parishes remained united for civil purposes. While Bloomsbury evolved into a leafy middle-class suburb, under the watchful eye of the Dukes of Bedford, much of the residue of the mother parish went rapidly downhill.

There had been a small Irish colony in St Giles for generations, possibly attracted there by the parish's reputation for generous poor relief. Now, between 1720 and 1750, there was a large-scale influx of immigrants from some of the poorest parts of Ireland. They crowded into deteriorating 17th-century houses patched up by unscrupulous middlemen, uncontrolled by apathetic ground landlords. The most infamously overcrowded area was Pitaunce Croft north of St Giles Church, later known as the Rookery, and treated in detail in Route 3.

Many incomers earned an honest living as costermongers or as Covent Garden market porters; others survived by prostitution or petty crime. St Giles became a byword for the worst excesses of urban degradation. Drunkenness was rife: the 18th-century gin-drinking epidemic was at its most virulent in St Giles, where (in 1751) one house in four reportedly sold spirits. Hogarth set his satirical engraving *Gin Lane* in the parish. The rot spread to neighbourhoods outside the Rookery such as Seven Dials. Commerce, of a sort, thrived in such places as old Monmouth Street, but most of the goods on sale were second-hand.

A haunt of thieves and receivers of stolen goods, St Giles was one centre of the crime-wave afflicting London in the early 18th century. Jonathan Wild and Jack Sheppard, among the century's best-known (English) criminals, both enter our story. The parish played a role in the last hours of many a convicted felon as he took his final cart-ride from Newgate gaol to the gallows at Tyburn: one (originally medieval) custom demanded a stop outside one of the local inns to receive a last drink, from the St Giles 'Bowl' or 'Cup of Charity'.

The district's dire reputation persisted through the 19th century, its evils causing consternation to a string of social commentators from Mayhew to Booth. Slum clearance in the second half of the century led to the construction of model housing blocks for the poor, at first through private enterprise, and later by a newly formed London County Council (LCC). Some of the worst slums were cleared as a result of Victorian road-building schemes. New Oxford Street (so named in a vain attempt to make it a shopping street as popular as Oxford Street) cut through the Rookery in 1844–47, unfortunately forcing its displaced inhabitants into already overcrowded areas. Some 40 years later, the Metropolitan Board of Works promoted the building of Charing Cross Road and Shaftesbury Avenue, these being (within our area) essentially widenings of existing streets. Later still and further east, Kingsway, a Victorian project completed only in 1905, swept away local slums, and bisected Great Queen Street which, as an offshoot of Lincoln's Inn Fields, had somehow survived as an enclave of middle-class respectability in an otherwise disreputable parish, to become a national centre of Freemasonry.

In 1900 St Giles and St George's merged with two easterly parishes to form Holborn, the smallest of the Metropolitan Boroughs; this, in turn, became part of the modern borough of Camden in 1965. During WWII, Holborn was among the most heavily bombed of all London boroughs; but on its western side, including St Giles, damage was comparatively light.

After the war, the main roads of our area were subject to the inevitable sprouting of office-blocks, Centre Point Tower being the most controversial example; some of the less inspired erections have now been more imaginatively refurbished. Recent decades have also, happily, seen the transformation of a very run-down Seven Dials area into the thriving tourist honeypot it is today. Fashion outlets and specialist shops are open seven days a week and Seven Dials has become a centre for strolling and diversion, recapturing its original spirit.

Much of its early architecture has been preserved and renovated. Large numbers of buildings in the area are Listed by English Heritage as of special architectural or historical interest, so we do not mention each one that is; however, where the Listing is recent or in any sense unexpected, we do.

Since 2010, 'InHolborn', a group promoting investment locally, has controversially sought to 'rebrand' the area, lumping St Giles together with Holborn and Bloomsbury under the bland name of 'Midtown'. The object of some derision, this has yet to catch on with the general public, and those with a sense of place and an interest in local history may hope it never does. At the same time, the historic parish name has been given a renewed prominence in the major new development known as Central St Giles (p 57), and there are even suggestions that Tottenham Court Road station be renamed 'St Giles'.

Of the parish's medieval roots and early development there are now only occasional reminders; but much remains from the 18th, 19th and 20th centuries to be discovered with delight as you walk through a district which (except for Lincoln's Inn Fields) was historically regarded as poor, yet which is rich in history.

The domain of the Leper Hospital

Circular walk from St Giles Circus
(see back cover for map)

We have already considered the history of St Giles' Hospital (p 8); this route traces its footprint and brings the story up to the present. We begin at the south-east corner of **ST GILES CIRCUS**, reached by bus or by Tube to **Tottenham Court Road station** (take exit 4, to emerge at the top of the steps under the huge bulk of Centre Point Tower, p 15). The underground station was formed by a merger of the Central London Railway platforms, opened in 1900, and the Hampstead Tube's 'Oxford Street' Station of 1907. The station is currently undergoing major changes, necessitated by the construction here of a linked station on Crossrail, the rail link through Central London between Maidenhead and Heathrow in the west and Abbey Wood and Shenfield in the east, due for completion in 2018. Since 1984, the station has contained abstract murals of glass mosaic installed to designs by Eduardo Paolozzi, which aim to symbolise the character of Charing Cross Road. Motifs include a saxophone (symbolising the local popular music trade), mechanical chickens and cows (fast food), and a man with a computer linked to his brain.

The hoarding to your left hides the massive construction site which is expected to give way to an open piazza by 2015. It covers the southern arm of the crossing before you, which has been known since 1921 as St Giles Circus. Until the early 1960s this was the meeting point of five streets: St Giles High Street (now hidden behind Centre Point), Charing Cross Road (leading south), Oxford Street (leading west), Tottenham Court Road (leading north) and New Oxford Street (on which you stand). The traffic lights installed here in 1930 were among the first in this country. The 1950s photograph (**[3]**,p 14) views the Circus from the opposite corner, before Centre Point was built.

In 1417, a gallows was erected at the intersection for the execution of the Lollard leader Sir John Oldcastle (c.1378–1417), the inspiration for Shakespeare's Falstaff. The Lollards were followers of the religious reformer Wycliffe; they used the fields around St Giles' Hospital as a secret meeting-place. Also at this junction, in the middle of the roadway, stood the St Giles pound for stray animals. It was brought here from a position in St Giles High Street (p 65) in 1656, and finally removed in 1765. There was also a cage, used as a temporary prison for humans. One of the 'features' lost to the 2011 redevelopment site was a desolate pool and fountains adjacent (and in similar style) to Centre Point, which marked the spot where until the 1960s St Giles High Street met Charing Cross Road at an acute angle. In the apex once stood the Crown Inn and brewhouse, established here by 1452, which gave its name to Crown Street, the precursor of Charing Cross Road. When the latter was laid out in 1886, the old pub was demolished and replaced by round-ended Imperial Mansions (actually comprising shops and offices).

Turn round and walk east along New Oxford Street, passing the foot of the Centre Point Tower. Immediately before the first traffic light, turn right under the bridge into St Giles High Street. A short distance ahead a road on the right feeds in traffic from Charing Cross Road, diverted while the roadworks block the entrance into St Giles Circus. Cross the road at the pedestrian lights to the first block on the south side of St Giles High Street; by this manoeuvre, you have crossed the line of

3 St Giles Circus. A 1950s photo taken from Tottenham Court Road. St Giles High Street is ahead on its original alignment. The two large blocks were demolished for the construction of Centre Point; the rounded one on the right was Imperial Mansions

recently vanished Andrew Borde Street. Dr Borde or Boorde (c.1490-1549), a Carthusian monk turned physician, was Suffragan Bishop of Chichester in 1521. He travelled widely in Europe, and is credited with sending 'seeds' of rhubarb back to England, though the plant was not cultivated in this country until the 1740s. The many books attributed to him include a *Dyetary* (of 1542) and a *Boke of Berdes* (beards) denigrating beards, published 1543. Boorde's colourful life led to his dying in the Fleet Prison, imprisoned for allegedly having once kept three loose women in his chambers in Winchester. Our interest in him is that in 1547 he was the probable last occupant of the Master's House of the St Giles Leper Hospital. This would have stood, surrounded by the hospital garden, just to the south of here.

Continue along **ST GILES HIGH STREET**. This thoroughfare was known until 1937 as High Street, Bloomsbury. In the neat Georgian shopping parade that was once here, No.46 housed the shop of Louis Panormo, described by Tallis in 1838-40 as 'the only Maker of Guitars in the Spanish Style'. With the opening of New Oxford Street in 1847 the High Street became something of a backwater, deemed too narrow for through traffic. In the present one-way traffic scheme introduced in 1961 it resumed its historical role as a major through-route, albeit for westbound traffic only.

The block to our right, prominently marked York and Clifton Mansions, bears all the hallmarks of planning blight, with derelict upper storeys. The ground floor houses a number of small restaurants. These included at No.52, from 1986 to 2011, the First Out lesbian and gay café-bar, where performer Amy Lamé was once a member of staff (she was subsequently chosen by Camden's mayor as his mayoress, 2010-2011).

Pass the entrance to an uninviting alleyway, one way into **DENMARK PLACE**. Previously Dudley Court, this was on the site of the 'White House' erected by Lady Alicia Dudley as a home for St Giles church's Rector. This may, in turn, have replaced the Master's House of the leper hospital. By 1792, and well into the 19th century, Dudley Court housed the chapel of the local Swedenborgian congregation. Single-storey **No.22** was a forge and smithy, believed to date back to the 17th century (**[4]**, p 16). The immediate surroundings were densely built-up. Old maps show a Rose & Crown Yard (1720), Farmer's Alley, later Farmer's Rents; while in 1871 Crown Place, Burnett's Buildings and Regent's Place were all contained within the area between the High Street and what became Charing Cross Road (then Crown Street). The 1888 Goad insurance map indicates new development in Denmark Place after Charing Cross Road appeared, and trades including

goldsmithing, silver casting, carpentry, and japanning. When Denmark Place started to decline is uncertain, but by the late 20th century a general air of sleaze and squalor had long pervaded the often rubbish-strewn alley. It gained notoriety with the deaths of 38 people in a fire at the Spanish and South American Clubs in August 1980.

Look back at **Centre Point tower**. This 33-storey, 398-ft high office block was designed by Richard Seifert and built in 1963-67, when architects loved to erect a prominent building to mark a traffic intersection or crossroads. From the outset this skyscraper was much criticised. Pevsner wrote that the LCC should not have permitted such a large building at a busy junction, and lamented the 'coarseness of the zigzag effect … and the pool with equally coarse shapes as fountains: who would want such a building as its image?' The block nevertheless received Grade II Listing (as an example of 20th-century architecture) from English Heritage in 1995. In the 1970s the building housed Centrepoint, a shelter for the homeless, but this moved elsewhere before the Confederation of British Industry chose to make the building its headquarters in July 1980, occupying 14 floors. These have now dwindled to 2; various business have offices on the floors other than 31-33, which are the abode of a smart restaurant and club run by the Paramount Group.

Take the next turning right into

4 Pre-WWI photo of the interior of the blacksmith's at No.22 Denmark Place

DENMARK STREET. This is famous as Britain's 'Tin Pan Alley', long connected with music publishing and management. It repays a close look because of the concentration of old houses here. Cross over to the corner of the south side and take in the view. Named in honour of the husband of Princess (future Queen) Anne, Prince George of Denmark (the wedding was in 1683), the street was developed in the late 1680s by Samuel Fortrey and Jacques Wiseman. According to Strype (1720), Denmark Street was 'a fair broad street with good houses well inhabited by the gentry'. Of about 20 houses completed by the early 18th century, eight survive, and are among the few terraced houses in London that are more than 300 years old, all being Listed.

18th-century occupants included Joseph Bramah, Charles Green, Jesse Ramsden and Caleb Jeacocke. Bramah started a workshop in the street in 1778 to manufacture the water closet he had just patented. He also patented locks, but his most important invention was the hydraulic press in 1795. The astronomer Charles Green, before becoming an assistant to two Astronomers Royal and then Acting

Astronomer Royal, worked as an assistant teacher at a school here. He was eventually charged to go on James Cook's expedition to Tahiti, to observe the transit of Venus (3 June 1769). Scientific instrument maker Jesse Ramsden was apprenticed in 1756 to mathematical instrument maker Mark Burton of Denmark Street. In 1787 he was to provide a 36-inch theodolite for General William Roy's project to check the longitude difference between the Greenwich and Paris observatories; this project was pivotal in the development of the Ordnance Survey. The orator Caleb Jeacocke, who attended the Monday evening meetings of the Robin Hood (debating) Society, and who was reported to have outwitted Edmund Burke and other notable MPs, died at his house in Denmark Street in early 1786. He began his working life as a baker's apprentice, before opening his own shop in St Giles High Street. He went on to be elected to the Skinners' Company and to become director of the Hand-in-Hand fire office.

In the 19th century, the north side of Denmark Street comprised mainly dwellings, with businesses concentrated to the rear in Denmark Place. The south side had trades associated with metalworking: sword cutler, silversmith, gunstock maker, bell hanger. The street had contained a number of publishers of sheet music in Victorian times, but it became most strongly associated with popular music during the 20th century, when it was dubbed 'Tin Pan Alley', like its American counterpart – West 28th Street, New York. By 1946, Denmark Street was home to at least 10 major music publishers and several firms managing popular entertainers. Today the majority of its shops sell musical instruments and keyboards.

Walk along the south side to look across at the north side, which presents an almost continuous row of instrument (particularly guitar) shops. Listed late-17th-century **No.27** has another entrance into Denmark Place. Listed **No.26**, adjoining, dates from the early 18th century; note its casement windows. **No.24** housed the 'Bioscope Department' of Moss Empires in the 1920s. The building had been replaced in the early 20th century by developer Walter J Fryer, who also rebuilt **Nos.4, 8, 19, 21** and **23-25**. No.21 has a huge window at first floor level with an unusually elongated fanlight. In the basement of red-brick **No.22** is the Tin Pan Alley Studio, where Manfred Mann made recordings in the 1960s, when at **No.20** a young Reg Dwight worked for 18 months for Mills Music as a 'general help and tea boy'. He showed little promise in this role but went on to achieve international stardom as Elton John. The house itself is Listed and dates from 1686-89.

No.19 was built as Wright House, taking its name from the man who did most to promote Denmark Street as the centre for popular music, Lawrence Wright. He moved into the street in 1912. He founded the magazine *Melody Maker* in 1926, and was prolific as a songwriter under the *nom de plume* Horatio Nicholls. Later, the firm Lawrence Wright Music moved from No.8 into No.19, which now houses the **Noel Gay Organisation**. This began life in 1938 as the Noel Gay Music Co., founded by Reginald Armitage, formerly organist at Wakefield Cathedral. He used the pen-name Noel Gay, writing a vast number of hit songs, including *The Lambeth Walk* and *Run Rabbit Run* and musicals such as *Me and My Girl*. The organisation, also known as Noel Gay Artists, is pre-eminent as an agent for broadcasters, journalists, comedians and musicians.

The north side of Denmark Street ends with a tall, late-19th-century apartment block, Shaldon Mansions: its main frontage (p 28) is in Charing Cross Road. Before crossing to it, examine the tiled floor in front of The Music Room at **No.11**. Here are the handprints set in cement of celebrities drawn to Rose-Morris, a celebrated maker of instruments, which moved into the building in 1983. This company had been founded in 1919 when two Rose brothers joined up with Victor Morris, and after occupying a series of premises in the EC1 area it opened its first West End premises in 1967 in Shaftesbury Avenue. It expanded into Nos.8 and 10, where it continues to trade, having relinquished the lease of No.11 in 2011.

The first floor of No.11 now houses a contrasting addition to the Denmark Street music scene: the Early Music Shop, which specialises in medieval, Renaissance and baroque musical instruments.

Return along the north side looking back along the south, which retains more of the street's 18th-century feel, as the original roofline is more in evidence. Nos.9&10 are both Listed, as are Nos.5-7. A previous occupant of **No.10** was Campbell Connelly Ltd, whose best seller was *Show Me the Way to Go Home,* and which moved here from Tottenham Court Road in 1926. A much earlier occupant was the non-musical Dr John Purcell, who died at No.10 in 1730; he wrote *A Treatise on the Vapours or Hysteric Fits* (1702) and *A Treatise of the Cholick* (1714). John Zoffany, the royal portrait painter, lived for a time next door at **No.9**, where, during the 1960s, the Café La Giaconda was much frequented by pop musicians: here David Bowie met his backing group, and the Small Faces voted to turn professional, signing a deal with Decca. No.8 was the base of the Billy Cotton Band just after WWII.

In 1976 the punk band the Sex Pistols moved into **No.6**, their manager Malcolm McLaren having bought the lease, and they composed and recorded their first hits there. In 2011 came the startling claim by two archaeologists in the journal *Antiquity* that caricatures of members of the band scrawled on the walls at No.6 might be considered as important historically as the images on the walls of the caves at Lascaux. The female pop trio Bananarama also lived at No.6 in 1981 and recorded their first hit in the same basement studio. How the owners of Zeno's Greek bookshop on the ground floor reacted to such music-making is not known. The bookshop had been there from 1973, having been founded in 1966 by Photini Constantinou and her daughter Monica Williams at No.122 Charing Cross Road. In 1990, the business moved to Fortess Road, Kentish Town as the Hellenic Book Service. Earlier, in 1897, we find the bookbinder Douglas Cockerell setting up his own bindery at No.6, before moving to Bloomsbury two years later.

No.5, sometimes attributed to the notoriously unscrupulous property developer Nicholas Barbon (d.1698), bears Denmark Street's only blue plaque, which commemorates the German-born engineer Augustus Siebe, who occupied the house in 1829 until his death in 1872. Here he established his family home, a workshop, and a shop window for his various mechanical devices. Most notably, he improved the smoke helmet used in fire-fighting invented by John and Charles Deane in 1823, and later developed it into a water-tight diving helmet, with a design superseded only in the 1950s by scuba-type equipment.

No.4 houses the Regent Sounds Studios, where the Rolling Stones recorded *Not Fade Away* in January 1964; here the Kinks had their first recording session, and Genesis recorded their first single here in late 1967.

The south side ends in the bland neo-Georgian brick pile at **Nos.1-3**, which until the end of 2011 housed a Job Centre; this was already an employment exchange in 1946, specialising in the hotel and catering trades. At original No.3, the engraver and printer Thomas Gaugain lived for four years from 1786; notable for his use of colour-printed stipples, he occasionally worked on paintings by George Morland. The mechanical engineer and iron founder George Medhurst had by 1800 established himself at original No.1 as a maker of scales and weighing machines. He invented the equal-balance weighing machine patented in 1817, used on many a shop counter and still as a heavy-duty platform for weighing sacks, carts and jockeys. He was also the first person to suggest pneumatic despatch.

Developers owning many of the houses on the north side of Denmark Street in 1975 sought planning permission to 'redevelop' the area, but these old houses were saved from this fate thanks to vigilant campaigning by the Tin Pan Alley Traders' Association.

Having regained **ST GILES HIGH STREET** we now approach the Palladian church of **St Giles-in-the-Fields**. An inscription on left-hand gatepost commemorates the former Metropolitan Borough of Holborn (1900-1965). St Giles was Holborn's civic church and the gate used to bear the Holborn coat of arms, but this has been removed (cf. p 70). The first building on the site, the St Giles Hospital Chapel or Oratory, served as a parish church from 1547, but was pulled down in 1624. A replacement church, in part financed by the generous Lady Alicia Dudley (p 21), was consecrated by Bishop Laud in 1630. The Fifty New Churches Act of 1711 led to the construction of the third, and present, building, completed in 1733. Its architect was Henry Flitcroft, his design for the church much influenced by the recently opened St Martin-in-the-Fields. Alterations were made to the church by Blomfield and Butterfield in 1875 and 1896 respectively. After relatively minor bomb damage in WWII, it was restored and redecorated in 1952-53.

Its splendid barrel-vaulted and columned interior is reached through a large porch which contains a number of interesting artefacts. These include the original wooden tympanum for the Resurrection Gate (p 20); a monument of 1930 honouring the sculptor John Flaxman; a mosaic after G F Watts, removed in 1970 from the exterior of the National School (p 53); and an initially puzzling blue plaque to George Odger, Labour leader 1820-1877, 'who lived and died here'. The inscription below explains that it was formerly on No.18 St Giles High Street. It faces the tombstone of

Richard Penderell (d.1672), moved here from the churchyard in 1922 to preserve its inscription. He was the Shropshire woodman who, with his four brothers, assisted Charles II to hide in the fabled 'Boscobel Oak' near their home after the Battle of Worcester. Richard later lived and died in Great Turnstile, off High Holborn.

Within the body of the church are further treasures, including the upper part of the three-decker pulpit once used by Wesley at the West Street chapel (p 40); a commemoration, probably by Inigo Jones, of the poet George Chapman, translator of Homer; and a memorial to the 2nd Lord Baltimore (p 101), unveiled by the Governor of Maryland in 1996. A 1669 effigy in white marble by Joshua Marshall depicts a recumbent, shrouded Lady Frances Kniveton, one of the five daughters and co-heirs of Robert and Lady Alicia Dudley. The author and press censor Sir Roger L'Estrange is commemorated by a memorial of 1704 ascribed to the Stanton workshop, which would have come from the second church. Also buried in the church is John Belasyse (p 97). Other monuments honour Dr William Balmain, who became principal surgeon to, and co-founder of, the colony of New South Wales in 1796; and Samuel Remnant, who died in Hampstead in 1835. Also worth noting is the elegant font of 1810 in classical style, attributed to Soane.

The 75 volumes of the parish registers include the names of over 150 people listed in the *Dictionary of National Biography*, among them Admiral Lord Rodney; the actor J P Kemble; Dr John Pell, the mathematician who invented the division sign; and Dr John Bulwer, creator of sign language for the 'deaf and dumb'. The engraver Wenceslaus Hollar was married in the church in 1653, as was the actress Frances Kemble in 1786, with Sarah Siddons as a witness. Baptisms included those of Catharine Sedley, the future mistress of James II; Mary, daughter of the poet John Milton, who for two years lived in eastern High Holborn; and, in 1694, of the future prime minister, Henry Pelham. In 1818, the church witnessed a triple christening: the two children of Percy Bysshe and Mary Shelley, and Allegra, the ill-fated illegitimate daughter of Lord Byron by Mary's stepsister, Claire Clairmont.

Continue along the street beside the church as far as the Grade II-Listed telephone box. High on the wall of the building beside it is a faded sign in the brickwork, just about discernible when the tree in front of it is bare, as "Continental Garage: Garages on hire; ouvert jour & nuit".

Unless the gates are locked, turn into **St Giles Churchyard**, opened to the public in 1891, and admire details on the church tower and steeple as well as the simplicity of Flitcroft's single-storey vestry building adjacent to the church's south porch. Two plague pits lie beneath the churchyard; here were buried many of those executed at the nearby St Giles gallows (p 13). Among the few surviving tombstones is the table-tomb of Richard Penderell. Others buried in the churchyard include George Chapman, translator of Homer (d.1634); fellow poet Andrew Marvell (d.1678); twelve of the Roman Catholic martyrs (including Oliver Plunket, Archbishop of Armagh) denounced by the villainous Titus Oates (p 103); and (probably) the highwayman Claude Duval. By 1803 the graveyard was full to overflowing, and the parish acquired a new burial ground at St Pancras Old Church. Back in the High Street, walk a little way further eastward. Here were four early dwellings known as the Spittle Houses, which after the dissolution of the Hospital in 1539 passed into the ownership of Katherine Legh. The house nearest the church became the **Angel**, which developed into a major coaching inn, with galleries to the rear. In 1720 Strype found it 'a Place of good Resort'. It was one of the inns offering the St Giles Bowl of ale (see also p 65) to convicts on their way to Tyburn. The convicted highwayman Jack Sheppard stopped here and took the cup. He is said to have smiled and said 'give the rest to Jonathan Wild' (the duplicitous thief-taker who had shopped him to the authorities). The old inn was pulled down in 1873 and replaced by today's building. If the doors of the inn's covered yard are open, it is worth looking in at its fine Victorian tiling. Outside the furthest door of the pub, granite setts form the pavement instead of the usual flagstones, perhaps to support the unloading of heavy beer barrels.

Retrace your steps to the church gateway and turn left into the alley beyond it. Originally called Little Denmark Street, this became **FLITCROFT STREET** in 1936. Flitcroft's name is carved on the frieze at the base of the church steeple, above the west door. On your left is the church's former main gate, moved here from the High Street in 1865, and known as the **Resurrection Gate** because of the bas-relief surmounting it: made in reconstructed Portland stone, this is a 1986 copy of the wooden original of 1687 (in the church porch), which in turn was based on Michelangelo's *Last Judgement* in the Sistine Chapel. The gate itself was manufactured in 1804 by G B Cooper of the West Central Iron Works in Drury Lane, when the St Giles area was a major centre of the ironmongery trade (as late as 1949, the district was still being described as the 'ironmongery capital of the world').

To your right, former workshops dated 1903 have been refurbished and now house media-related firms. Here for many years, at No.4, was an 'Italian warehouse' of Messrs Crosse & Blackwell. Ahead of you, to the left of the path, is a brick building also of 1903 with an extraordinarily narrow but huge taking-in door, purpose-built for Elms-Lester Bros, painters of theatrical scenery, as can be seen in the inscription above. Though badly damaged in the Blitz, the premises were taken over in 1944 by the renowned 'scenic painter' Tod Kingman, who named them Key Studios. Recycling the name of the original occupants, today's **Elms Lesters** Painting Rooms serve as conventional artists' studios, though theatre scenery is still occasionally painted here. The building occupies the site of St Giles's first National School, opened here in 1830 and later transferred to Endell Street (p 53). Facing it is the forbidding **No.6,** dating from 1850, refurbished in 1881, and once part of Thomas Marshall's tin-box factory. By the 1930s it housed the Minerva Club, remaining a social club well into the post-war years. It is now home to Paul McAneary Architects, a practice founded in 2007 and already winning awards.

Proceed to the anti-cycling barriers. On the wall to the left of these is a small brass plate inscribed 'Craig Hayden lived and then died in Flitcroft Street, 26 May 1971 – 6 June 1997'. Hayden was a homeless man, a long-time pavement-dweller here, always friendly and popular with passers-by. Soon after his death the brass memorial suddenly appeared, erected by an unknown hand.

The path now veers to the right and becomes a narrow street. This portion of Flitcroft Street was formerly named Lloyd's Court. Here stood the St Giles Vestry House, home to the parish beadle, and from 1815 Shelton's Charity School (see p 77). Also here, in 1871, were a ragged school and a mission house of the Biblewoman movement (cf. p 74), presided over by Mrs Eliza Ann Spiller.

In the early 1990s some of the old industrial buildings in Flitcroft Street were under threat of demolition; they have instead been retained and have undergone 'regeneration'. On the right, **No.8** was once part of the tin-box factory just mentioned; it later housed a firm making fenders and other 'hearth furniture', and after WWII a stereotype foundry. Next on your right is a large metal gate, giving access (when open) to **Book Mews**. This winds its way into an area known in the 18th century as Eight Bells Yard, and then fronted by an Eight Bells public house, where bell-ringers would have relaxed after their exertions in the belfry at St Giles, which has a peal of eight bells. More recently, Book Mews served as an unloading bay for the defunct bookshop Borders formerly in the Charing Cross Road (p 28). Pulse Films, a film content production company, known for adverts for such products as Kronenbourg lager, became a major occupant of the Mews in 2010. Here in earlier times was the main residential building of the leper hospital – its 'capital place or mansion'. After 1545, this was converted into a residence by its new owner, John Dudley (Lord Lisle). As Dudley House, it was later home for many years to Lady Alicia Dudley (see also p 19), the abandoned wife of

Robert Dudley, the grandson of Lord Lisle. A most pious lady and a great benefactress of the parish, she died here aged 90 in 1669, and the mansion passed to the dissolute Duke of Wharton. His house and garden were soon to be swept away in the building of Denmark Street (p 16).

Next to the gate leading into Book Mews is a Victorian Gothic arch surmounted by the monogram 'WA' and the date '1878' far above it. This was the warehouse of the wholesale ironmonger William Addis. Ahead, Flitcroft Street continues as a footway to join Charing Cross Road. Look along it. On the right is a larger building of yellow stock brick that in late Victorian times served as an iron-bedstead factory. Beyond that, and extending behind, were further premises of Crosse & Blackwell. Described in 1846 as 'oilmen by appointment to the Queen', the food manufacturing partnership was a major employer in the Soho/Charing Cross Road area from the 1830s to the 1920s. Here, on the north side of what was then Lloyd's Court, stood their pickle factory, while their candied lemon works occupied the south side. An unusual music-hall named Alcazar opened in the 1920s in the disused candied lemon works, promoted by the impresario Lucien Samett. Entered from Charing Cross Road, the establishment offered all-day entertainment with a continuous sequence of variety acts. The audience would wander between the

three stages set up in the long, narrow hall, as one turn ended and another began. Besides the paying public, the Alcazar was frequented by West End theatre managers on the lookout for talent; admitted free, they used the place as an audition space. Samett's experiment was a failure and the Alcazar soon declined into a 'Fun City', with slot machines and dubious-sounding attractions entitled 'Beautiful Artists' or 'Posing Models'.

Passing the stage door of the Phoenix Theatre (p 22) on your right, walk along **STACEY STREET,** named in 1878 in memory of a 16th-century James Stacey, who built two houses here on what is thought to be the site of the leper hospital's orchard. The street was first built up in the 17th century and named Brown's Gardens after a gardener called Brown who rented a plot next to the churchyard. The left-hand side of Stacey Street was residential until it suffered bomb damage in 1941; modern railings there now form an attractive surround to the Phoenix Garden (see below). The west side was occupied in the early 1900s by a warehouse of the locally important plate-glass merchants Alfred Goslett & Co Ltd (after whom Goslett Yard on the Westminster side of Charing Cross Road is named). **The Alcazar** flats now on this side of the street were built in the 1990s for the Soho Housing Association and named after the former music-hall.

A former Phoenix tavern in Stacey

Street gave its name to **PHOENIX STREET**, into which we turn. First on your right at **No.1A** are stylish, early-21st-century flats faced with wood and metal cladding which have supplanted the former Curzon Phoenix Cinema, a featureless modern building which had the merit of promoting film as an art form, until its closure in 1998. Next door is the **Phoenix Theatre.** Its façade incorporates the mythical bird and a terracotta centrepiece featuring four tightly twisted columns crowned by Composite capitals, a style favoured by Sir Giles Gilbert Scott, who worked on the building with Bertie Crewe. The theatre opened in 1930 under C B Cochrane's management with a production of *Private Lives*, one of many Noel Coward plays that it has staged. Until the 1980s, it specialised in repertory productions, attracting many stars of stage and screen: Diana Rigg and John Thaw in Tom Stoppard's *Night and Day*, and Penelope Keith and Keith Michell in Bernard Shaw's *The Apple Cart* are 1970s examples. Since 1991 it has staged the musical *Blood Brothers* by Willie Russell. Just beyond the theatre's entrance at the corner of Charing Cross Road, the **Phoenix Artist Club** was previously the theatre's dressing and rehearsal rooms, transformed into a wine bar and restaurant in the late 1970s, whose walls and display window are adorned with memorabilia supplied by club members.

Back in Stacey Street, after a few steps we turn left into **NEW COMPTON STREET**, originally known at its western end as Stidwell Street, a corruption of Stiddulph Street (after Sir Richard Stiddolph, who was granted a licence to build on pasture ground near the Hospital in 1671). Strype, in 1720, calls the street 'Stedwell Street', and finds it 'very ordinary both for buildings and inhabitants'. Many houses were rebuilt in 1775-76 (but none survive), when the street was renamed after Henry Compton, the Bishop of London, who in 1676 created the nearby Soho parish of St Anne. The street was originally a continuation of Soho's Old Compton Street, from which it is now cut off by a huge office block entered from Shaftesbury Avenue and backing onto Charing Cross Road (*see* Caxton Walk, p 28). In the 19th century New Compton Street was a mixture of small shops and houses, with a wire factory and warehouse heralding the arrival of the electrical specialties soon to colonise the neighbourhood. Ironmongery and music publishing businesses were also here in the 1940s.

The post-WWII story of the street's north-west side is one of car parks and local politics. A bombsite on the Stacey Street corner operated as a car park until 1984, when the Covent Garden Open Spaces Association took it over and developed it into the pleasant **Phoenix Garden**, which won a Shell Better Britain Campaign Award in 1985; it was officially opened in June 1986 by Frank Dobson, the local MP. Its meandering plant-lined paths, made up of bricks or flagstones, lead to small ponds or secluded benches. It was appreciated by a former Director General of the CBI, witness the inscription on a seat, 'Digby Jones takes time to smell the flowers'.

Alongside the garden is **ST GILES PASSAGE**, an ancient 'churchway', renamed from Church Passage in 1937. Old maps show a few houses here, while directories record rag merchants and a bookbinder at various times. Living at the three addresses in the 1871 census were people from Ireland and France; two of the residents, a pickle maker and a pickle labeller, would have been employed by Crosse & Blackwell.

Beyond St Giles Passage on the north side of **NEW COMPTON STREET**, a terrace of small 18th-century houses was pulled down in 1966. Attempts at rebuilding them produced protracted wrangling between local landlords and Camden Council; eventually the Soho Housing Association built **Pendrell House**, a development of flats and maisonettes, on the site. Because the area once lay within the precincts of the old leper hospital, English Heritage organised an archaeological dig before the flats were built. Their projecting railed balconies are best viewed from across the street.

The eastern end of New Compton Street covers the site of Kendrick's Yard, described by Strype as 'a place chiefly taken up for coach houses and stablings'. In his novel *Jack Sheppard*, fancifully based on the highwayman's life, Harrison Ainsworth cites Kendrick's Yard as the eastern approach to the St Giles Roundhouse, through the roof of which his hero makes one of his legendary escapes. The parish's earliest Roundhouse did indeed exist somewhere near here, its walls bulging so badly that it resembled an upturned beer-barrel; a circular doorway at first-floor level served as the perfect 'bung-hole', completing the illusion. Ainsworth was seemingly unaware that this building was demolished soon after 1690, some 30 years before Sheppard embarked on his criminal career, and that a replacement had meanwhile been erected farther east.

To the right, on the south side of New Compton Street, are the backs of buildings on Shaftesbury Avenue (see below): the Odeon cinema, and three refurbished office buildings more pleasing to the eye than were their precursors.

On regaining St Giles High Street, turn right to reach the junction with **SHAFTESBURY AVENUE**. Here we find one of Camden's four air-pollution monitoring stations, masquerading as an advertising column. It was erected in 2002, replacing equipment previously on the triangle closest to the Shaftesbury Theatre.

Pause here and look right. The building line on the right-hand side

follows the old leper hospital boundary. Shaftesbury Avenue lies over an ancient trackway known as 'Le Lane'. As the north-western boundary of Neale's Seven Dials development (p 29) this became Monmouth Street – not to be confused with its nearby present-day namesake (p 29). Duncan Campbell (*c*.1680-1730), a soothsayer who claimed to have been born in Lapland, took a house here. He established himself in business as a soothsayer and a novelty, a deaf mute who could converse. His popularity eventually waned, but he was involved in the production in 1720 of *The History of the Life and Adventures of Mr Duncan Campbell* by Daniel Defoe, and was presented at court to George I.

Clothing was once a staple trade of old Monmouth Street. In the early 18th century it was noted for its lace and finely embroidered coats. Lady Wortley Montagu, the society hostess, wrote of the street in her diaries. Soon afterwards its commerce had declined into the selling of cast-off clothes, often third- or fourth-hand. 'Monmouth Street finery' became a byword for tawdriness. Dickens described the street as the 'burial place of the fashions', devoting a whole chapter of *Sketches by Boz* to imaginative musings on its trade in old clothes. The pavements were lined by rows of boots and shoes for sale, the work of the street's population of (often Irish) shoe-binders. They lived and worked in dark,

crowded cellars accessed only by ladders, transforming utterly outworn footwear into saleable products. Contemporary writers regarded these troglodytic folk as a virtual sub-species; one compared their appearances on the surface to 'otters coming up to breathe'. The thoroughfare was renamed Dudley Street in 1845. Its poor yet vibrant street-life was captured in a well-known print by Gustave Doré **[5]**, published in 1872, not long before all was replaced by a sanitised Shaftesbury Avenue.

Opened in 1886 as part of a mid-Victorian road-building scheme, Shaftesbury Avenue attracted firms then at the forefront of technology. The corner block at **Nos.179-199** and Nos.65-67 St Giles High Street was, for many years, home to the electrical firm Philips, principally supplying lamps, x-ray equipment, industrial and electrical welding and cinema apparatus. The company provided the original floodlighting for St Giles church. Century House, the block's dull post-WWII incarnation, was refurbished in 1996 for the Standard Life Assurance Co. to the designs of Cummings Marsh & Rolfe Judd and renamed **Endeavour House**. The ground floor nearest us (No.199) was then occupied by lighting retailer Christopher Wray until 2008, when the stylish Italian interior design company Molteni and C Dada opened its UK flagship store. Walk past the entrance doorway (No.189), above which is the present editorial office of *The Bookseller*, which continues its association with the district (cf. p 81). The far side of the block houses Forbidden Planet, which describes itself as the 'cult entertainment megastore'. Fronted by a general hardware and DIY shop, glass-fronted Lindsay House follows at **Nos.167-177**.

The opposite (south-east) side of Shaftesbury Avenue was built up quickly after the road opened. At **No.180**, until it closed in 2002, was Ray's Jazz Shop; Ray Smith (d.2011) had worked at the former Collett's jazz and folk shop at this address. The terracotta designs just under roof level – with abundant use of the sunflower motif – are reminiscent of those used by James Hartnoll for his housing projects, but as far as we know this is not one of them. The most prominent building here sports a red brick and terracotta façade; this was originally the *Nouvel Hôpital et Dispensaire Français*. Established to offer medical aid to French-speaking foreigners, it moved here c.1890 from Leicester Square. The building later served as the Shaftesbury Hospital (part of St Paul's Hospital, p 50) until it closed in 1991. When it was remodelled as a hotel accessed from Monmouth Street (p 50), the Shaftesbury Avenue entrance of the Grade II-Listed premises was filled in.

5 Dudley Street, previously the original Monmouth Street (Gustave Doré, 1872)

The French Hospital was the birthplace in 1916 of the artist Robert Buhler. Three years later the painter Harold Gilman died there, a victim of the post-war influenza epidemic, as did anthropologist Emil Torday (1875-1931). To the right of the former hospital, equally attractive and also in red brick, **Leader House** (No.166) accommodates a Thai restaurant.

On the Avenue's north side, on your right, a striking new development at **Nos.151-165** replaced former Dial House, a drab brick edifice of 1948, demolished in 1996. The Museum of London undertook an archaeological evaluation of the site, seeking evidence of the location of Lundenwic (p 8) and of the old St Giles Hospital precinct wall; there were no conclusive finds. Completed in 1999 by Jarrah Properties with the Devereux Partnership of architects, the building is officially Shaftesbury House - see the bronze plaque at waist height at the extreme right - but it is more prominently labelled simply as 'No.151' in giant illuminated white glass numerals inside the tinted glass façade. It is partly occupied by a branch of the Polish bank PKO. The attractive rounded corner at St Giles Passage rises into a kind of turret above the sixth floor.

Surviving opposite, despite wartime damage to its lancet windows, is a narrow red-brick chapel, which since 2004 has been the Soho Outreach Centre of the **Chinese Church in London**. Previously known as the Shaftesbury Avenue Chapel, it was built in 1887 as the Soho Baptist Chapel (see the terracotta inscription), subsequently occupied by a congregation of Particular Baptists who had migrated from the Providence Chapel in Gray's Inn Lane via Conway Street, Fitzrovia and then Gower Street (1843). They moved to Shaftesbury Avenue in 1917, renaming the building the Gower Street Memorial Chapel, which remained its alternative name until its eventual closure. Activities here once included a Dorcas Society, which made clothes for the poor.

On the corner of Mercer Street opposite, at **No.164**, once stood Shaftesbury House, the HQ of the Shaftesbury Homes for Boys and the 'training ship' *Arethusa* (boys leaving the homes were typically encouraged into naval careers). The charity had its earliest roots in the ragged school founded in the Rookery in 1843 (p 59), and later moved to Broad Street (p 63), while its immediate precursor was the home for homeless boys subsequently opened in Great Queen Street (p 91). Lord Shaftesbury, after whom the Avenue is named, eventually presided over the institution. The charity continues today as Shaftesbury Young People. The National Farmers' Union (NFU) had its headquarters at No.164 after moving from Knightsbridge in the 1990s, and before relocating to the National Agricultural Centre at Stoneleigh, Warwickshire in 2006.

Cross to No.164 by the pedestrian crossing to get the best view of the **Odeon (Covent Garden) cinema** on the north side. Designed by T P Bennett & Sons, it opened as the Saville Theatre in October 1931. The first owner, Mr K H Lane, preferred not to name the theatre after himself, instead plucking a name at random from a telephone directory. Particularly special are the ten medallions just below the roof line entitled *Art through the ages*, and a 130-ft bas-relief frieze depicting *Drama through the ages*, for which Gilbert Bayes, the creator of both, received a sculpture award. The theatre's opening show was *For the Love of Mike*, a musical comedy. Most of the productions were in similar vein until the mid-1950s, when classical plays (some televised) were staged by actor-manager John Clements. The theatre was also renowned for hosting performances by visiting dance companies and by foreign entertainers such as Yves Montand and Marcel Marçeau. Later managers included Bernard Delfont, who tried to change the theatre's name to the Gaiety, and Brian Epstein (cf. p 30), during whose time the Saville doubled as a pop music venue: Sunday gigs featuring some now legendary names began in November 1966. After Epstein's suicide 9 months later, his brother Clive took over. Actors appearing at the Saville over time included Doris Hare, Stanley

Holloway, Peter Ustinov and Alan Bates. One of the last productions, Brecht's *The Resistible Rise of Arturo Ui* launched Leonard Rossiter's career, and the very last was *Enemy!* by Robin Maugham, with a young Dennis Waterman in the cast. The theatre was eventually acquired by EMI, who converted it into a comfortable and spacious, if undistinguished, two-screen cinema, which opened in December 1970 as the ABC Shaftesbury Avenue; it later became an MGM cinema, before assuming its present name. None of the original interior décor is now visible.

Cross back to the north side and continue westwards. Beyond Stacey Street is **No.121**, until recently occupied by Pages, trading hereabouts since 1834 in catering equipment and fine tableware; the shop is now run by Bristol-based Nisbets, in the same line of business. Next door, terracotta-adorned **No.119** houses 'Angels', part of Angels & Bermans, costumiers to the entertainment industry, where fancy dress can be hired. Across the Avenue at the junction with Earlham Street (p 43) is **No.144**, which was for many years the woodwind and brass shop of Bill Lewington; it is now home to Fopp Ltd, an independent music store. On the corner above first-floor level is a stone carving (c.1890) of a female bookbinder, a reminder of the building's original use, the premises of Zaehnsdorf, bookbinders and conservators to the British Museum. The firm was founded in 1842 by Joseph Zaehnsdorf and received Royal appointment in 1902.

We have reached **CAMBRIDGE CIRCUS,** the north-eastern quadrant of which is in Camden. This was the pivotal point of the Victorian road scheme that gave birth to both the Avenue and Charing Cross Road. Under the Metropolitan Street Improvements Act of 1877, plans for the building of Shaftesbury Avenue and Charing Cross Road were drawn up by Joseph Bazalgette, engineer to the Metropolitan Board of Works, and George Vulliamy, its architect. By contrast with the earlier building of New Oxford Street, when the displaced populace was left to find its own salvation, the new Act required replacement housing to be provided for 3,044 'persons of the labouring classes'. The MBW was reluctant to purchase more land than necessary, and the Camden stretches of both thoroughfares were essentially widenings of existing streets. Shaftesbury Avenue was opened in 1886; February 1887 saw the official opening by Prince George, Duke of Cambridge (a cousin of Queen Victoria) of Charing Cross Road and of Cambridge Circus, which until then had been provisionally named Shaftesbury Circus. Although a boon to traffic, both new roads were architecturally disappointing, lined (with some honourable exceptions) by a hotchpotch of often second-rate buildings, and comparing unfavourably with the LCC's elegant Kingsway development of only two decades later (p 89). The planting of trees along these roads did something to improve the ambience.

Cambridge Circus replaced an earlier junction of five narrow streets, known popularly in Victorian times as 'Five Dials', by analogy with nearby Seven Dials, though there were no sundials here. One of the five old intersecting streets was Moor Street, most of which still exists, on the Westminster side of the Circus next to the Cambridge pub; it once continued a little further eastward, thus briefly intruding into the parish of St Giles. On this site, from 1775, was the chapel of the Église Suisse. After it moved to Endell Street (p 53), the premises were taken over, in 1855, by Bloomsbury Chapel, as the headquarters of its Domestic Mission. This was led by the celebrated Baptist preacher George M'Cree, whom Lord Shaftesbury dubbed the 'Bishop of St Giles'. Earlier still on the same Moor Street site was the French Change, 'an old house with pillars before it', as J T Smith described it in *Nollekens and his Times* (1829). This was a meeting-place for the many Huguenots who had fled to England and settled locally after the revocation of the Edict of Nantes; here they would gather to socialise and talk business.

Now turn north along the east side of **CHARING CROSS ROAD**, which here forms Camden's western boundary.

6 Nos.114-116 Charing Cross Road in 1904, originally built for Crosse & Blackwells

This was once part of the main highway northward from Whitehall to Hampstead. Named in ancient records as Oldstrate or Eldestrate, it was known by 1746 as Hog Lane. Half a century later it had become Crown Street, from the Crown Inn (p 13) which then stood at its northern end. So it remained until widened as part of the new Victorian street.

The restaurant on your right, with entrance in Cambridge Circus, includes as part of its premises **No.84**, formerly the second-hand bookshop of Marks & Co, immortalised in Helene Hanff's wartime correspondence with the proprietors, published under the title *84 Charing Cross Road*. The shop closed in the late 1970s, as have most of the Road's independent book shops, which could not survive the dramatic rises in West End rents and competition from the Internet.

Cross now to the Westminster side of the street and continue north to view the buildings on the Camden side. Note the brilliant red-brick and terracotta block of mansion flats at **No.90** by James Hartnoll, who named it **Trentishoe Mansions** after a Devonshire hamlet. Built in 1891, the block is adorned with pedimented gables, a Chambord-style turret, and on the string course, acanthus leaves and *JH* insignia – all hallmarks of Hartnoll's style. The building incorporates at **Nos.92-94** Macari's music shop, established in 1958, which also has a branch in Denmark Street. Between Macari's and Blackwell's, the academic bookshop at **No.100**, is a paved area known for postal purposes as **Caxton Walk;** this is the rump of truncated New Compton Street (p 22) and is immediately opposite Soho's Old Compton Street.

Former businesses along this stretch of Charing Cross Road have included electrical engineering and accessories, music publishers, musical instrument retailers, booksellers (including, on the Westminster side, the famous Foyle's), and theatre-related concerns, most notably Anello and Davide, theatrical footwear specialists, at former No.96. Past Phoenix Street (p 22), the attractive Charing Cross Road entrance of the **Phoenix Theatre** has decorative mouldings, and plain columns with Composite capitals incorporating human faces. Across Flitcroft Street, at Nos.114-116, is **Flitcroft House**, a 5-storey block (**[6]**, p 27) originally built as 4 storeys in red brick and stone by Roumieu and Aitchison for Crosse & Blackwell in 1888, but now painted white. Round-headed windows with human-face plaques at 2nd-floor level give the building a Florentine flavour. This building later housed the Selmer Company of

London, which by the outbreak of WWII was the UK's leading musical instrument company, having originally started on and outgrown the first floor at no.126. In the 1930s, the company was the first to sell amplification equipment, eventually of its own manufacture, and also sold Lowrey organs, Hofner guitars and Fender guitars and amplifiers. Here the jazz singer and washboard player Beryl Bryden, then an employee at the shop, met the jazz trumpeter Humphrey Lyttelton buying his first cornet. **Nos.118-120**, described by the *Survey of London* as a 'good and unaffected modern building', was from the late 1990s until 2009 occupied by the bookseller chain Borders, but after that company went into administration it became, together with Nos.122-124, a TK-Maxx retail outlet. The latter building has fine rubbed-brick decoration.

Beyond Denmark Street at **No.128** (present-day Rock Stop Music), Adrien Wettech, the Swiss clown known as Grock, formed a partnership with the music publisher Leon Silberman in 1916, until they fell out in 1919. They composed a hit song called *My Devon Girl*. Two doors further is the entrance to another Hartnoll mansion block, **Shaldon Mansions** at **No.132**, a striking 'German Renaissance' composition in dark red brick dressed with stone, featuring grotesques, scrolls and strapwork. Still inscribed on a stone plaque dated 1889 on its north side is its original

name, 'Halberstadt Mansions', origin unknown. The more patriotic Devonshire name of Shaldon was substituted when WWI broke out.

Shaldon Mansions constitute the northernmost remaining property in Charing Cross Road, the north end of which has seen two phases of demolition, first during the 1960s with the advent of Centre Point, when publishers George Allen at No.156 were displaced and James Hartnoll's Bude Mansions were pulled down. More recently demolished, with the start of the Crossrail development, were the grey-bricked Nos.142-146, built 1888, and stone-fronted No.148 of the same date but with a more theatrical design. No.142 once housed the Music Copyright Association for the Suppression of Piracies.

Cross back over and follow the curved slip road into St Giles High Street. Behind the hoarding to our right we can see the hotchpotch of buildings which make up what remains of Denmark Place.

Cross at the lights to walk round and under Centre Point to regain St Giles Circus.

Route 2
Seven Dials
& Endell Street
Circular walk from St Giles Circus
(see back cover for map)

*The first part of this Route covers
Seven Dials and its surrounding streets.
The second part (p 47) explores the
streets abutting Endell Street.*

Route 2(a) Seven Dials

From the south-west corner of New Oxford Street at its junction with Tottenham Court Road, walk east past the entrance to Centre Point Tower and turn right into St Giles High Street, as in Route 1 (p 8). Continue past the parish church to the corner of Shaftesbury Avenue. Turn right and in a few yards cross over by the pedestrian crossing to the far side of **MONMOUTH STREET**. Turn right again and take in the prospect.

The street here was called Great St Andrew Street until 1938, when it merged with Little St Andrew Street (its southern continuation) to form Monmouth Street. The new name recalls an earlier street which lay along the line of present-day Shaftesbury Avenue (see p 23) and was probably named after Charles II's illegitimate son the Duke of Monmouth, who from 1682 lived in a large mansion on

the south side of Soho Square.

Here we are on the edge of the area known as **Seven Dials** (bounded by Shaftesbury Avenue, West Street, Shelton Street and Neal Street), at the centre of which seven streets converge. Now a popular and attractive shopping area, for centuries it had a reputation for poverty and crime.

This was far from Thomas Neale's mind when, during the reign of William and Mary, he started laying out the streets on open meadowland. The field had been known for centuries as the Marshland, otherwise St Giles' Field, a stretch of marshy land enclosed by a ditch. A Parliamentary Survey in 1650 showed that it had a handful of tenements and a conduit which provided water to the Exchequer offices in Whitehall. By the 1660s the land was also called Cock and Pye Fields, after a tavern of the same name that stood by what is now Shelton Street, at its southern edge.

In 1671 Charles II issued a proclamation forbidding the building of tenements here, that might 'choak up the air of His Majesty's palaces and park and endanger loss of water which by expensive conduits is conveyed from those fields'. This remained in force for 20 years, but was largely ineffective: sporadic building continued on the fringes of the land, much of which was cluttered with rubbish and night soil from London's streets. By 1691 the Marshland was the last remaining open

field south of High Holborn. But not for much longer. The Crown granted it to Thomas Neale and by 1693 he was leasing it for building. In the process the 'great ditch' which surrounded it was arched over.

Neale was Master of the Mint under Charles II and Groom Porter to the Crown, a post he retained through the reigns of James II and William and Mary until his death in 1699. As Groom Porter, he was responsible for controlling gambling at Court, where he had to provide cards and dice and arbitrate in disputes. In 1694 he organised a lottery-and-loan scheme for the Government to help the war effort, on the security of a new Salt Tax, which raised £1 million. Neale enriched himself from his office, which included licensing or suppressing gaming houses. His wealth enabled him to act as a building speculator, in which he rivalled the rapacious Nicholas Barbon.

Inspired by French urban-planning models, Neale's scheme was for streets radiating out from a central *rond-point*. This plan astonished contemporaries. John Evelyn recorded in October 1694 that 'building was beginning neare St Giles's, where seaven streetes make a starr from a Doric Pillar plac'd in the middle of [a] Circular Area'. The unusual layout provided a larger number of houses and site frontages than development around a square (for which there was little room on the site) and maximised rents, which were then charged per foot of site frontage. But as a speculation it was ultimately a failure. Neale had been granted a freehold but he also had to buy out two existing leases of the Marshland, by offering £4,000 cash and a yearly rent for a lease that expired in 1732. This was a very substantial financial commitment and Neale sold his interest in 1695. The rest of the development was carried out by individual builders, but only four streets are recorded as having been built up by 1708. The whole project was complete by about 1714, but the poor quality of the houses led to a rapid deterioration in the status and condition of the area soon afterwards. As early as 1720 Strype said it was 'filled with abundance of Poor'. In the late 1730s, the then owner, James Joye, broke up the freehold, selling off the triangular sections separately. In the absence of a single freeholder, there was no-one to enforce Neale's restrictive covenants. The area became increasingly commercialised as the houses were subdivided and converted into shops and tenements. But many houses still occupy the original Neale building plots and a number retain original fabric behind remodelled or rebuilt façades.

Now proceed towards the Seven Dials monument, passing **Nos.9&11** with stucco surrounds to its windows. The shop **Mysteries** specialises in the occult and the alternative, giving psychic and tarot card readings. St Giles has never lost its reputation for occultism and strange practices, being home in the 18th century to numerous astrologers and some infamous quack doctors.

At **No.13** a plaque was unveiled in September 2010 by the singer Cilla Black in memory of her manager Brian Epstein, whose first London office was here in 1963-64. Epstein, of course, catapulted the Beatles to fame, and was affectionately known by John Lennon as 'the fifth Beatle'. The plaque was paid for by the Seven Dials Trust, its first heritage or 'People's Plaque'.

Opposite is the smart **Covent Garden Hotel**. The hotel is housed in the former French hospital, whose title *Nouvel Hôpital et Dispensaire Français* (p 24) is clearly visible in the pale red terracotta. There is still a French flavour to the immediate area because the hotel faces at **Nos.19&21**, a chic French restaurant, **Mon Plaisir**, sporting an enormous tricolour. The restaurant has been here for over half a century, opening at No.21 in October 1951. The French atmosphere is perhaps appropriate because there was a strong Huguenot presence in the Seven Dials district in the 18th century. For example, living in Great St Andrew Street around 1750 was the Huguenot watchmaker Francis Barraud. With his brother Paul he established a firm that was later famous as chronometer makers and survived until late in the 19th century as Barraud and Lund. On the site of Mon Plaisir was once No.12 Great St Andrew Street where Robert Smith died in 1841, worth £400,000; a smith by name and vocation, he was also a speculative builder, erecting almost 200 houses in Hampstead Road and owning several properties in the Seven Dials area. The notice of his death in *The Times* said that he was a miser who didn't speak to his neighbours, cleaned his windows only once a year and 'was of the most niggardly and miserable habits'.

Turn left down the white-painted alley (on whose left-hand wall there is a Banksy-style art work) and enter the colour and bustle of **NEAL'S YARD**. On Neale's plan this was shown as King's Head Court, but had received its present name by the time of Rocque's map of 1745. In 1840 a fire destroyed a cowshed for six cows. It was started deliberately; at that period any one giving a 'call' at any fire station received a shilling reward. In 1847, the Seven Dials ragged school opened in the yard, with a separate school for girls three years later by the entrance from what is now Monmouth Street.

Right up until the 1970s the yard's buildings **[7]** were connected with the activities of Covent Garden Market and included premises for wheelwrights and packing-case manufacturers. The market closed in 1974 but the food connection has been maintained, largely because the hippie Nicholas Saunders (1938-1998), a leading light in the campaign to save Covent Garden from comprehensive

redevelopment, bought **No.2**, a former
banana store, and set up the Wholefood
Warehouse. This launched a culinary
craze, and Neal's Yard is now packed with
wholefood cafés and shops selling organic
food and other New Age products. At first-
floor level are dining rooms, and below,
tables spill out into the yard. The **World
Food Café**, on the left, in a warehouse
overgrown with plants, was opened in
1991, with Saunders' help. It bears an
unofficial blue plaque *"Monty Python,
film producer 1976–87"*. Michael Palin and
Terry Gilliam bought these offices to serve
as studios and an editing suite for Python
films and other projects. Neal's Yard offers
other delights, with several alternative
health establishments such as the **Neal's
Yard Remedies**, opened by Saunders in
1981 as the Therapy Rooms. It pioneered
natural remedies in the UK and continues
to promote a holistic approach to health and
beauty, on a rather more commercial basis.

Where the yard opens out, bear right,
between the two buildings that form
Neal's Yard Salad Bar, begun in 1982 by
Saunders, who is commemorated by a black
plaque over to the left. Via the passageway
that runs through the restaurant **Souk**

Medina, regain **MONMOUTH STREET** between **No.31** and **No.33**, two shops run by the Irish fashion designer Orla Kiely. Away to our right is **No.27**, dating from the late 17th century with an early-19th-century shop front. It houses the Monmouth Coffee Company, a sister company of Neal's Yard Dairy (p 46), both set up in 1979, again by Saunders.

Across the street the two shops at **Nos.14&16** were granted on a 30-year repairing lease in 1757 to James Whittle and Samuel Norman, who were high-quality furniture makers, noted for carved and gilded looking glasses and pier tables. Along with No.18, these were the only old buildings on the western side of Great St Andrew Street to survive the slum clearance development of Shaftesbury Avenue (p 23).

That side is now dominated by the early-20th-century, refurbished **Mountbatten Hotel**. Cross over to it. The Shaftesbury Hotel, its predecessor, opened before WWI as a facility for 'men of slender resources', and was hailed at the time as 'a new departure in hotel life'. Its large corner site of 6,000 square ft spread into neighbouring Great White Lion Street (now Mercer Street), where it also housed a technical school for boy boarders aged 15-18. The entrance there lay opposite a café run by James Kitten, born in Sierra Leone. His establishment was the subject of a 1926 article in *John Bull* headed a 'Terrible Negro Haunt', which called for its

closure, claiming it was a drugs den where white women [prostitutes] 'shamelessly consorted' with 'coloured wastrels'. Kitten sued for libel but lost the case, closed the café and ended up bankrupt.

The Mountbatten Hotel covers the site of No.42 Great St Andrew Street, which was the fictional location of Mr Venus's shop in Dickens' *Our Mutual Friend*. In *Sketches by Boz*, the novelist refers to a real shop at No.6 (now No.33), Pitt's Toy and Marble Warehouse, whose once famous toys included 'Slender Ben'. At No.7 (now No.31) had stood the workshop of Stephen Rimbault, a clockmaker of Huguenot descent, noted for his 12-tuned Swiss timepieces. He was based here from 1760 to 1781. When John Zoffany, the future royal portrait painter, first settled in London and was starving in a Drury Lane garret, Rimbault employed him to paint clock faces with landscapes and movable figures.

Look back to the east side. On the brick façade of **No.35**, now a fashionable second-hand clothes store, is an old painted sign for 'pictorial postcards and general stationery'. Until recently the well-known funeral directors France & Sons had a branch at **No.41**, but their century-and-a-half connection with St Giles is now severed. In Victorian times they were based around the corner at No.9 Great White Lion Street. No.41 dates from the mid-19th century; in 1852 an oil-and-colour shop then on the site, run by a Mr Levy,

8   Seven Dials in 1780 (painting attributed, possibly wrongly, to William Hodges, now lost)

collapsed, seriously injuring the proprietor's wife. Next door is the **Crown**, which says it has been trading on this spot since at least 1700, and forms one of the wedge-shaped buildings that bound Seven Dials. The present building has rusticated stucco Corinthian pilasters and a cornice decorated with anthemiums. Pevsner & Cherry state that it dates from 1865 despite the light-blue plaque bearing the date 1833, when records show the pub was indeed rebuilt.

We are now at **SEVEN DIALS** proper. Note that the replica column in the centre has six rather than seven dials: Neale's original plan, submitted to the Surveyor-General Sir Christopher Wren, was for six streets. Little White Lion Street (since renamed as part of Mercer Street, by the side of the Cambridge Theatre) was then added, leaving two of the streets converging on one angle. The junction must always have been rather confusing, and one feels for the pedestrian referred to in John Gay's *Trivia* in 1716:
Here oft the Peasant, with enquiring Face Bewildered, trudges on from Place to Place.

The column was removed in 1773 (see **[8]**, painted a few years later) by order of the Paving Commissioners to

prevent undesirable elements congregating round it. The *Morning Chronicle* called it a 'rendezvous for blackguards and chimney-sweepers'. Local legend has it that a mob helped tear it down, in a vain hunt for treasure rumoured to have been buried beneath it. Nearby stood a pillory, which witnessed some brutal stonings; John Waller, charged with perjury, died here in 1732.

The column had been purchased by the architect James Paine and was taken to Sayes Court in Addlestone, Surrey, where it lay neglected until 1822. Its stones were then re-erected, surmounted by a ducal coronet, on the green at Weybridge, as a memorial to the late Frederica, Duchess of York (sister-in-law to George IV); she had died in nearby Oatlands two years before. The dial stone was used as a mounting block by the Whip inn on the green; it is now outside Elmbridge Museum, Weybridge.

Various attempts were made from 1907 to return the column to its rightful position, but Weybridge refused to give it up. In the 1980s an appeal led by David Bieda was launched to raise £50,000 for a replica. A five-year campaign by the Seven Dials Monument Charity (now Seven Dials Trust) was eventually successful, although the replica cost four times as much. The Portland stone column, with its six dials painted blue, is based on the original designed of 1693-94 by Edward

Pierce, then England's leading stonemason, who worked with Wren. Pierce's drawings were kept in the British Museum, allowing architect A D 'Red' Mason to produce an exact copy. It was erected by trainee masons working for Whitfield Partners, who raised and lowered all the stones by hand over a two-and-a-half month period. The 28-ton monument sits on top of an unseen giant concrete stool above the main sewer and other services.

The new pillar was unveiled in June 1989 by Queen Beatrix of the Netherlands, as part of the Anglo-Dutch celebrations to mark the tercentenary of the accession of William and Mary to the English throne. If you cross the road carefully, you can see that in a circular ring set into the steps around the base of the column are listed its many benefactors, including the architectural historian Sir John Summerson, the opera singer Janet Baker and the Comyn Ching Company (p 41).

It has been suggested that Seven Dials was used by Hogarth as the setting for his picture *Gin Lane*, though authorities disagree (see also Dyott Street, p 60). To cope with the demands of immigration, flimsy wooden buildings were erected in every available space in courtyards behind the brick-built houses. They were overcrowded and inadequately drained. *Sketches by Boz* described the people of the area in the 1830s as 'dirty men, filthy women, squalid children' and it is possibly

9 *"The Morning Toilet"* Illustrated London News, 5 Sep 1874. Beautifying animals before selling them in the West End

the slum named 'Tom-All-Alone's' in *Bleak House*. Dickens, as a small boy, had always been 'supremely happy' if taken for a walk around 'the Dials', at once repelled by its poverty and attracted by its vibrancy. His biographer John Forster has Dickens exclaim 'What wild visions of prodigies of wickedness, want and beggary arose in my mind out of that place!' Newspaper reports in the 1840s talk of the streets and pavements swarming with pigs, poultry and ragged children, and windows patched with rags and paper. In the mid-19th century the district was frequented by sellers of various commodities: cats and dogs; old boots and old clothes; and birds and birdcages. There was a Sunday morning bird market, and on the 1861 census several residents of Great St Andrew Street were involved in the bird trade [9]. Itinerant workers, attracted by the nearby fruit and vegetable market in Covent Garden, could make use of the many rather unsavoury lodging houses [10]. One, at what is now Nos.5-11 Shorts Gardens (the street, p 46, to the right of the Crown), was Tom Farmer's, but better known as 'The Kip', where until the end of the 19th century residents slept on a rope (sitting down leaning on a rope which was

untied at dawn). Troublesome customers were thrown out and tied to a barrow to await a policeman, who would wheel them to Bow Street police station. It remained a lodging house until well into the 20th century.

The Crown was only one of several elaborately decorated gin palaces facing Victorian Seven Dials. The next corner clockwise was occupied by another called the Bunch of Grapes, in memory of which the tiled façade of **Seven Dials House**, its refurbished successor, is pleasingly adorned with grape motifs. Note its octagonal cupola. On the Cambridge Theatre site (p 43) a third pub, the Temple Arms, stood until the 1870s, when it was converted by the St Giles Christian Mission (p 55) into a coffee tavern; this doubled as the mission's 'Seven Dials Station', presided over by a redoubtable Miss Ling. Just back from the corner where now stands the Mountbatten Hotel, there was yet another hostelry known as the King Henry the Eighth. It fell down in May 1811, killing or severely injuring several people, but was rebuilt and closed in the late Victorian period.

Seven Dials was also long the haunt of chapbook vendors and publishers. In the early 19th century there were several such publishing firms in Great St Andrew Street, including that of Johnny Pitts (d.1844). As well as ballad printing, Pitts ran the well-known toy shop mentioned above. Some people believed that Pitts was

actually a female, who had begun work as a 'bumboat' woman on the Thames. As a printer, he or she was the arch-rival of Seven Dials' most famous and successful chapbook seller, James 'Jemmy' Catnach (1792-1841). He founded his business in 1813 at Nos.2 & 3 Monmouth Court, which once lay off the north side of Little Earl Street (now Earlham Street) to our right. Catnach was born the son of an impoverished printer in Alnwick, Northumberland and took to selling broadsheets, but on an unprecedented scale. He paid writers, usually anonymous, a shilling for the words, which were then normally set to a well-known tune. The lyric was typeset, illustrated with a little woodcut, in a vigorous if crude design, on the cheapest paper available. They were then sold in the streets, usually for a penny, by 'patterers', who would perform as well as sell their wares. Catnach paid his employees in the pennies that he took, and reputedly made weekly trips to the Bank of England in a hackney coach with sacks of coins. His sheets capitalised on the sensational, and were sometimes hoaxes. In 1818 a print suggesting a Mr Pizzey of Clare Market made his sausages from human flesh caused a riot. Crime was his best-selling subject. He commissioned 'last dying confessions' to be sold under the drop at public executions, causing disappointment if there was a last-minute reprieve. Although crude and opportunistic,

10 "Low lodging house, St Giles's", newspaper illustration, 1872, probably from *The Graphic*

the broadsheets played a major role in developing a literate public. Reacting to the events and fashions of the moment, Catnach made broadsheets the popular chronicles of the times. In 1839 he retired to South Mimms, but collapsed and died of jaundice on a visit to his shop in Monmouth Court two years later. The business was taken over by his sister Ann Ryle and was still running in the 1850s, when Henry Mayhew chronicled the life of the patterers among a host of other street sellers in his *London Labour and the London Poor*.

There was much clearance in the Seven Dials area from 1840 through to the 1880s, but several battered earlier terrace houses survived. In the mid-19th century, conveniently situated public toilets started to appear, such as the octagonal and spacious WC erected here in 1858. By the time Shaftesbury Avenue was laid out, Seven Dials was on its way to becoming a more wholesome, if shabby, working-class area. After Covent Garden Market closed, Seven Dials was declared a Housing Action Area in 1977; and over the next seven years every vacant residential property was put back into use, and major private housing schemes and new businesses were

encouraged. In recent years the area has become very fashionable, with boutiques, craft shops, restaurants and wine bars, promoted as Covent Garden's 'hidden village'.

The buildings on the corners opposite the Crown were erected in the late 1980s in a post-modern idiom, with their striped brickwork and glass drum. **Fielding Court**, on the right, replaced a petrol station. The musician and music producer Dave Stewart, of Eurythmics fame, was an early resident, on the top floor. The building on the left is by Terry Farrell, and houses Vidal Sassoon's hairdressing salon. Cross to the pavement in front of it, stopping to look at the bollards which bear the motif of a deer with an arrow in its side. This is the old emblem of St Giles, referring to his legend as a friend to animals.

Leave the mini-circus and continue down the southern part of **MONMOUTH STREET**. Until 1938 this was Little St Andrew Street. Born at No.1, on the site of Fielding Court, was the artist and designer Robert Anning Bell RA (1863-1933). He was to design the façade of the Horniman Museum and mosaics at the Palace of Westminster. After WWI he became professor of design at the Royal College of Art. No.1 became a 'medical hall' by 1870, when its chemist owner was prosecuted for 'habitual carelessness' in preparing medicines for the poor. His untrained successor was also prosecuted

in 1878 for signing death certificates in the name of a doctor.

In 1924 Little St Andrew Street was one of the first roads in London to be made one-way, to ease congestion around Covent Garden market. The Victorian urinal in the roadway at Seven Dials was removed. The traffic flow was from south to north, changed to its current direction of north to south in 1935.

There is a profusion of colourful window-boxes hereabouts, the result of a millennial community project to re-create the 'Hanging Gardens of Seven Dials', as Victorians called the earlier efforts of resilient locals to enliven their drab environment through 'window horticulture'.

On the right at No.40 is the **Two Brewers**. There has been a pub of that name here since the early 18th century. The present building retains the original plan but was rebuilt in the 19th century and refaced in tiles in the 1930s. Cross over to the pub. Two doors along, **No.44,** which dates from the 1790s, formerly housed Pollock's Toy Museum and shop, founded by Marguerite Fawdrey (1912-95) in 1954, after she purchased Benjamin Pollock's stock of English toy-theatre prints. It has been said that she pioneered the revival of the Covent Garden area, before she moved north to Fitzrovia in 1969.

Stay on this side of the street but look across to **Nos.53&55**, dating from c.1720 but refronted; these have interesting dormer

windows in the roof. **Nos.57&59** are taller houses with a modillion cornice in brick, and now house a music shop which retains a delicate *art nouveau* wrought-iron screen in front of the door. This was made by the ironworkers Comyn Ching (p 41); it was once the main entrance to their large premises behind. **No.63** used to be No.20 Little St Andrew Street, which until the 1860s housed the White Swan public house. It had a large club room, where the masonic Lodge of Prudence and Peter was set up in 1740 and met until 1797. It is contemporary with **No.61**, which was built in 1699. **No.67** retains a painted sign on its brick surface, announcing that this was the shop of B Flegg, saddler and harness maker, established in 1847. In the 1970s No.67 housed the Anthropos Gallery, at the time 'the only European gallery devoted to Eskimo art'. It was set up by Satish Chander Kapoor, who had had a distinguished academic career as a professor of philosophy but had amassed a large collection of Inuit art while teaching in Canada. **Nos.73-75**, on the corner, form a sympathetic post-modern rebuilding of earlier houses.

Turn right into **TOWER STREET,** which took its name from a long-lost tavern. Laid out in the 17th century, Tower Street was home from 1688 to about 1701 of the highly fashionable flower painter Jacob Bogdani. In 1694 he painted flower decorations for Mary II's Looking-glass

Closet in the Water Gallery at Hampton Court. His patrons were leading aristocratic families, e.g. William Cavendish, 1st Duke of Devonshire at Chatsworth House.

Tower Street's status deteriorated later and it became one of the district's poorest streets, shown in black (the worst category) on Charles Booth's 1880s poverty map. Today, the street is much more prosperous, its east side (beyond the small street Tower Court, see later) being enlivened by **Beadworks**, 'the original London bead shop, founded 1967'. Before that, at **Nos.19-22**, is an early and ambitious example of a London Board School, dating from c.1874, and built in a Jacobean style, with a 5-storey bell-tower. Adorning the yellow stock-brick walls are carved stone plaques featuring national emblems and allegorical figures in praise of literacy. In the late 1980s, the building was converted into a silversmith's warehouse; it now houses Andrew Lloyd Webber's Really Useful Company.

The school has an important place in education history. During the 1890s, the school's manager Margaret Frere determined to find out why so many of the children there were underfed and badly clothed, by visiting their homes. Her work led to the establishment of the Charitable Children's Fund in 1899. She was subsequently co-opted onto the LCC Education Committee in 1907, and served on the Children's Care Subcommittee

from 1909 until it was disbanded in 1925. School care services lasted until 1970, when they merged with the school attendance service to form the education welfare service.

On the site of the school, former No.19 was the first business address from 1822 of the printer and once-famous pornographer William Dugdale (1800-1868). Opposite, at **Nos.4-10**, is a solid, red-brick Victorian commercial building, now converted into flats, bearing two stone plaques. The first suggests, implausibly and misleadingly, that this was once a charity school; the second reveals the truth: that the block was built in 1878 as a printing works for one John Strangeway. Our researches have revealed that Mrs Palmer's Charity was the ground landlord of the property, and that its rents originally helped endow charity schools in the neighbouring parish of St Andrew, Holborn. Next door is a 1980s block, built for the former GLC, and converted to house the **Actors' Centre** originally founded in 1978 by a group of actors including Sheila Hancock and Clive Swift. Its early home was at the YMCA in Tottenham Court Road; in 1995 it relocated to the present building which was opened by Sir Anthony Hopkins. Its patrons have included Lord Olivier, Sir Alec Guinness, Sir Alan Bates, and now Julie Walters. The Centre is the UK's foremost resource for actors, comprising five rehearsal studios, and holding at least

1700 workshops and classes each year. The adjoining **Tristan Bates Theatre** is named in memory of Alan Bates' son, a promising actor who died in 1990 aged 19; the theatre hosts contemporary productions.

Now turn right into the northern portion of **TOWER COURT**. Nos.5-8 are late-19th-century houses, with shop windows altered for domestic use, as is No.10 beyond the rear of the Two Brewers (p 38) which intervenes. Tower Court was once known as Lumber Court, in turn derived from an earlier Lombards Court. Victorian Lumber Court housed a colony of butchers, served by a Butchers Arms pub. In the late 19th century, the Booth poverty survey notes the presence of 'thief prostitutes' in Lumber Court and Tower Street.

We turn left into **EARLHAM STREET** alongside another bead shop, which was until 2002 the shop of A S Portwine & Son, a family firm of butchers that had been in Seven Dials since at least 1790 (see the preserved roofline inscription). This portion of Earlham Street was called Little Earl Street until 1938. From Monday to Saturday there is a bustling street market here, appealing to those with an interest in artisan crafts – a pale reflection, however, of the deafeningly noisy, lamp-lit meat market held on Saturday evenings a century ago. These days, there are no pubs on this stretch of Earlham Street, but we know of three in 19th-century Little Earl

Street: the Rose & Three Tuns, the Duke of Newcastle and, not to be confused with a namesake at Seven Dials (p 43), the Grapes. Fashion shops have recently begun to invade the street. Another family firm that ceased to exist in the early 21st century was F W Collins & Sons, the ironmonger's at **No.14,** which was founded in 1837. Twenty years later, the first Fred Collins invented 'Elastic Glue' the advertisement for which has been retained by the shop's latest occupants, **The Vintage Showroom,** selling vintage menswear. The third Fred Collins, who died in 1989, was actively involved in opposing the destruction of the Covent Garden area. For three decades from 1956, **No.10** was the base of the publisher Max Reinhardt, who acquired and expanded the Bodley Head; he persuaded J B Priestley and Graham Greene to join his board of directors. Syd Barrett of Pink Floyd fame lived at the former No.2, where he wrote material for his own and the group's first albums.

Turn left at Shaftesbury Avenue past the **Marquis of Granby** (built in 1886 by Wylson and Long), and left again along **WEST STREET** (the western boundary of the parish of St Giles). This narrow street originally formed, with St Martin's Lane and Hog Lane (p 27), part of the main road leading north from Whitehall. Only the eastern side of the street is in Camden, but this is the more historic. Clients of the two smart restaurants on the Westminster side of the street and of the chi-chi handbag showroom at **Nos.36-38** would doubtless be horrified to learn that late-Victorian West Street was described in Charles Booth's notebooks as 'a street of pickpockets, burglars, pimps and prostitutes'. At **No.24** is the former West Street Chapel, which was originally built in 1700 as a place of worship for Huguenots and named La Pyramide de la Tremblade, probably after a village near Rochefort in western France. It was leased from 1743 to 1791 by John Wesley, the founder of Methodism: he and George Whitefield both preached there regularly, while Wesley's sister Emily lived in the chapel-house. The blue plaque erected by the World Methodist History Society in 1980 replaced a bronze tablet stolen some years before. The chapel façade was rebuilt in the early 19th century, by which time the building served as an Anglican chapel-of-ease, with a school for 200 poor children. In 1888 the chapel was acquired by the parish through public subscription, and as All Saints Church served the poor of St Giles with free seating for 1,100; it also served as a base for the Anglican Seven Dials Mission. Secular uses followed in the 20th century: in the 1920s, the ground and first floors were let for ballet instruction under Margaret Craske, and later Anna Stafford Northcote (Severenska). In the 1940s, the Tiller Girls rehearsed there. In the late 1980s, after years as a warehouse, the building was occupied by the London School of Classical Dance, where Margot Fonteyn and Michael Soames are said to have also rehearsed. A media company has now moved in.

We next come to a pair of theatres by the architect W G R Sprague. A former public house, the Fishmongers' Arms, gave way to the **Ambassadors Theatre**, built in 1913. It staged plays and musical revues in repertory, continuing to entertain during WWII. Its programmes read like a *Who's Who* of 20th-century theatre, featuring Hermione Gingold, Peter Ustinov and Max Adrian, to name but a few. The theatre's main claim to fame is Agatha Christie's record-breaking *The Mousetrap*, which opened on 25 November 1952, transferring to the St Martin's Theatre next door on 25 March 1974 and still running in 2011. During the 1990s, the Ambassadors staged productions of the 'Royal Court Upstairs' while the Royal Court's Sloane Square premises were being rebuilt.

The start of WWI delayed construction of the **St Martin's Theatre**. Built as a companion to the Ambassadors, it is, however, more elaborate, with Ionic columns. Like its neighbour, it has lost many of the original vases and cartouches that once adorned the parapets. The theatre opened under C B Cochrane's direction on 23 November 1916, with *Houp La!*, a 'comedy of music'. Other productions have included three plays by

John Galsworthy and Arnold Ridley's *Ghost Train*, and of course *The Mousetrap*. Close to the Upper Circle entrance, a blue plaque commemorates 50 years of performances of *The Mousetrap*.

Beyond the St Martin's, and around the corner, **No.8** is wedge-shaped, with a plain Dutch-style gable and an early shop front (though not as early as the surely facetious plaque inscribed *Built 1692* would suggest). High on the next building is a 1691 St Giles-in-the-Fields parish boundary mark, incorporating crossed ragged staffs, deriving perhaps from Alicia Dudley's association with Warwickshire (coat of arms: the bear and ragged staff).

On the corner is **Nos.2-6**, built as Motograph House in 1913, when it was the HQ of the Motograph Film Company specialising in features and documentaries. The TV pioneer John Logie Baird worked from the upper floor of Motograph House from 1926 to 1928. His 2TV 250-watt station was licensed in August 1926 and he began transmitting experimentally from here that autumn, 3 years before his work with the BBC. Here he demonstrated noctovision (an apparatus for seeing in the dark by invisible rays) and also phonovision (televising by gramophone – one needle for sound, another for picture). Now Guild House, it houses the HQ of the actors' trade union **Equity**. It bears a plaque celebrating the centenary of the cinema in 1997 and, specifically, the

contribution of Sir Alec Guinness.

Guild House abuts Upper St Martin's Lane, which lies in Westminster. Cross it diagonally to the left to enter **SHELTON STREET**, the south side of which is also in Westminster. On that corner once stood the Cock and Pye tavern, which lent its name to the eponymous Fields that began to be built on in the 1690s. Thereafter the pub is not mentioned in the records. On the line of Shelton Street was a medieval country footpath alongside the Cock and Pye Fields, or the Marshland as they were then known. By 1650, when the Marshland was surveyed by Parliament, there were 'three tenements of timber and Flemish wall, with thatched roof' on the north side of the footpath, adjoining a one-roomed conduit. More building spread along the lane in the 1670s, when St Giles village rapidly developed with the influx of immigrants after the Great Fire. It was known as Castle Street until 1938, when it was renamed after William Shelton, a St Giles vestryman at the time of the Great Plague, which hit St Giles severely. Shelton bequeathed enough money in 1672 to clothe aged parish paupers every year and to educate 50 children of the poorest sort in a school, now closed, which he founded in Parker Street (p 74).

House numbers here have changed several times. The original numbering of Castle Street was consecutive but was amended in 1874 so that the St Giles side

had even numbers commencing at the far, east end. In 1938 the numbering of renamed Shelton Street was reversed, the buildings being given odd numbers running from this west end.

In the early 19th century almost all the business premises at this west end of the street housed carpenters and furniture shops. These old shop fronts have now been renovated. Among them was a long-established firm of metalworkers called Comyn Ching, which traced its history back to Joseph Gostling, ironmonger of Castle Street in 1723. The firm, British despite the Chinese-sounding name, expanded by the mid-20th century to cover **Nos.15-21** and the land behind, up to Monmouth Street and Mercer Street, on whose corner they once had a forge. Theirs was a very successful business which included fitting out the Titanic and other luxury liners, as well as many public buildings. They produced ironmongery for Royal Parks and pioneered gas lighting in London, for example installing the gas-lamp columns around Buckingham Palace in the 1830s. The company moved in 1979 to Golden Lane (Finsbury) but for a decade from 1985 had an architectural ironmongery showroom here.

On your left, between No.13 and No.17, is an opening into **Ching Court**, alternatively known as the Comyn Ching Triangle. It is a gated private place but usually open to the public during the day. A delightful, calm, triangular space, sloping from the north, it is framed at the three corners by modern infill, some details of which give a slightly oriental feel, but also recall the style of Charles Rennie Mackintosh. It was created in 1982-88 by Terry Farrell & Co. and named after the firm that had occupied much of the site. There are seven luxury flats included in the development, with balconies and roof terraces. Farrell tactfully consolidated the original work, supplied a taller new building in inoffensive pastiche to each of the three corners, and opened up the interior of the block for public use. It is unclear what the space is for, except perhaps to relax on the wooden bench carved in a Chinese style and shaded by palms. The corners of the Court have convex shapes, echoed in the steps to the several back entrances to the houses along Monmouth Street. On the right the space reveals the backs of late-17th-century buildings in Mercer Street. Two have pantiled loft workshops, possibly for Huguenot weavers who had escaped from France.

Return to Shelton Street and admire the restored late-18th-century shop fronts on **Nos.17&19**, which are Grade II★ Listed and bear little lion heads. In the 1950s and 1960s many of these shops housed hot-dog stalls, stocked up by men, generally Italians, before plying their trade around the West End. That chronicler of London life, Geoffrey Fletcher, drew the scene on a typical Sunday afternoon.

At the corner with Mercer Street, pause and look ahead along Shelton Street to the backs of Victorian warehouses that used to service Covent Garden market (fruit and vegetable merchants, box and basket makers). They cover the site of No.38 Castle Street which in the 1870s contained the wholesale piano warehouse of F Hund & Sons, a company awarded a silver medal at the Great Exhibition for its iron cottage pianos, direct from Stuttgart. The tall, cavernous buildings beyond, replete with hoists, were once part of the Woodyard Brewery.

Sometime during the 17th century, a timber yard on the Westminster side of Castle Street was taken over by John Shackly as a cooperage. On his death in 1722 his son carried on the business as a cooper and small brewer. In 1739 William Gyfford assumed control, taking his brother Joseph into partnership and developing a large brewery which they named Woodyard. Harvey Christian Combe (Lord Mayor, 1799-1800) took over the Woodyard in 1787 with his brother-in-law Joseph Delafield and other partners, and the business became known as Combe's brewery. In the 1840s Delafield's son Edward, a junior partner, frittered away £100,000 on the Theatre Royal, Drury Lane and a certain Belgian singer. Combe amalgamated with Watney & Reid in 1898 and the Woodyard Brewery closed in 1905, when production moved to Mortlake. The buildings on either side were connected from the 1860s by high-level cast-iron bridges. Beneath the main building, a series of tunnels was made so that beer barrels could be transported to local pubs without fear of theft.

Across the road to our right there is a small wall plaque over the corner doorway, showing a crowned woman. This 'demi-virgin' is the sign of the Mercers' Company, who owned the ground stretching to Long Acre to our right (all in Westminster) since at least 1391, and who gave their name to **MERCER STREET**. To our left the cobbled stretch (in Camden) was known until 1938 as Little White Lion Street. No.12 was the childhood home of Charles Boon (1877-1943), the founder of the romantic fiction publishers Mills & Boon. Its site now lies under the theatre building which takes up the whole of the east side.

Cross over and walk up that side, to get a good view back to a group of late-17th-century dwelling houses at **Nos.21–27**, with small wooden entrances and whose attic windows and pantiled roofs we noted in Ching Court. No.23 was converted in the late 19th century into a warehouse, with a symmetrical gabled frontage. The others have window frames flush to the brickwork, in central London a tell-tale sign of building work before the Building Acts of 1707 and 1709. As in

Monmouth Street and Shelton Street, the house numbers are, since renovation, very prominently displayed on painted wooden blocks. Up until the 1990s Comyn Ching held most of these properties.

As you reach Seven Dials, look carefully up the wall of the theatre to your right: behind the Borough of Holborn street-name plate you can just make out the street's original name, Little White Lion Street, carved in stone.

We are now at the entrance to the **Cambridge Theatre**. Clean-lined and airy, it was designed in 1930 by Wimperis, Simpson and Guthrie with an eye to modernity. Serge Chermayeff was involved in the design (he later worked on the De La Warr Pavilion in Bexhill, and on Gilbey's headquarters in Camden Town), and the auditorium has concealed lighting, an early example of progressive German ideas. The Cambridge originally alternated theatre with opera, ballet and film. In the 1960s 24-year-old Albert Finney scored a hit here in Keith Waterhouse's *Billy Liar*. The National Theatre's 1970 season starred Laurence Olivier as Shylock in Jonathan Miller's *Merchant of Venice*. More recently there has been a succession of hit musicals. The theatre holds nearly 1300 seats. The decor is *art deco*. Take a quick look at the very fine foyer, which includes, on the wall immediately beneath the dome, a frieze by Carl Toms depicting naked athletes.

The theatre stands at the entrance to

EARLHAM STREET, the section east of Seven Dials known until 1938 as Great Earl Street. The original name of Earl Street was probably chosen to give a cachet to the address; the prefix was added to distinguish it from other streets similarly named. In the 18th century this was home to John Turmeau (bap.1756), a painter who specialised in the production of pictures created with human hair and who exhibited two landscapes made of hair at the Free Society of Artists in 1772. His son John (1776-1846) was to achieve some fame as a miniaturist. In the 19th century trade here was mainly in second-hand goods, and street directories rarely bothered to record the street. Earlham Street achieved notoriety in 2011, when the lobby group Republic applied to hold a 'Not the Royal Wedding' street party; the request was turned down by Camden Council after receiving objections from Shaftesbury plc, the locality's major property owner.

On the opposite corner was one of the pubs facing Seven Dials. This was the Bunch of Grapes, whose replacement building we passed earlier. It was licensed as a pub until 1919. During the 1920s it was home to a number of clubs that were prosecuted in turn for selling alcohol without a licence. In September 1927 another club successfully applied to use the premises, claiming it was for theatrical and artistic people who would present no

trouble. This was the Cave of Harmony, founded in Charlotte Street (Fitzrovia) a few years before. Its owners were a young Elsa Lanchester (later famous in films as the Bride of Frankenstein) and her partner, Harold Scott. At the club they performed one-act plays and sang cabaret songs. The Cave of Harmony was a popular meeting place for London intellectuals, including H G Wells, Aldous Huxley and Evelyn Waugh, but Elsa closed it down in late 1928 after she took up with Charles Laughton. Agatha Christie was no doubt influenced by the area's reputation for questionable clubs when she wrote *The Seven Dials Mystery*, published in 1929.

Proceed along Earlham Street. Past the Cambridge Theatre, at **Nos.36–38**, are two early-19th-century shops. The doorways have geometric fanlights, shutters and panelled doors. Beside **No.40** is a large wooden goods entrance, which leads down into a yard containing the **TSQ health spa and food emporium**, in converted warehouses that give onto Shelton Street behind. In the 18th century there were two yards here full of tenements, Duke's Court and Earl's Court, but these were removed during the Regency as Combe's Brewery expanded.

Nos.42-46 is a large building, once called Seven Dials Warehouse. Note the big-cat insignia above its black-painted entrance, which was the insignia of the paper merchants Lepard & Smith, based here from the 1920s. It now hosts a number of organisations including the Covent Garden Community Association's Seven Dials Club, founded in 1973. By the side of No.46 there was once a turning that joined up with Shelton Street: Sweep's Alley, named after the soot house that stood along it in 1760. It was stopped up after Combe and Delafield bought it in 1799. They built a warehouse on the site that is now home to **Belgo Centraal**, a Belgian-inspired restaurant and beer hall, which makes full use of the cavernous cellars. If the gates of Belgo Centraal are open, peer down into the cellars below and whet your appetite, observing the huge display of cooked foods being prepared in the kitchen. Another eating place making use of former warehouse premises is the **Detroit** bar, back across the road at No.35. Throughout the 1970s and 1980s No.35 was part of the art gallery of the picture-framing firm of Blackman Harvey. At that time there were a number of galleries in the street.

Opposite us is the 250-seat **Donmar Warehouse** theatre, in the same building as **Thomas Neals** shopping arcade. (The 1990s sign for the latter, surmounted by an enormous hoist, shows *Thomas Neal's*, but the apostrophe has now been jettisoned.) The theatre is housed in what was the vat room and hop warehouse for Combe's brewery. At the end of the 1920s the premises became a colour film laboratory of the Raycol British Corporation, whose two-colour additive system had fallen out of favour by 1933. The building (until 1938, No.10 Great Earl Street) was then used as a banana-ripening depot for Covent Garden Market. The Donmar gets its unusual name from Donald Albery, impresario, and his friend the ballerina Margot Fonteyn. They purchased the former warehouse in 1961 to convert it into a private rehearsal studio for the London Festival Ballet. From 1977 until 1981 the Royal Shakespeare Company made the Donmar its main London home, and during the 1980s the theatre became a base for Britain's most innovative touring companies. The Donmar was redeveloped into its present form in the early 1990s when Sam Mendes became Artistic Director, a post he retained until 2002 when Michael Grandage took over.

At **No.41** was the Freedom Brewing Company, set up in 1995, when it was the UK's only micro brewery producing lager. It moved out in 2004 to Staffordshire in order to expand its production. At the far corner of the street is **No.43**, an 1870s former warehouse. With other warehouses in Neal Street and Shelton Street, the building was a focus for the renewal of the Covent Garden area. In the 1970s, when wholesale redevelopment seemed likely, it fulfilled a much needed role as rented accommodation for local community groups, shops, galleries and studios. From May 1967 the ground floor housed the British Crafts Centre, which hosted many exhibitions until it moved out in the mid-1990s to Percy Street, Fitzrovia, having been renamed Contemporary Applied Arts.

No.43 is now yet another clothes store, as is the building on the opposite corner of Earlham Street. Inside the latter the exposed iron columns of the old Woodyard brewery building are much in evidence. Before WWII this housed the stores of the International Correspondence Schools (ICS), founded in the US in 1890, one of the first internationally recognised schools for distance learning, whose British headquarters were in Kingsway (p 89). In the early 1980s, the building was taken over by the Seven Dials Gallery, owned by Christina Smith, a founder of the Covent Garden Community Association and by then a local entrepreneur.

We are now in a cobbled pedestrianised area, always bustling with people. This is at the foot of the Camden section of Neal Street, with its short Westminster section to our right leading down to Covent Garden proper. The pub here is the **Crown & Anchor**, bearing a date 1904, although there has been a tavern of that name on this site from at least 1760. It was then much smaller, and throughout the 19th century stood next to a bakery on the corner with **SHELTON STREET**. This leads off to the east. Proceed along it a short way. Adjoining the pub is a Dutch-style warehouse with prominent taking-in doors, and past Nottingham Court (p 47) a smaller Victorian warehouse at **No.41**. After WWII both were used as stores by Odhams Press, which was based on the whole block opposite (in Westminster) until 1969, when it was closed down by Robert Maxwell. The block was subsequently redeveloped as shops and residential flats, bisected by a passage called Odhams Walk. On the Camden side, beyond No.41 is a large 3-storey mixed development, extending round the corner into Endell Street (p 48), and incorporating roof gardens. It was designed by the GLC architect F B Pooley and built in the early 1980s. Most of the ground floor was then used by the London Ecology Centre, based here for a decade before its move to Clerkenwell, and the environmental charity Common Ground. This was founded here in 1982 by Sue Clifford and Angela King, aiming to promote "local distinctivenes" (a phrase they coined). It has done this through tree dressing, Apple Days, nature guides and parish maps celebrating the value of the ordinary and the everyday in people's lives. It moved to Shaftesbury, Dorset in the mid-1990s, when an application to open a huge restaurant on the site was turned down as detrimental to the small-scale nature of the businesses in the area, a decision upheld on appeal.

Return to the Crown & Anchor and turn right up **NEAL STREET**. In medieval times this was a footpath along the edge of the Marshland. It was one of the first streets to be developed by Thomas Neale, who called it King Street, and it was known as such until 1877, when it was renamed to avoid confusion with the King Street in nearby Covent Garden. The street commanded higher rents than those of the smaller streets off Seven Dials. Strype in 1720 called it 'a very large and handsome Place with good houses'. By the 19th century it was full of shops and businesses, this southern end closely associated right up to the 1970s with the nearby fruit and vegetable market. In 1898 Booth noted a concentration of costermongers, and berated the Vestry for the state of this and other streets nearby for the mess of crushed fruit and pea pods, packing cases and loose straw, not swept away.

Neal Street became traffic-free in 1984, when it was planted with trees and wooden bollards. It has since become a mecca for lovers of shoes and fashion with several exclusive labels and boutiques. On the right, Nos.26-32 date from 1903, built speculatively and originally used as empty-box warehouses for Covent Garden Market. **Nos.26&28** became the Neal Street Restaurant, which opened in No.26 in 1971, the brainchild of the designer Terence Conran. His design studios were then next door in No.28, which was bought in 1982 by Christina Smith, Conran's former secretary. The year before, that champion of Italian cuisine and purveyor

(by royal warrant) of truffles, Antonio Carluccio, became the manager of the restaurant, and in 1989 its owner. At the time he was Conran's brother-in-law. The celebrity chef Jamie Oliver began his professional career under Carluccio at the Neal Street Restaurant, which closed in 2008. **No.32** was the home and office of the Modernist architect HT ('Jim') Cadbury-Brown (1913-2009). He was here from the mid-1960s until 1982. His most prominent building is the Royal College of Art, close to the Royal Albert Hall.

Whilst remodelled externally, Nos.27-37, on the opposite side, form part of the late-17th-century development of Seven Dials. At **No.31** is **Food For Thought**, a vegetarian restaurant established here in 1974 and family-run since 1977. It has a small late-18th-century fanlight above the side door. **No.33** was once No.43 King Street. Here from 1804 until 1831 the young Edward John Dent lodged with his cousin Richard Rippon, a watchmaker, whose trade he learned. Dent's own company was to become one of the most famous clockmakers in the world, installing the clocks at the Palace of Westminster (notably Big Ben) and the clocks at King's Cross and St Pancras stations. In the 20th century No.33 was until the early 1980s one of the premises of the barrow-making firm of Ellen Keeley (see below), and in 1987 became home to Wayne Hemingway's Red or

Dead fashion business, where one could purchase high-heeled Dr Martens boots. Hemingway later opened a flagship store a short way along at Nos.41-43.

Turn left into **SHORTS GARDENS**. On a 1691 plan of Seven Dials the street between King Street and Seven Dials is shown as Church Street, since it was to lead to a church. This was never built and the street was developed as Queen Street; it was known as such until 1906 when it was renamed as a continuation of the road to the east. It was at first inhabited by gentlemen. In the 1790s the instrumentalist, singer and conductor Benjamin Jacob (1778-1829) was living at No.13 Queen Street and No.17 housed John Davy the printer, before his move to Long Acre in 1820. But by mid-Victorian times the street had gained an unenviable reputation. It was described in 1865 as follows: 'here are principally thieves' kitchens, and lodging houses, with here and there a low villainous looking public house, one or two rag, bone and metal warehouses, and a low gambling house known as a Dolly shop'. We have already mentioned the Kip (p 34). Charles Booth, in 1898, called the street 'very rough' and the state of some of its tenements 'about as bad as it can be'.

All rather different today. Across the road, an amusing water clock is attached to **No.21**, formerly the Wholefood Warehouse. The clock was placed here in 1982 by Hunkin and Plant, aquatic horologists. It is, sadly, no longer working; when it was, the minutes were counted by the rising water level in the vertical tube. On the hour, water was released to rise through various containers, causing watering cans to water, flowers to open and bells to chime. Turn briefly (left) into roofed-over **Cucumber Alley**, masquerading as an official Camden street. The former alleyway here was called thus on Rocque's map of 1745, but later came to be known as Neal's Passage, until obliterated by warehouses in the 1870s. In the filthy cellar of former No.1 Neal's Passage (alternatively No.15 Great Earl Street) the hanged body of a six-year-old child, Richard Jeffery, was found in 1866; his father was convicted of his murder.

Cucumber Alley is part of a large galleria of shops called **Thomas Neals** that is housed in a yet another former banana warehouse, whose iron columns have been retained. They support a shallow brick vault in the arcade, which gives onto a triangular top-lit space on two floors. Suspended here is an intriguing sculptural light fitting featuring outsize light bulbs. The development was undertaken by architects RHWL (Renton Howard Wood Levin Partnership), who improved a whole section of the conservation area – as far as Seven Dials House (p 36), overlooking the column. After work began in 1989, Saxon remains were uncovered, dating from the mid-8th century, when the centre of inhabited London lay to the west of the City, around the Strand and Aldwych ('old port'). A four-month dig found traces of wattle-and-daub houses and evidence of iron-working on the site. This was the northernmost evidence yet of Saxon London (Lundenwic).

Go back out into Shorts Gardens s. Cross the road diagonally to your left, to admire the huge British cheeses in the window of **Neal's Yard Dairy** at No.17. Begun in Neal's Yard itself in 1979, as yet another project of Nicholas Saunders, the business moved here in 1992 and now also has premises by Borough Market. It transports cheeses across the globe. Now turn and walk past the southern entrance to Neal's Yard; a short way up on the right-hand side is the original independent skate-board shop, **Slam City Skates**. This opened in 1988 and until 2007 also housed Rough Trade records; its basement ceiling was covered in the signatures of visiting bands. On the near corner with Neal Street, from 1751 until the late Victorian period, stood a pub with the enigmatic name the Two Spies, possibly a Biblical allusion to an Old Testament reference to two spies in the Book of Numbers, 13:23.

At this point you can regain your starting point by walking up the remaining stretch of Neal Street to Shaftesbury Avenue. Alternatively, continue the walk to explore Endell Street and its environs.

Route 2(b) Around Endell Street

From Neal Street walk east along a short stretch of **SHORTS GARDENS**, on either side of which were once the grounds of William Short, gardener of Gray's Inn, who in 1590 purchased land between Drury Lane and the Marshland, fields known as Newland. The Short family were prominent parishioners of St Giles' until Thomas Short sold the property around 1690. The street that developed was always rather poor, Strype in 1720 calling it 'of no great resort or thoroughfare'. In 1865, missionary George Hatton (see p 55) noted a colony of organ grinders here. In fact they were all living in the same house, No.13, where the 1861 census records 25 Italian 'street organ grinders'. Shorts Gardens remained primarily residential until the late 19th century, after which it contained numerous fruit warehouses until Covent Garden Market closed in 1974.

The building on the left-hand corner was the base in the 1960s and 1970 of the film director Michael Crosfield. In 1977 he decided to convert his film editing studio into a shop selling English copper. He had been married to the South African writer Noni Jabavu, who in 1961 became the first woman and black person to edit a literary magazine, the *New Strand*.

On the right-hand corner is **Nottingham House**, built in 1925 by the Society for Improving the Conditions of the Labouring Classes. It was opened as St Giles Buildings. By the entrance is a dedicatory plaque, unveiled by Princess Louise, Duchess of Argyll. The block was built over the site, among others, of a pub called the Horse & Groom, in Neal Street from at least 1760 until 1909 when its licence was not renewed. Walk a short way down the next opening on the right to see the back of the housing development, which was given a make-over in the late 1990s.

We are now in **NOTTINGHAM COURT**. It was laid out in 1710 and named after Daniel Finch (1647–1730), son of Heneage Finch (p 93), 2nd Earl of Nottingham and First Lord of the Treasury, a leading Tory and a distinguished resident of the parish. The carver and furniture designer Matthew Lock was based here in the 1740s, when he was one of the first to introduce the Rococo style to England. Nothing remains from the Court's early years, but at the far end are small late-19th-century terraced houses opening directly onto the paved passageway. Based at Nos.4-7 until 1983 was the noted book-bindery of W T Morrell.

Just behind Nottingham Court, until the early 1980s, was one of the premises of the market-barrow-making firm Ellen Keeley, established in Ireland in 1830. The Keeley family came to England at the time of the potato famine and made their homes in Nottingham Court. James Keeley invented and produced the costermonger's barrow, like a shop on wheels. He also developed the donkey barrow, once a familiar sight in London. Ellen Keeley also had premises in Neal Street (p 45) and Shorts Gardens. Shortly before Covent Garden Market moved out, the Keeley family diversified into hiring out their barrows as film props; Keeley Hire (now based in Hoddesdon) is a major prop hire company.

The Keeleys' Irish background is instructive, because Nottingham Court had a concentration of Irish people in the 19th century. For example in 1861, of its 337 inhabitants just over a quarter were born in Ireland and many others had Irish surnames. Most household heads were labourers or costermongers. An extensive fire in 1870 left many destitute; George Hatton successfully appealed for funds. Booth labelled the court black on his Poverty Map, his lowest category, and had not changed his mind by 1898. After revisiting it, he considered it the worst street in St Giles, full of 'Cockney Irish' who, while 'not immoral', would steal when they got the chance and 'bash in the heads of policemen'.

Back in Shorts Gardens, on the other side of the road, is another court, now refubished. Cross the road for a closer look, and note the four sculpted heads terminating the arch of **Matthews Yard** (shown as Mathews Yard on OS maps). This was one of the GLC's last developments, completed under the London Residuary Body in 1987 and built by the Elliott Group. For most of its existence the alleyway, with its poor tenements, had been known as King's Head Yard.

Continue and reach **ENDELL STREET**. The street was laid out after the 1842 Streets Improvement Act by Sir James Pennethorne, an architect now best known for his involvement in improvement schemes such as New Oxford Street. Endell Street was intended to aid traffic circulation to and from Waterloo Bridge. It followed the line of a street called Old Belton Street, first laid out in 1683; this was continued northwards by New Belton Street, linking up with Bowl Yard that led into Broad Street. Endell Street was renumbered in 1877.

Roughly where we are standing stretched the grounds of a mansion off Drury Lane that was leased by William Short in 1623 to Esmé Stuart, Duke of Lennox. The Duke's widow lived here until 1637. During the reign of Charles II, the property became the town house of Sir John Brownlow, Bt, of Belton House, Lincolnshire. After he ceased to live in the house around 1682, Brownlow let plots of land for building and Belton Street was formed. The *Victorian* street that replaced

it was named after James Endell Tyler, then Rector of St Giles. His parishioners insisted on naming the new street after him, but he modestly declined to let it be called by his surname, permitting only his relatively unknown middle name.

Now turn right and pass **No.37**. On this site was No.8 Old Belton Street, the birthplace of the watercolour artist 'Bird's Nest' Hunt (p 80). **Nos.33&35** had a long connection with cinema. It was the HQ of the British and Colonial Kinematograph Company film producers from 1911-1924, and then became a film warehouse. There was another film company, Poetic Films Ltd, here in the early 1960s when it also housed the Endell Street Preview Theatre.

The **Cross Keys** at No.31 has one of the handsomest pub fronts in the area, swathed in hanging plants. There has been a pub licensed here since at least 1760, but the present building dates from the mid-19th century and bears cherubs holding crossed keys, in stone. The interior walls are literally covered in prints and bric-a-brac, of which the landlord is an inveterate collector. On display are a brass privy, a stuffed fish, and a selection of framed signed letters by footballer David Beckham. In the 1860s the pub adjoined a Burton brewery to the south, damaged by the extensive fire in Nottingham Court in 1870.

At **No.27** is the 'little crystal shop', **Buddha on a Bicycle**, which was in Neal's Yard until 2008, as 'New World'. It houses

a room for therapies, yoga and meditation classes. The Campaign for Single Homeless People, CHAR, was based here in the 1970s. On the site of the shop next door (inexplicably now marked **No.17**) used to stand No.3 Old Belton Street. Its domed back room, 16 ft by 9 ft, was lined with blue-and-white Dutch tiles and contained a large tank that was known in the 19th century as Queen Anne's Bath **[11]**; by popular tradition she used to bathe here. Ratebooks show that it was certainly used as a bagnio in George II's reign when occupied by Daniel Hahn, otherwise Holme. The bath was fed by an iron-rich medicinal spring which, when the bath was exposed in 1845 on the construction of Endell Street, was claimed to have its origin in Highgate (although local legend put its source at the nearby Bowl tavern). A contemporary plea that the bath be made available to the poor fell on deaf ears. The premises were then taken over by an ironmonger, John King, who cut off the spring and used the bath for storage.

The modern buildings to the corner of Shelton Street replace houses that were totally destroyed in WWII bombing; other parts of St Giles largely escaped major damage. They are part of the mixed development of the early 1980s that we noted earlier (p 45). Opposite is a block of 4-storey brick terraced houses which date from the formation of Endell Street. Look across the road to them. **No.20**, on the

11 "Queen Anne's Bath", anonymous drawing, dated 1851 but drawn in 1844

corner of Betterton Street, was home in the 1880s to Nathaniel Westlake (1833-1921), a leading Gothic Revival designer who specialised in stained glass.

Facing it across Betterton Street at **No.22** is the Painted Glass Works, built in 1859-62 by Robert Jewell Withers for the firm of Lavers and Barraud, whose name is still visible at second-floor level. Westlake became a partner in the firm in 1869 and its sole proprietor in 1880. Pause to admire the façade. Withers was a church architect, and it shows in the building's Gothic windows and multi-coloured brickwork. Note the crow-stepped gables and corbelled-out dormer windows. The huge end window has stained glass by Brian Clarke, added when the building was successfully converted to offices in 1983 (earning a Civic Trust award).

Retrace your steps, looking across the road at the east side. Past the Glass Works is the Jacobean-style façade of a former hospital, at **No.24**, behind which is an ultra-modern building housing the Hospital Club. Designed for those in the creative industries, and launched in 2004, this was founded by Paul Allen (co-founder of Microsoft) and the musician

Dave Stewart (of Eurythmics fame). The building contains an HD TV studio, recording studio and gallery, as well as bars and a restaurant. The club prides itself on its philanthropic ventures, which have included the establishment of the Camden Arts and Business Consortium, a youth arts charity that has developed the careers of such performers as the vocalist Ms Dynamite.

The original building dates from 1849. It was erected for the British Lying-In Hospital, which moved here from nearby Betterton Street (p 79). Here, in 1873, the nurse Zepherina Smith (née Veitch) qualified as a midwife and devoted herself to improving the status and efficiency of midwifery. In 1881 she formed what became the Midwives' Institute (and the Royal College of Midwives in 1948). Another leading light in the profession, Dame Rosalind Paget, trained as a midwife at the hospital in 1885. She was to use her wide circle of social and professional connections to push successfully for the registration of midwives in 1902 and to raise money for the Institute. The jazz singer Evelyn Dove (1902-87) was born at the Lying-in Hospital, which closed in 1913.

St Paul's Hospital for Urological Diseases, begun in Red Lion Square, Holborn in 1897, transferred here in 1923, two years later than planned owing to financial problems. It became a postgraduate teaching hospital within the newly formed NHS in 1948, having merged with St Peter's, Westminster. St Paul's set up Britain's first artificial kidney unit, opened in 1959, and the first dialysis in the UK was performed there in 1961. The mathematician James Mercer (1883-1932) and the actress Diana Wynyard (1906-64) both died in the hospital, which closed in 1992, when its services moved to the Middlesex. The building then lay derelict before renovation as the Hospital Club, started in 1999.

Cross over to it and take time to admire the façade. The segmental pediment above the entrance bears two dates – 1897 (foundation) and 1921 (intended move here) – while along the side wall in Shorts Gardens one can see strapwork surrounds to the windows and two rather fierce-looking carved corbels.

Cross Shorts Gardens. The brick-faced council flats beyond, with prominent balconies, are called **Dudley Court** and were opened in 1983. Designed by Powell and Moya, this was one of the last major housing schemes in central London. Enclosing a communal courtyard, the flats are reminiscent of interwar LCC blocks.

The flats cover the site of the buildings of the parish workhouse, here from the 18th century. In 1725, the two parishes of St Giles-in-the-Fields and St George's Bloomsbury took over a site that stretched from Shorts Gardens to Vinegar Yard (see p 53), and over the years expanded the workhouse to incorporate adjacent properties, resulting in a confusing and poorly arranged complex. By 1777 the workhouse could accommodate over 500 people. St Giles and St George's retained special parish status after the passing of the 1834 Poor Law Amendment Act and continued to use the workhouse, to which was added in the mid-1840s a badly built infirmary on the north side of Vinegar Yard. In the course of building work a burial ground was uncovered, and able-bodied inmates were used to clear the bones of some 2,000 people. This caused an outcry, though it was nothing compared to that provoked by articles in the medical journal *The Lancet* in 1865, investigating conditions in London workhouses and their infirmaries. The report revealed a catalogue of appalling conditions in the workhouse, into which over 900 paupers were crammed, and called for the infirmary tto be condemned. Thirteen years later a new infirmary was erected alongside Shorts Gardens, with a square 5-storey tower, designed by William and Arthur Beresford Pite. The rest of the workhouse was then rebuilt in a grim and forbidding Gothic style and named Dudley House. Its male wing fronted Endell Street. In 1895, the purchase of a run-down court of houses in Shorts Gardens allowed a further infirmary block to be added at the east of the site, and in 1902 a new building, containing a receiving house for children and a nurses' home, was erected on Broad

Street to the north.

A now famous photograph of a prematurely aged pauper slumped in a doorway with another woman's baby in her arms, was taken on the steps of the workhouse in Shorts Gardens and published in Thomson and Smith's *Street Life in London* (1877). She was characterised as a 'St Giles crawler'. As the book made clear, these 'wrecks of humanity' were 'old women reduced by vice and poverty to that degree of wretchedness which destroys even the energy to beg. They have not the strength to struggle for bread, and prefer starvation to the activity which an ordinary mendicant must display. As a natural consequence, they cannot obtain money for a lodging or for food'.

The workhouse closed in June 1914, when the two parishes became part of the Holborn Poor Law Union. In May 1915 the premises were requisitioned by the War Office for use as a military hospital (see below). In the early 1930s the Post Office used two floors of the building, while the Ministry of Health had pathology laboratories on the upper floors. The building was damaged in WWII but afterwards became home to the Public Health Laboratory Service (until its move to Colindale) and then to the Supplies Division of the Ministry of Works until its demolition in 1978. The rest of the north side of Shorts Gardens, from the workhouse to Drury Lane and as far north as High Holborn, was, until 1905, a barrel-washing works (Broad Street Cooperage) owned by Combe & Co. of the Woodyard Brewery (p 42). Its huge site was auctioned in 1906.

Continue along Endell Street alongside Dudley Court, looking at the opposite side. On the corner, at **No.47** is **Rock and Sole Plaice**, which boasts that it has been in business since 1871, which would make it London's oldest fish-and-chip establishment. The shop itself has been rebuilt and on this spot in the 19th century was the London Medical Mission, which aimed to treat the poor and preach the gospel. It was founded in 1869 and merged with the London City Mission in 1950. It had a clinic in Nottingham Court (p 47) until the formation of the NHS.

Nos.53-59 form a group of late-18th-century buildings, modernised in the mid-19th century by the addition of stucco and heavy segmental pediments above the first-floor windows. The buildings survive from the west side of New Belton Street. **No.53**, in a then rather seedy Endell Street, was from 1945 the studio of the flamboyant photographer Angus McBean (1904-1990), very popular after WWII and throughout the 1950s. He focused on the world of theatre and was famous for his surrealist portrait studies of celebrities. He photographed The Beatles for the cover of their first album, a shot he recreated in 1970 for their retrospective record. **No.61**, with its tall red-brick pilasters, still bears the name of Latchfords, the firm of timber merchants that occupied the premises until 1999. Each window used to have heavy wooden louvres to aid the seasoning of timber. After Latchfords left, the yard behind was converted into apartments, called Ventana Court.

Attached to the wall of Dudley Court at this point is a nicely carved **plaque** put up in 2008 in memory of the Endell Street Military Hospital which, it points out, was the only British army hospital to have been entirely staffed by women. Soon after the start of WWI two doctors, Flora Murray and Louisa Garrett Anderson, both suffragettes, set up the Women's Hospital Corps to provide medical care to wounded soldiers. Snubbed by the British establishment, they were helped by the French authorities to open a hospital in Paris. Their work was belatedly recognised by the War Office: in 1915 they were invited to become army officers and given the former workhouse premises to convert into the Endell Street Military Hospital. Lifts, electricity and modern cooking apparatus were installed. Many of the wounded soldiers needed immediate surgery, and it was not unusual for up to 30 men to be operated on every day. The two doctors still found time to give weekly lectures to their staff on women's rights. They were both awarded a medal at Buckingham Palace in the first investiture of the OBE on 27 September 1917. At the hospital, Helen Chambers introduced a new antiseptic treatment, Bipp (bismuth-iodoform-paraffin-paste), which precluded the need for daily wound dressings, and which greatly reduced infection. The novelist Beatrice Harraden, whose highly successful book *Ships that Pass in the Night* (1893) coined the phrase, was the hospital librarian. After the patients were demobbed in late 1919, the hospital closed and was handed back to the War Office in 1920. The hospital had treated over 26,000 patients.

Just beyond the plaque, modern Dudley Court covers the site of Christ Church, which fronted Endell Street. It was built in 1845 in the Early English style in 1845 **[12]** to designs by Benjamin Ferrey, then a leading neo-Gothic architect who had studied alongside Pugin. Its 1,000 seats were all free (i.e. there were no rented pews) – then a tell-tale sign of a poor area. It had a 120-ft steeple, making it quite a landmark, until it fell down on being struck by lightning in 1887; it was not replaced. The church closed in 1929, when its parish was reunited with St Giles. It was subsequently demolished, but the furniture and fittings were taken to the new church of St Michael, Tokyngton (near Wembley).

The church's north wall abutted an ancient yard, known in the 17th century as Greyhound Court, taking its name from the Greyhound pub in Broad Street. After that became the Crown, the alley was known as Crown Court, then Vinegar Yard, and latterly Vinegar Lane. A deed of 1707 states that there was 'formerly a faire brick house standing' alongside its southern end, owned in the 1660s by Dudley Short, and here in 1725 the earliest buildings of the workhouse were erected. At its corner with Belton Street stood the Guy Earl of Warwick pub, swept away as so much on this side by the creation of Endell Street in the 1840s.

Nos.63-69 opposite us form a late-18th-century terrace, a further survival from New Belton Street. **No.71**, dated 1887, displays stone swags above the second floor, and at ground level has a decorative stuccoed entrance into a yard housing several businesses.

Beyond is a large interwar block, **Nos.73-77**, initially called Beckwood House. Here until 2008 were the offices of RHWL architects, whose projects have included the development of Thomas Neals and the renovation of the former Midland Grand Hotel at St Pancras International. The engineers Scott Brownrigg are its present occupiers. In the 1880s former No.75 housed the stained-glass firm Worrall & Co., examples of whose work can be seen at Cardiff Castle.

Set into the wall on our right are the remains of a once free-standing drinking fountain. It was donated by Sir Marmaduke Langdale in 1859, but is now defunct.

Next on the opposite side is the **Église Helvétique,** as the Église Suisse or Swiss Protestant Church is currently known. Built in 1853-54, to the designs of George Vulliamy, it replaced earlier premises at 'Five Dials' (p 26). English Protestants in the mid-19th-century demanded Gothic for their churches, but the Swiss Protestants, who still use the church, were given a building in late Palladian style. Since its opening in February 1855, the church has been a hub of London's Swiss community. It was refurbished in 2009.

No.81, formerly a shop, was transformed in 1927 when it became the Children's Theatre, set up by a young Australian actress, Joan Luxton (real name Mrs J Lowson). The troupe performed folk songs and sea shanties and one-act plays, mostly written by Margaret Carter. The performances were rapturously received by children and critics alike. The company included the actors Geoffrey Wincott and Norman Shelley, who were both later associated with radio broadcasts of *Winnie the Pooh*; the former voiced Eeyore while the latter was the bear himself. Shelley was also rumoured to have impersonated Churchill for radio broadcasts during WWII. The company moved out in 1931, the 125-seat auditorium proving too small, and during the 1930s had a number of

seasons at the Embassy Theatre, Swiss Cottage. No.81 became home to the Caravan Club which ostensibly offered tea dances. However, its owners were sentenced to imprisonment with hard labour in October 1934 for running what the judge termed a 'vile den of iniquity'.

Behind No.81 was the St Giles Evening Institute for Women, which moved here from Tower Street (p 38) in 1916 and which closed in the early 1960s.

On the site of this end of Endell Street was Bowl Yard, behind the Bowl tavern (p 65), formed by 1680. The yard had a rather unsavoury reputation by the late 18th century, when it was known for its trade in stolen goods. In the 1830s it housed a factory producing Grimstone's Eye Snuff (p 65). At first, Bowl Yard led into Shorts Gardens by a narrow passage, but afterwards the entrance was widened, and the southern part of the thoroughfare was named New Belton Street, Belton Street proper being distinguished as Old Belton Street. In 1845-46 both were widened on the east side to form Endell Street, and the still remaining portion of Bowl Yard at the northern end was swept away.

The Bowl's brewhouse survived until 1846, on the corner where now the imposing **No.83** stands. This is the former St Giles National School, designed in 1859 by Edward Middleton Barry, shortly after he had finished the Royal Opera House and had taken over his late father Charles' practice. In a lively Gothic style, it is the architectural highlight of our walk. Note the asymmetrically placed gable and the second-floor windows between arches, supported by polished Purbeck marble columns. On a constricted site Barry designed what was then an unusually tall building of five storeys, to accommodate 1,500 children. It had a soup kitchen and an industrial school in the basement, infants on the ground floor, masters and mistresses above, then a girls' school, and at the top the boys'. Its playground of just 40 ft square had to cope with the 900 children who enrolled on the first day. The school closed in 1963, after which the building was colonised by squatters, who were evicted by 200 policemen in the 1969 Endell Street 'Siege'. In the 1970s it became a YMCA hostel, until purchased in 1982 by St Mungo's, London's largest homeless charity. The building was renovated by Peter Barber Architects and reopened in December 2008 as a hostel for 53 homeless people. A mosaic based on G F Watts' *Time and Death followed by Judgement*, presented to Canon and Mrs Barnett in Whitechapel in 1884, had graced the exterior from 1925 to 1970, before its removal to the south porch of St Giles Church (p 18).

We have reached the **Oasis Sports Centre**, entered from High Holborn. It includes a swimming pool (partially open-air) with badminton and squash courts and other sports facilities. Baths and washhouses were put up on this spot in 1853 by the two parishes of St Giles and St George. The later Bloomsbury & St Giles Baths included two indoor swimming pools. These were extended in 1900-02, but demolished as antiquated in 1937, to be replaced by an open-air swimming pool. The Oasis, designed by the Holborn Borough Architect S A G Cook, opened in 1960; it now lies behind the 1990s frontage of High Holborn's Berkshire House (p 66).

Cross the road to the former National School building and follow it round to the left, to reach a row of early Victorian buildings on the corner of **SHAFTESBURY AVENUE**. These shops at **Nos.190-204** were formerly part of King Street (as Neal Street was originally called). They date from the 1840s when the north-east end of King Street was improved, at the same time that Endell Street was created. For a few decades they were numbered as part of Broad Street but were left standing when Shaftesbury Avenue was laid out and were incorporated into the new street. **No.196** was the base in the early 1960s of the Institution of Works Managers. At No.194 is **Arthur Beale**, the yacht chandlers, which traces its origins to a company of ropemakers on the Fleet River at the start of 16th century. In the early 1780s the original No.4 King Street, roughly on this site, was briefly home to a free dispensary for poor children, set up by George Armstrong (1720-89), a Scottish physician whose work initiated the scientific study of paediatrics. He had previously run a dispensary at Red Lion Square, Holborn. The cost of providing the service ruined him.

We now attain the corner of present-day **NEAL STREET**, which is worth another look from this end. At Nos.80&82 **The Punjab**, the first Punjabi restaurant in London, was opened by Gurbachan Singh Maan in 1951, four years after he set up business in the City. After his death in 1994, his grandson expanded the business into No.82. Parts of the building are said to date from the 1650s, before the street was laid out; there is a building shown here on Hollar's contemporary drawing, at the edge of development along High Holborn.

No.78 is the **Astrology Shop**, which offers horoscopes and compatibility profiles while you wait, and claims to be both the first and the largest shop in the world dedicated solely to astrology. It has a mid-19th-century shop front, but the building itself, since stuccoed and painted, dates from the late 17th or early 18th century. Note the attic workshop windows. The old vaults of a 17th-century wine merchants still exist here, beneath what had by 1723 become a pub called The Fountain that closed exactly two centuries later. In 1815, in evidence given on the subject of beggars in St Giles to a parliamentary committee, the pub was said to be the haunt of many beggars, including one Granne Manos, usually in gaol, who to ensure a good taking never wore shoes and scratched his legs to make them bleed. 'Negroes' made up a visible proportion of London beggars at the time, often referred to as 'St Giles blackbirds' because of their prevalence in this area.

At No.74 was a foundry run by the Stevenson family since at least 1812; it was bombed in WWII. In the 19th and early 20th centuries this northern part of Neal Street contained several metal-working firms. **No.70** is the Birkenstock shoe shop, opened here in 2004. The first shop dedicated to selling such shoes had opened in 1995 at No.37, as an offshoot of the Natural Shoe Store. This company had pioneered the brand in Neal Street, when it opened its shop at No.13 (in Westminster, and still in business) in the late 1970s. At the side of **No.68** is a private entrance (marked No.68A) leading to a storehouse at the rear, which used to be small chapel. On the 1720 parish map there is a building at the end of a yard off King Street called Martin's Alley. A United Free Methodist chapel by the earlier 19th century, it later became the King Street Mission Hall, the first base of Bloomsbury Chapel's Domestic Mission (see also p 26). From 1863 it served as the mission hall and soup kitchen of the Young Men's Society for the Relief of the Poor, a small band of young middle-class men, mostly from the Bloomsbury congregation, who devoted their spare

time to visiting the needy of Seven Dials. In 1867 they broke away from their parent church and, led by law stationer George Hatton, established the non-denominational, and eventually enormous, St Giles Christian Mission. When this moved its headquarters to what is now Keeley Street (p 103), it left behind in King Street a home for orphan girls. Continue as far as **No.64** on your left, which was purchased by the GLC in a sorry state in 1977. They found that although Listed as early-18th-century, it actually dated from the 1690s and retained its original panelling, most of which had to be stripped out in the restoration. It has an early-19th-century shop front and a mid-19th-century cast-iron bracket for the shop sign. In the mansard roof are dormer windows.

Further down the street, on the opposite side, the second shop from the corner with Shorts Gardens, **Nos.41-43**, was home from December 1976 to the Roxy Club, run by Andy Czezowski specifically to promote punk music. Every major punk band apart from the Sex Pistols played here. It closed in early 1978 as rents started to rise in the area after the closure of Covent Garden Market. At the start of the new Millennium, the building was the flagship store of the Red or Dead fashion house. On the same side, opposite us at this point, is **No.55**, a small late-Victorian red-brick warehouse, vaguely Dutch, with its scrolled gable and loading platforms.

Retrace your steps to the northern end of Neal Street and pause at its junction with Monmouth Street and Shaftesbury Avenue. This corner is the conjectural site of what was probably St Giles' earliest place of refreshment and entertainment. At one time owned by Herbert de Redemere, the leper hospital's cook, the inn was known in the thirteenth century as 'Le Croche Hose', from the crossed-stockings trade sign (like a St Andrew's cross) used by hosiers. It had ceased to exist (or been renamed) before the reign of Henry VIII, and there is no sign of it on Elizabethan maps.

As you take in the views down Monmouth and Neal Streets, ponder the significant changes the area has seen since the 1970s. The GLC's conversion of the central market building into a specialist shopping centre, which has become a hugely successful tourist attraction, led to the transformation of a large area around the market. What had been fruit and vegetable warehouses, hardware stores and workshops now offer an astonishing array of small specialist shops and cafés thronged with colourful tourists enjoying the still more colourful goods and services on offer.

From here it is a short way up
St Giles High Street back to St Giles Circus.

Route 3

London's spinal cord

Linear walk from St Giles High Street
to Kingsway (see back cover for map)

Make your way to the south-west corner of New Oxford Street, at its junction with Tottenham Court Road, either by Tube or bus. With the north side of Centre Point towering above on the right, walk east. Cross a double set of traffic lights under the bridge and immediately turn right along the far side of the road. We are now at the present western extremity of **ST GILES HIGH STREET**; this Route follows its northern side (for the south side see Route 1). Until the 1960s the street ran diagonally across the Centre Point site. The modern roadway was a product of an abortive 1960s traffic scheme, in which the surviving rump of neighbouring Lawrence Street finally disappeared. Continue past **Nos.16-18**, which in 2011 house an exhibition about the Crossrail project (p 13). The pioneer British trades unionist George Odger (1820-1877) lived at the earlier No.18. He was head of the London Trades Council when the Trades Union Congress was formed and the first President of the First International. A blue plaque to his memory was moved into St Giles Church when his house was demolished.

St Giles High Street is a continuation of Holborn, the Roman road from London to Silchester in the west. The Anglo-Saxons knew it as the 'broad military road', i.e. one that was wide enough for an army on the march. In 1248 Henry III ordered the road to be paved 'from furthest Oldeborne [Holborn]' to St Giles-in-the-Fields village. Early-18th-century licensing records locate several public houses in a St Giles street named The Causeway; as it was never marked on any map, we do not know where it ran, but its name presumably recalled an early roadway raised clear of adjoining swampy ground.

According to an assessment of 1623, there were by then 97 houses along or off the north side of the High Street. But the village long remained a semi-rural outpost, surrounded by market gardens and pastures, and it was not until the mid-1700s that there was continuous ribbon development between here and the City. In the late 17th century the district had been part of the 'West End' of London, favoured by prosperous City merchants and wealthy nobles for their residences, but they were soon to move further west. The area to your left, known as Pitaunce Croft in the Middle Ages (and later as Church Close), began a steady decline into the slum later known as the St Giles Rookery. When James I sold St Giles manorial land to the Earl of Southampton to enable him to enlarge his Bloomsbury estate, the Pitaunce

Croft was not included in the sale, and so would never become part of the leafy district to the north.

In the 18th century the High Street and Broad Street, its eastward continuation (see p 63), became unfashionable, witness the lower poor rates paid by residents living west of High Holborn. They were, however, built up with typical Georgian terraces, as depicted in the street scene published by John Tallis in 1838-40 (for a portion further east see p 66), lined at ground-floor level by shop fronts with many-paned windows. Shopkeepers, small manufacturers and professional men lived above their businesses with their families and apprentices. This way of life gradually disappeared during the 19th century. By then (and until 1937), the road was known as High Street *Bloomsbury*, the suffix evidently added in an attempt to create a better image. On Charles Booth's poverty map of 1898, the buildings lining the street were marked in red, suggesting that its inhabitants were still of the middling sort; and even the nearby side streets were coloured in pinkish tones, indicating occupation by skilled workmen.

By the 20th century, and especially after WWII bombing, the area was distinctly shabby. Geoffrey Fletcher, in *London's Pavement Pounders* (1967) thought of these streets as the northern end of Bohemian Seven Dials. He wrote with nostalgia of 'the Swiss-German café, a relic of the Kaiser's Berlin and King Edward's London in combination: four old Germans in white moustaches and aprons were stationed behind the long marbled topped counter and each would pass your order for smoked sausage and sauerkraut to the other, like buckets at a fire, to the last man who executed it'. This establishment, along with a dozen other European eating-places, had gone by the 1980s.

Reach **EARNSHAW STREET**. Cut through in 1850 from the newly opened New Oxford Street, it was at first called Arthur Street; Queen Victoria's seventh child, Arthur, had been born in that year. At this southern end the new street cut through the spacious yard of the timber merchants at No.14 High Street, whose entrance Tallis charmingly depicts. Arthur Street was renamed in 1937 in honour of Thomas Earnshaw (1749-1829), the inventor of the modern chronometer escapement and balance, whose workshop was at No.119 High Holborn.

The calm presence of the parish church (p 18) opposite is in marked contrast with the enormous, garish new building complex opposite called **Central St Giles**, which was the name of the local ward till 1965. Clad in glazed terracotta tiles, each of the development's 13 street-facing façades presents a wall of colour 10 storeys high, in one of four singularly unpleasant dirty-looking hues, a nauseous fruit cocktail of lime green, orange, lemon yellow and strawberry red – all intended to bring brightness into a previously drab area. The complex's residential block entered from Earnshaw Street, Matilda Apartments, takes its name from the medieval queen who founded the nearby leper hospital. It contains just over 100 flats, half of them offering affordable accommodation for Camden key workers.

The immediate predecessor of Central St Giles was St Giles Court, a brick-built block of Government offices designed by Lewis Solomon, Son & Joseph and erected in 1952. Before the new development was started in 2006, the Museum of London undertook an archaeological dig which produced some 11th-century pottery and fine 17th-century pottery, indicating both the longevity of occupation of the site and the high status of local residents then. Over the next two centuries, the quality of the finds progressively deteriorated.

Cross Earnshaw Street and continue along the north side of **ST GILES HIGH STREET**. By the 1880s the houses here were occupied by a printer, a cabinet maker, a hairdresser, a cheesemonger and an ivory-carving business. No.10 was occupied by Alfred Greenland, provision merchant (speciality: bacon), who remained here until just before WWII. Also here was the London Nelson Club and Institute. By this time few families still lived above their shops; improved transport links had allowed them to move to the suburbs and escape the smoke from coal fires that so afflicted central London.

Now walk ahead to the first passage into **Central St Giles**. Here stands one of two commissioned pieces of street art. This 3m-high persimmon-coloured figure is by Steven Gontarski. Glossy and doughnut-like, it is called *Ob 8*. Behind in the open piazza, note the two pin oak trees, the tallest 18m high, grown for 80 years in a tree nursery in Houtvenne, Belgium. They are intended to bring the development together. Continue along the High Street and enter the complex via the main entrance.

Its height was informed by Ken Livingstone's London Plan of 2004, which was based on the forecast of an increase in London's population over a 15-year period equivalent to the entire population of Leeds. The height restrictions on buildings in central districts, such as the Tottenham Court Road 'intensification area', were therefore abolished. Completed in summer 2010, this was the first project in England by the Italian architect Renzo Piano and his Building workshop. (The Shard by London Bridge will be another.) It aimed to provide 2,000 new jobs within the intensification area, and offers double the density of the offices it replaced. The horseshoe-shaped commercial block covering three sides of the site has 10 floors, 8 of which have floor plates of 4,000 square metres. Each floor boasts a winter garden, and the top four have roof terraces with 360° views of London.

Another commissioned sculpture here, an amorphous clay and bronze object by Rebecca Warren, is supposedly a 'non-gender specific figure' but is entitled *William*. Ahead on the right through revolving doors is the informal work lobby, an entirely new concept. The public may use its space and the cafés on the

ground and mezzanine floors.

Leave the complex by the north exit from the piazza, which sports colourful chairs arranged in circles, to emerge in **BUCKNALL STREET**. This was so named in 1877 after Ralph Bucknall, who was made a St Giles vestryman in 1675 and was prominent in parish affairs until his death in 1710. Running through the heart of the Rookery, the street was earlier known variously as Church Lane and Church Street. Once approaching it from the north was Carrier Street; and off the latter's east side was a diminutive Ivy Lane (or Ivy Street, see map on p 2 (frontispiece), home to the Rat's Castle, a notorious all-male haunt of thieves.

The Pitaunce Croft is shown as fully built-up on Strype's parish map of 1720, but over the next 100 years it was further developed by small-scale entrepreneurs disregarding any regulation by the ground landlords. The area deteriorated and became known as the Rookery because its denizens were packed in like roosting birds. The Philological Society's *European Magazine* states in 1824: "The place is called the Rookery, and extends from Tottenham Court Road on the west to Charlotte-street [now Bloomsbury Street] on the east, is bounded by Holborn on the south, and [Great] Russell-street on the north. This is one of the greatest receptacles in the metropolis for wicked characters". Similar words appear in

Sketches by Boz, while John Timbs' 1877 *Curiosities of London* describes it as "one dense mass of houses through which curved tortuous lanes, from which again diverged close courts – one great mass, as if the houses had originally been blocks of stone eaten by slugs into small chambers and connecting passages. The lanes were thronged with loiterers; and stagnant gutters, and piles of garbage and filth infested the air."

The fronts of houses had been opened up to allow access to gardens, cellars were dugout **[13]** and slum buildings were erected to house the ever growing population of labourers, migrants and petty thieves, vagabonds and prostitutes. In 1780 most of the estimated 20,000 Irish living in London were in St Giles. The locality was then variously nicknamed 'Little Dublin', and 'the Holy Land', alluding to the inhabitants' Catholic faith. In the early 1800s more Irish came to escape famine in Ireland. The generous poor relief provided by the parish was a great attraction. Many came as labourers for seasonal work on farms, but stayed on as workers in the building and brewing industries. The sensationally grim accounts of contemporary journalists should not blind us to the fact that many Rookery inhabitants were industrious people, struggling to earn an honest crust in menial occupations.

In the 1840s most of the area was

pulled down to make way for New Oxford Street, obliterating Buckeridge Street to our north. This actually caused further deprivation: the Royal Statistical Society found that 5,000 people had lost their homes and that streets just outside in the affected area had seen a 76% increase in population. Church Lane had an average of 23.5 occupants in the 1841 census but by 1851 this had risen to the even more scandalous 51.5.

The surveyor tasked with rebuilding the sewers in and around the Lane reported in 1849 that the conditions were a perfect disgrace to a civilised society. Unscrupulous landlords (and landladies) achieved large incomes from a complex system of letting and subletting. Some had destroyed privies in many of the houses in order to avoid the cost of emptying the cesspits. By the time the sewers had been rebuilt in 1854, many of the destitute had moved on to other poor areas such as Somers Town.

Proceed east along Bucknall Street, shortly passing on your right a large delivery bay. South of this was the site of 17th-century Eagle & Child Alley, later superseded by Victorian Clark's Buildings, which led from the High Street into Clark's Mews and to Hampshire Hog Yard, the one-time property of the Hampshire Hog inn. In Clark's Mews was the bacon-curing plant of Mr Greenland (p 57), set up in the 1880s. On the site during WWII was a piggery, whose animals survived

14 The brick arch unearthed in 2006 on the site of the St Giles Rookery and recorded as an escape route for ruffians from the Rookery. © Museum of London Archaeology

on scraps brought by civilians. Houses in Clark's Buildings were renovated c.1860 for occupation by just one family in each unit, by the Society for Improving the Conditions of the Labouring Classes. Two decades later, Nos.9-15 on the west side had become a police barracks, known by the 1920s as a police section house. By 1940 the police had left and six years later No.9 became the temporary home of Borough of Holborn Club and its two separate social centres for adults and young people. In 1952, Clark's Buildings and the whole block of surrounding properties were pulled down to make way for St Giles Court.

DYOTT STREET intersects at a crossroads. Generally regarded as the Rookery's most notorious street [14], it survived both the destruction of the Rookery and WWII bombing. It was known initially as Maidenhead Close or Maidenhead Lane. The first houses were built along it on the Pitaunce Croft before 1672 by Henry Bainbridge, whose daughters married gentlemen named Maynard, Buckeridge and Dyott. The first recorded building in the Lane was the eponymous Maidenhead Inn, which stood at the foot of the opposite (left-hand) side. It was already trading in the reign of Elizabeth I, and in its early days was used as a parish meeting place; but by the early 19th century it had declined, together with the Lane.

The street had become Dyot Street by the 18th century and along it was the relatively grand Dyot House, home in 1782 to Philip Dyot; this had by 1830 degenerated into a brothel, later a common lodging house recorded by Mayhew in 1850. It has long since been demolished. No trace remains either of the Presbyterian Dyot Street Chapel that was erected in the early days of the street. Thomas Cotton (1683-1746) was a minister of the chapel, as was Joseph Read in 1695, but otherwise records are scant.

Dyot Street was renamed George Street in the mid-1820s. The licentious behaviour in the lowest of the local taverns and gin shops, such as the Noah's Ark, the Robin Hood, the Turk's Head and the Black Horse shocked even the most hardened observer. One cause of the debauchery was the availability of cheap gin, or 'jenever'; in the early 18th century the government had allowed low tariffs on the manufacture of English gin in an attempt to block the importation of French brandy. In St Giles, every fourth house was said to be a gin shop. Though the famous engraving by Hogarth entitled *Gin Lane* is no longer thought to represent a particular location, some have claimed that it shows this street in 1751, for Hogarth has placed in the centre of his picture a distant view of the characteristic steeple of St George's Bloomsbury, then visible from here. Poverty encouraged drunkenness but could also foment unrest. Dyot Street was home in the early 1790s to a Jacobin club, and a Rights of Man Society, who met 'at the sign of the French rebels'.

The Maidenhead Inn and the lower east side of George Street were pulled down in 1834, and the site was used as a stone-yard by the Vestry until two religious buildings that we shall describe later (p 61) were erected on it, facing the future Shaftesbury Avenue. At the time the Avenue was begun, in 1877, a quieter George Street (re)gained its present name, Dyott Street. Nos.7-8 became home to the Anglican St Giles Mission House and Institute, which survived into the 20th century as St Giles Church House and Club.

On the north-west corner of the crossroads, and undergoing refurbishment in 2011, is Victorian **No.12**, latterly home to the publishers Whitakers. Joseph Whitaker (1820-95), the founder of the firm, and the son of a London silversmith, was apprenticed at age 14 to a bookseller in Fleet Street. Starting his own business, he launched *The Bookseller* in 1858 and ten years later first published his well-known Almanack. The firm published it every year from 1868 to 1997, when it was sold to The Stationery Office (A & C Black are its publishers today). The trade periodical *The Bookseller*, though disposed of in 1999 to the Nielsen media group, is still edited locally (see p 24).

Continue past the crossroads into the short remaining part of **BUCKNALL STREET**, which as the staggered junction suggests is a combination of two old streets. This eastern end was Phoenix Street until the 1840s, when it became part of Thorney Street, which at that time extended a little further east. On the way it crossed Plumtree Street (built c.1686 by one Henry Plumtree), which later became a southward extension of Bloomsbury Street. The landscape painter John Linnell (1792-1882) was born in Plumtree Street, the son of a woodcarver, frame-maker and picture dealer.

You emerge into one arm of **SHAFTESBURY AVENUE**. Built in 1877-86, the Avenue was made to fork here into separate branches, which today carry two one-way streams of southbound and northeast-bound traffic. High Holborn cuts across both at Princes Circus (p 63) to your right.

Await a gap in the southbound traffic, and cross with care to the paved triangle between the two carriageways. Take a brief look at the south-facing buildings to your left. Several private detective agencies were based locally in the 1930s (cf. Nos.219-231, below), and **No.245**, beside the rear of the Crown pub, housed the delightfully named enquiry agents Mole & Mole. The pop star Yusuf Islam, born in 1948 and baptised Steven Georgiou, but better known as Cat Stevens, lived as a boy at No.245. Though his Cypriot father Stavros was Greek Orthodox and his mother Ingrid a Swedish Baptist, the young Steven attended St Joseph's Roman Catholic School (p 86).

The frontage of the buildings on the east side of the northbound roadway is bisected by the egress from Grape Street (p 65). South of this junction, above the shops at Nos.212-222, are **King Edward Mansions**, originally built as mansion flats, but converted into offices after WWII and now known as Sovereign House. North of Grape Street, attractive turrets add interest to the terracotta façade of Nos.228-234, part of **Queen Alexandra Mansions**. Built in 1902-08, they are Listed Grade II by English Heritage, who express the view that they are almost certainly by Charles Fitzroy Doll, surveyor of the Bedford Estate at the time. Doll was responsible for designing many Bloomsbury developments, including the Russell Hotel; a local man, he was also the district surveyor and twice mayor of Holborn (1904-05 and 1912-13). The **Bloomsbury** public house on the corner with New Oxford Street (No.236 Shaftesbury Avenue) is definitely his work, built in 1904. The 'heritage pub' plaque above the door is an encouragement to explore what remains of its original Arts and Crafts décor – the fireplaces on the ground and first floors, the cornice behind the bar on the ground floor, and some panelling to the first-floor.

Turn now to face the southbound branch of Shaftesbury Avenue and admire the large rose window of what Pevsner called 'the white brick neo-Norman' **Bloomsbury Central Baptist Church**. Thus renamed in 1905, but originally known as Bloomsbury Chapel, the Grade-II Listed building was designed by John Gibson and built in 1845-48 as a speculation by the railway magnate Sir Samuel Morton Peto, MP. The church was the first Baptist meeting-place to stand prominently on a London street as a visibly ecclesiastical edifice: earlier Baptist meeting places had been tucked away down back alleys or in upper rooms. Faith Bowers recounts in her history of the church, *A Bold Experiment*, that when Peto sought to lease the land from the Crown, the First Commissioner of Woods and

Forests objected because Nonconformist chapels were too dull: he liked a church to have a spire. 'A spire?' exclaimed Peto 'My Lord, we shall have two!' Twin spires did indeed grace the towers, until they were demolished in 1951, declared unsafe after wartime damage.

The church has responded throughout its history to social changes in the community; for most of its life it has seen a constant loss of members to the suburbs. Until 1870 the chapel basement housed a mid-week Day School which provided a good, cheap education for the children of the 'respectable poor'. In 1914 the original large gable was removed and a storey built above the chapel to provide extra accommodation for activities. After WWII it was felt that the church should be a central Baptist meeting place rather than just a local church, so that unlike other Baptist churches, which are self-governing, 'Bloomsbury' reports to the London Baptist Association, which has offices on the top floor. As part of a refurbishment in the late 1990s, the church's Sanctuary was updated and a Friendship Centre created in the basement, now open to all from Monday to Friday between 10 and 4.

In the mid-19th century, in what was then called Bloomsbury Street, three places of worship stood here side by side, a civilising influence in a neighbourhood previously known for the depravity of its inhabitants.

To the north, on the site now occupied by the brown-and-pink-marble-faced No.55 New Oxford Street, was the Bedford Episcopal Chapel, a proprietary Anglican establishment dating from 1771 and erected by Samuel Micke on a piece of land demised by the Duke of Bedford for a period of 101 years from 1765. The covenants stated that the chapel should not be consecrated, and that only preaching and reading prayers and psalms in the Book of Common Prayer were allowed. The chapel remained standing for some years after the end of the lease, during which time the minister was the controversial Rev. Stopford A Brooke, an Irish man of letters who had seceded from the Church of England in 1880 and preached here as a Unitarian minister from 1876 to 1895. His publications included studies of Shakespeare, Milton, Tennyson and Browning.

To the south of the Baptist chapel stood the Huguenot Protestant Episcopal Church of the Savoy, which moved here from the Strand in 1845 to a new building designed by Ambrose Poynter. Founded to serve French expatriates, this church enjoyed a grant in perpetuity made by Charles II in 1675. Worth some £200,000 by 1884, in that year the Lords of the Treasury decided that the church no longer had a legal claim to assistance.

Sandwiched between the church and its Baptist neighbour was the French Protestant School of Westminster, first founded in 1747 to educate girls descended from Huguenot refugees. It closed when its church was pulled down in 1925 and replaced by the present, Grade-II-Listed **No.233**. Designed (c.1929) by Leo Sylvester Sullivan, this was originally named Museum House. Early occupants here were Britannia Batteries Ltd, who promptly renamed it Britannia House. Pevsner described it as 'modern commercial, all verticals with Egyptian detail. It stands side by side with the Baptist church, and the two together look like an Osbert Lancaster drawing'. The recently restored carved details, including sun god symbols and a pharaoh's head, were probably by Henry Poole.

South of Britannia House is a late-Victorian building at **Nos.219-231**, with a pleasing cone-capped corner turret, originally built as flats and named Ashley House. After its ground floor and basement were occupied by the Daimler Motor Co. in the 1890s, the block changed its name to Daimler House, and it later became Exide House, when it was occupied by battery manufacturers. In the 1930s, No.231 housed both the Fitch Detective Service and the World Association of Detectives.

On the corner to the east is the **Shaftesbury Theatre** at No.210, with its 'jolly rotunda' mentioned by Pevsner. The present building was erected in 1911, designed as a theatre for melodrama by

Bertie Crewe, a pupil of the famous Frank Matcham. It was called the New Princes Theatre, as there had been a previous Princes Theatre on the site, built in 1888. Memorable productions in the 1920s were Sarah Bernhardt in *Daniel* and Fred and Adele Astaire in Gershwin's *Funny Face*; there were seasons of Diaghilev's *Ballets Russes* and Gilbert & Sullivan operettas performed by the D'Oyly Carte company. Later artists appearing there included Evelyn Laye, Maurice Chevalier, Michael Redgrave and Peggy Ashcroft.

In 1961 the theatre was saved from closure by the Save London's Theatres Campaign. Two years later the interior was reconstructed by Jack Hilton and renamed the Shaftesbury, a theatre of that name just west of Cambridge Circus having been blitzed in WWII. *Hair* opened in 1968 and was a triumphant success, but just as the theatre was due to celebrate its 1000th performance, the ceiling fell down. The building was rescued from demolition by 1973 by the efforts of Alec Guinness and Paul Scofield, amongst others, and still retains its wonderful interior. It was Listed in 1974. By the 1990s the theatre was known as the Shaftesbury Theatre of Comedy and run by a syndicate of famous theatrical names. Later in the decade it was temporarily taken over by the Royal Opera House while the latter was being renovated. Further renovations to the Shaftesbury took place in 2006.

The road junction here is the unlabelled **Princes Circus**, officially so named in 1958 in memory of the Princes Theatres. However, in February 1990 Camden Council agreed to the request of Ian Albury, the theatre impresario, to change it to *Shaftesbury Circus*, on condition that he pay all the council's reasonable costs. To date, this change has not been effected.

The triangular road island ahead contains a defunct Romanesque drinking fountain in polished red granite, now encaged and inaccessible. It was donated to the St Giles Board of Works via the Metropolitan Drinking Fountain & Cattle Trough Association, and erected in 1897 to mark Queen Victoria's Diamond Jubilee – though not here. For a century it stood at the north-eastern tip of Shaftesbury Avenue, facing the Bloomsbury pub. Soon after its relocation here, it was surrounded by railings, installed in 2002.

The busy thoroughfare to the east was renamed as part of **HIGH HOLBORN** in 1937. This portion of the old Roman road was variously known in the 18th century as the Broadway or Broad St Giles, before settling down in the early 1800s as Broad Street. Until Shaftesbury Avenue arrived and sliced off the corner, Bloomsbury (late Plumtree) Street met Broad Street at a right-angled junction here. West of the junction, Broad Street once turned briefly south to terminate at an end-on junction with old Monmouth Street (p 23). The

wide roadway there was known in the late Georgian period as Broad Place.

At No.19 Broad Street, just west of the junction, stood the St Giles and St George's Ragged School & Refuge. This school had been founded in 1843 by London City missionaries above a cowshed in Streatham Street (north of New Oxford Street). When the cowshed was pulled down, the school used a succession of temporary premises in Dyott Street and Seven Dials. Then in 1852 a 'freehold carcase intended for a gin palace' (the closed George IV pub) was acquired at No.19 Broad Street and fitted up as schools for boys, girls and infants. Soon, dormitories were opened to provide shelter for a few destitute boys and girls, and the institution became both school and refuge. Interestingly, Sunday worship for the boys was in the gallery of the nearby Baptist chapel, while the girls went to Anglican St Giles. Numbers grew, and in 1855 the 60 boys by then in residence were moved to No.17 Arthur (now Earnshaw) Street, leaving the girls behind in Broad Street. Five years later the boys moved on again to the new Home for Homeless and Destitute Boys in Great Queen Street (p 91). The eventual fate of the girls' refuge is unclear.

Nearby, the 1720 parish map shows an isolated block of buildings in the middle of the main highway. These were the parish almshouses, five two-roomed brick dwellings erected in 1656 to house aged

64

15 Middle Row, Bloomsbury, looking west towards the spire of St Giles-in-the-Fields. Artist 'WP', c.1830

widows, who were each allowed 7 farthings a day besides 'coal and other bounties'. The village pound, which previously occupied this site, had been moved to what we now call St Giles Circus (p 13). The almshouses were moved in their turn, in 1783, to Lewknor's Lane, now Macklin Street (p 86).

Here also stood another isolated block of houses known as Middle Row **[15]**. In 1675 a Lady Katherine Cope is recorded as living there, but by 1835 it was a less prestigious address, the central position in the Row being occupied by Apted's, 'fresh and shell fishmongers'. It was known as Middle Row *Bloomsbury* to distinguish it from the more famous Middle Row similarly incommoding traffic at the far end of High Holborn a mile away (see *Streets of Old Holborn*). Middle Row Bloomsbury was pulled down in the 1840s to allow Endell Street to be cut through (see "Proposed Route to Waterloo Bridge" on map, p 2).

Facing you, where Endell Street now emerges, lay early-17th-century Bowl Yard (see also p 20). Bowl Yard was already beginning to be built on in 1623 when owned by a Mr Barber, vestryman of St Giles. Behind his house was an open space known as the 'Great Garden', while facing the main road on the west side of the yard stood the Bowl Inn and Brewery, the first version of which was built here in 1623 on Canter's Alley. John Merritt was the landlord in 1654, but the inn was demolished in 1661 to make way for new premises. It presented criminals on their way from Newgate to Tyburn with a free bowl of ale to dull their apprehensions; in time it became only one of several inns on the route along Holborn and Oxford Street to be associated with this custom (see p 20). Legend had it that the inn contained a medicinal spring, which supplied a pool known locally as Queen Anne's Bath (p 48).

By the 19th century, Bowl Yard was reached by a covered way burrowing through part of No.37 Broad Street (**[16]**, p 66) Here James Chamberlain made and sold 'eye preserving spectacles of superior materials & manufactured upon unerring principles, at half the price usually charged by other opticians.' Two doors to the east, at No.39, was the shop of William Grimstone, the sole inventor of an eye snuff, which claimed on the façade to restore sight and cure headaches and to be 'patronised by his late Majesty, the Lords of the Tresury *[sic]*, the Duchess of Kent, and the Royal Family'. This was evidently meant to encourage clients to use eye snuff rather than go to the inconvenience of wearing spectacles.

Now cross the eastern arm of Shaftesbury Avenue and walk east to reach the stage door of the Shaftesbury Theatre on the corner of **GRAPE STREET**. Retaining a flavour of the Edwardian period, this quiet street is worth a short detour. Dating from 1905, this is a truncated and realigned version of earlier Vine Street, both names being allusions to the vineyard belonging to the St Giles Hospital property called 'The Vyne', which is thought to have flourished in this area. The left-hand side of Grape Street is mostly lined by King Edward Mansions (p 61), whose west wing we encountered in Shaftesbury Avenue; the two wings taper to meet near the top of the street. Opposite are Queen Alexandra Mansions (see p 61), where the drama critic James Agate (1877-1947) died in his mansion flat at No.7. Well known in his day, he is now mostly forgotten but for his diaries. Published from 1935 in nine volumes, and entitled *Ego 1* to *Ego 9*, they describe his hedonistic lifestyle and reflections on the intellectual life of the period. During WWII Agate was the Literary Advisor to Metro-Goldwyn-Meyer British Studios. Until 1942 he had lived in Fairfax Road, West Hampstead.

Grain rather than grape was distilled on the east side of 19th-century Vine Street. William Currie, distiller, was based here in the 1820s, and in 1830 Charles Tanqueray, the son of a Bedfordshire clergyman, established his Bloomsbury Distillery here. His particular brand of London gin was soon exported worldwide, and the distillery

thrived until it merged with Gordon's in 1898, when production moved to Finsbury. Still the best-selling gin in the USA, Tanqueray has been mentioned in several popular songs, including the recent *You Know I'm No Good* by Amy Winehouse. No.7 Vine Street was the base in the 1860s of the famous soap manufacturers Yardley.

Back on the east corner with **HIGH HOLBORN**, at **No.167**, the Cuban flag announces that this is Cuba's Embassy and commercial office, housed in a terracotta-faced building that before WWII was a showroom for Amami shampoo.

Look across to the south side of High Holborn. To your right, on the site of 18th-century Salutation Yard, stands **Berkshire House**, an office block of 1961 incorporating the Oasis Sports Centre (p 54) and, at first, a rebuilt Oporto Stores pub on the corner, which has since closed. The original hostelry took its name from General Wellesley's recapture of Oporto, Portugal in May 1809 during the Peninsular War. The ground rent on the reconstructed pub was set at 'one quart of finest English ale to be paid by the brewers every Midsummer's Day' until 2060.

This stretch of High Holborn is not very prepossessing now, but as Broad Street it had a long history, mostly of taverns. One of the westernmost was the Greyhound, later known as the Crown, part of whose

66

property at the back was taken in the 18th century to form the workhouse (p 50); and to the east was the Swan, here from at least 1360. 19th-century successors were the Rose & Crown at No.46 Broad Street and the Spread Eagle at No.56.

To the east of Berkshire House is a mirror-glass-fronted modern box at **No.175**, otherwise called The Place. Its 7th floor houses the offices of Roubini Global Economics, chaired by Nouriel Roubini, *alias* 'Dr Doom', the American economist who famously predicted the credit crunch of 2008. On this site, an early Lamb Alley gave way to the later (inexplicably named) Lascelles Court and Lascelles Place, short terraces of working-class houses; the latter had an iron-barred entrance to Vinegar Yard (p 53) and was still directory-listed in 1930. At that time the Broad Street frontage was shared by offices of the Ministry of Health and George Care's boot-tree and last factory, reflecting High Holborn's transition from small specialised enterprises to the corporate office blocks of today.

Next, at **No.178**, is the 'High Holborn Residence' of the London School of Economics, 13 brick-faced storeys of student accommodation opened in October 1995 (architects, IKA Project Design and Development). The previous building here was the Westminster Ophthalmic Hospital, which moved here in 1930 from William IV Street (next to the old Charing Cross Hospital), serving from 1946 as the Holborn branch of Moorfields Eye Hospital. Here in the previous century, at No.57 Broad Street, were the offices of the Vestry and Guardians of the United Parishes of St Giles and St George Bloomsbury, combined for secular purposes; and also the Registrar's office for births, deaths and marriages for St Giles.

The opening beyond the hall of residence, once named Cock Alley, led in the 19th century to the cooperage department of Combe's brewery, employing 450 workers and covering a large area behind, stretching south to Shorts Gardens (p 47). Sandwiched between the cooperage entrance and the corner building in Drury Lane (ahead), and surviving until WWII, was a small pub, the Brown Bear, the successor to an earlier Bear inn. On its site once stood a forge, leased in the reign of Henry II by Hugh the Smith from the leper hospital of St Giles, which then owned all the land here; the forge (like the Hospital) had disappeared by the time of Queen Elizabeth I.

Continuing east along the north side, we pass the site of No.10 Broad Street, to which the father of landscape artist and etcher Samuel Palmer brought his family to live in 1820 after the death of their mother. Towering unnoticed above us, and with an entrance at present-day **No.166** – where we halt again – is the high-rise north annexe of the Travelodge hotel opposite on the corner of Drury Lane (p 77).

We have now reached a spot described in the 13th century as 'by the Cross at Aldewych'. A stone cross called the Aldewych Cross stood here, with an adjacent cottage in Broad Street opposite the entrance to Drury Lane, then known as the Via de Aldewych. (see also **[21]**, p 82). Nearby was the *fons communis* or common spring, which supplied local houses with water. How long the cross and spring survived is unknown, but there is a possible reference to the spring in a petition dated 7 July 1637 from the inhabitants of St Giles' Town complaining of the stopping up of a 'fair, large and open well in ye saide town'.

Ahead on the left, the neglected, oppressive Modernist block, with long bands of Portland stone and glass, was built for the General Post Office by E T Serjent in 1961-69 as its West Central district sorting office. Later it was used for storage purposes by the British Museum, and permission was given in 1999 by Camden Council for a change of use to include a museum study centre, a fitness club and hotel accommodation. In 2011 it is still unoccupied, except when hired out for the occasional fashion shoot. In November 2010 it was subjected to an invasion and damage by an all-night, internet-fuelled 'rave' lasting 18 hours and called the Scumoween Squat Monsters Ball.

In the early 1860s the Pneumatic Dispatch Company's underground railway, a pneumatically operated parcel tube, ran about 5 ft below the road surface from Euston via Euston Road, Tottenham Court Road (thus skirting the Bedford estate), St Giles High Street and High Holborn, to the main post office at St Martin-le-Grand near St Paul's. Described by Derek Bayliss in *The Post Office Railway* as one of the blind alleys of Victorian technology, the tube was abandoned within a few years and was bought by the GPO in 1921 to house telephone cables; it also carried gas pipes. Early on 20 December 1928 a workman climbed down a manhole to inspect gas pipes there with the aid of a cigarette lighter. The resulting explosion and another one minutes later at the corner of Grape Street and Broad Street, plus a third explosion the following day, ripped up the roads and damaged buildings 80 metres to the east and as far as Denmark Street to the west. The damaged roads and the Princes Theatre were closed for many weeks.

No harm seems to have come to the deeper Post Office Underground Railway, newly opened for letters and parcel traffic in December 1927. Running from Paddington to Whitechapel, the line called at Mount Pleasant and Tottenham Court Road sorting offices en route, curving sharply south and then north again to pass beneath the West Central office. Dwindling volumes of mail led to the closure of the line, by then renamed Mail Rail, in 2002. It was, however, mothballed for possible reopening should circumstances change.

Cross Museum Street. In its previous incarnation, on the same site, the sorting office lent its name from 1938 to nearby **WEST CENTRAL STREET**, viewable from here turning off the west side of Museum Street. The L-shaped street, bending north to meet New Oxford Street, was formerly Hyde Street, itself a combination of parts of earlier Duke and Brewer Streets. Maps show Brewer Street leading to a brewery in 1746 and to Carrick's Distillery by 1828. On the south side of Brewer Street in the later 19th century, were Holland & Hannen, a notable building firm later merged with Cubitt's. Most of Hyde Street, its longer eastern arm, now lies under the sorting office. The Presbyterian minister and Biblical scholar Edward Harwood died at No.6 in 1794. At No.12 lived the comic actor John Emery, once well-known on the London stage for his portrayal of Yorkshiremen; he died there in 1822. At this time there was an academy at No.22, with an extensive library, run by Rev. Peter Fenn. This was an assumed name, the schoolmaster being found guilty in 1828 of passing a forged £50 note, and transported to Australia.

Just visible today on the north-east corner of West Central Street is a black-painted nightclub called **The Den**, housed in a former goods-receiving depot of the London & North Western (later LMS) Railway.

Continue east along the original **HIGH HOLBORN**. We have now left erstwhile

Broad Street behind, and the highway is noticeably narrower; locals referred to this stretch of road as 'The Narrows'. One of the main reasons behind the construction of New Oxford Street was to alleviate the traffic congestion here. In September 1874 the Metropolitan Board of Works proposed that the road name be altered to 'Holborn', but residents of Holborn vigorously opposed this suggestion and it was dropped. 'High Holborn' probably originally meant the higher part of the Roman road which led up from the 'bourne in the hollow', i.e. the lost River Fleet, whose valley has been spanned since 1869 by the Holborn Viaduct (way off to the east from here).

On the south side, at **No.181A** are the head offices of Thames and Hudson, the respected publishers of art books. The firm was founded in 1946 by Eva and Thomas Neurath, both refugees from Nazi Germany, at nearby No.244 High Holborn, moved to Bloomsbury in 1956 and in 1999 transferred here into offices designed by John McAslan. The large modern windows allow one to view the interior.

At No.181 is **Esavian House,** its name derived from the Educational Supply Association which occupied the building from 1925 to 1960. Its 'ESA' logo is liberally applied to the façade on the upper floors. The ground floor has become today's West Central Post Office. On the north side we pass the site of

No.167, which in the 1890s was the 'No.2 Bessbrook Home & Employment Agency', providing shelter and work for sandwich(-board) men. According to Charles Booth, who interviewed the home's Secretary, James Keates, there were 2,000 such men in London, recruited from the ranks of 'drinking clerks, valets and footmen... the ne'er-do-wells of civilized society', often out of work in rainy weather and preferring to go fruit picking in the summer. Beyond at No.158 was the meeting-place before WWI of the Holborn Artists' Club.

Kelly's Directories were published across the road at Nos.182-184, on the near corner of Smart's Place, from 1893 to 1922. Later occupants included Charles Fox, theatrical costumiers and wigmakers, before WWII, and the publishers Harrap's thereafter. Published today, from modern, mirror-glass-fronted Arab Press House at **No.184**, is *Asharq Al-Awsat*, a leading pan-Arab daily newspaper founded in London in 1978.

Opposite, and unlabelled at this end, is **Dunn's Passage**, marked on a 1746 map as Dumb's Alley. Now open to the sky and gated, it was once a very narrow pedestrian tunnel. Lining the west side, behind No.154 and extending through to the then No.485 New Oxford Street, was the Dunn's Passage Factory. Already disused by c.1849, it was acquired by the Oratorian Fathers to house a ragged school. This group of secular priests – Oxbridge

graduates and Tractarian converts of John Henry Newman – had volunteered to take part in 'an experiment in education for poor Irish Destitute children'. A report on the school suggested that most of the 500 places were taken by the offspring of respectably poor parents ambitious for their children's education. The boys were taught by the Brothers of St Joseph; the girls and infants by six Daughters of Compassion, members of an Anglo-French Servite order who had arrived from Cuves in eastern France to learn English and take up missionary work. In 1857 the school moved to new premises in Charles (now Macklin) Street (p 86). Based at No.154 at the same time was the (Catholic) Shoe Black Society of St Vincent de Paul, which dressed poor boys in uniforms and sent them out to earn a living brushing and polishing the footwear of passers-by in return for a penny.

Restoring the premises to industrial use was a versatile Yorkshireman named George Bussey, who came to London in 1851. He would later become notable as London's largest maker of sports equipment, from tennis rackets to cricket balls and footballs, but his early career in St Giles was as a gun-case maker. After spells at No.173 High Holborn, and then in Arthur (now Earnshaw) Street, he installed himself (in 1859) in Dunn's Passage, from where he applied for his second patent for cartridge carriers. By 1869 Bussey had moved south of the river to Peckham, where he

established a new works and a firearms museum. Next to move into No.154 was Henry Moorse, an early manufacturer of 'photographic apparatus', whose business remained here for forty years.

No.190, opposite, covers the site of a passage known from the 17th century as Harrow or Wild Boar Alley and later replaced by a Black Horse Yard. The modern block houses the qualification-awarding firm Edexcel and other subsidiaries of Pearson Education. The previous block on this site was for much of the 20th century the headquarters of Odhams Press (p 45). At the earlier No.192, from c.1848, was the 'Musical Bouquet Office', printers and publishers of popular music, run at first by Charles Sheard, and then by his son, also Charles; the firm moved c.1897 to No.196 Shaftesbury Avenue.

Walk on past the site on the left of the long-closed Windsor Castle at No.152. **No.146** houses a bar serving Thai food with the name of Brown Sugar, where the long-established Three Compasses pub used to be. The latter has been rebuilt as a unit of the present Commonwealth House, a building in the angle ahead where High Holborn meets the east end of New Oxford Street.

On reaching the junction, look across to the recently well restored edifice on your right, now known as **Holborn Hall**, actually a combination of two matching buildings erected twelve years apart. The west wing is the former Holborn Town Hall. Its foundation stone remains, laid on 27 October 1906 by William R Small, MD DSc FRS ED, Mayor of Holborn. Its architects were Warwick and Hall, and Pevsner described it as having bold baroque details and generous finishes typical of Edwardian public buildings. Restoration of the building (which had before that been empty for 12 years) was completed by Garnett and Partners LLP in 2004, when they were the recipients of a Camden Design Award. Adorning the balcony is the Borough of Holborn coat of arms, resplendent in its original colours; the heraldry includes a representation of a hind, the emblem of Saint Giles. The old main door on the right leads to eight sets of offices; at weekends entry to the lobby is barred by the old Holborn Borough wrought-iron gates. The middle door to the left leads into the Shanghai Blues Chinese restaurant and bar.

The earlier-built east wing stands on a site previously occupied by the offices of the St Giles District Board of Works. Still labelled 'Public Library', it was designed by W Rushworth and opened in 1894 as the St Giles' (Free) Library. After six decades as the Holborn Central Library, it served finally as Camden's High Holborn Branch Library until its lamented closure in 1987. Pevsner mentions 'the double oriel and pretty French Renaissance ornament'. The front door is now closed but still bravely embellished with an 'SGL' monogram. Alongside is the foundation stone, this one laid by 'the Noble Herbrand', the 11th Duke of Bedford who became Holborn's first Mayor. To the left of the former library a modern gate guards the narrow entrance to the old Green Dragon Yard, which we describe in Route 4 and to the front door of **No.198**, the third development on the site and known as The Connection.

Now cross the end of New Oxford Street in front of the **Holborn Tower** at Nos.137-144. Old No.145 High Holborn, which was destroyed when New Oxford Street cut through in 1844-47, was the birthplace in 1813 of the radical Henry Vincent, a leading figure in the Chartist movement, who because he was a powerful orator chiefly active in Wales and the West Country was dubbed 'the Demosthenes of the West'. By coincidence No.144, which stood on the corner of Bury Place, served briefly as the HQ of the National Land Company. This was founded in 1846 by the Chartist leader Feargus O'Connor to buy rural land to be made available to working-class men, who could thus become property owners and so electors in county seats. A few settlements were established, such as 'O'Connorville' at Heronsgate near Rickmansworth, plots being allocated by ballot. But the project was a disaster: those who moved in proved too poor to pay any rent, let alone buy their plots. The company was wound up after only five years by Act of Parliament in July 1851.

On the west side of Holborn Tower is an inscription recalling the Women's Freedom League. Founded in 1907 in neighbouring Barter Street, this moved in 1916 to No.144, where it remained until after WWII. Its founder members were three prominent suffragists – Edith How, Teresa Billington and Charlotte Despard – who set it up as an alternative to the Women's Social and Political Union run by the Pankhurst family (whose headquarters were in Kingsway, p 89) after the Union's change of policy from peaceful protest to a campaign of vandalism. No.144 also housed the Minerva Press, the League's publishing arm, and the Emily Davison Club, named after the suffragette who threw herself under the king's racehorse during the Derby of 1913. Based here, too, for many years, was the Psychic Press. On the ground floor was the London Savings Bank, but by 1955 the Good Earth restaurant and club had taken its place.

In 1959 Nos.137-144 were demolished for the construction of New Oxford House (now Holborn Tower), designed by L Blease and J A Rawlinson for the Co-op Permanent Building Society, a constituent of Nationwide Building Society.

During building works in 1961, part of a Roman tombstone was found on the Holborn Tower site, only 25 ft below the present road surface, in the backfill of a sewer trench. Dedicated to Caius Pomponius Valens, born in Colchester, the beautifully carved inscription is now in the British Museum.

A King's Head public house is known to have traded on the site of No.142 at least as early as 1667. On 24 August 1764 it fell down at about 3 pm; the only person to die was a 'tippling tailor' named Murphy. The tavern was rebuilt with the same sign, and lasted until demolished when New Oxford Street was constructed.

We have reached Bloomsbury Court, on whose west corner stood another large 18th-century pub, the Compasses. On the east corner, where the Nationwide branch now stands, was the site of the short-lived British Museum tube station on the Central Line, opened in 1900 but closed only 14 years later and moved east to link with Holborn station on the Piccadilly Line. Holborn station was completely rebuilt in 1930-33, and only then did 'British Museum' finally close. Above it were the offices of British Museum Station Chambers (later Museum Station Buildings), which attracted a mixed bag of occupants, the British Esperanto Association rubbing shoulders with the makers of Socleano Soap.

Look across now to **Nos.199-206**, redeveloped by Sidney Kaye, Eric Firmin and Partners in 1978. Retained was the Grade-II-Listed frontage of **Nos.199-201**, built 1869-70 by W J Trehearne as a factory and showroom for George Kent, inventor of a patent knife-cleaning machine and other domestic gadgets. The building, in Italian Renaissance style, is now Grade-II Listed. The ground floor has modern shop fronts between columns, displaying games and model kits. This well-known model shop was formerly kept by Beatties but is now occupied by Model Zone, who also use **Nos.202-203**. No.202 previously housed the Leica camera specialists, R G Lewis Ltd, a long-standing business still thriving today, though at nearby No.29 Southampton Row. An innovative venture, the High Holborn shop was opened by Norman Lewis, using his father's already well-established name. From 1931 Norman began travelling and later became a well-known travel writer. He married Sicilian Ernestina Corvajo and they lived for a few years with her gregarious family in Gordon Street (Bloomsbury) in a house full of animals and birds. Norman Lewis wrote 33 books, most memorably *Naples 44*, describing the effect of the Allied invasion of the port and the fierce resistance of the Germans. His 1968 article in *The Sunday Times* deploring the extermination of the native Indian population in Brazil led to a change in the law of that country.

Now offices, the upper storeys at Nos.202-204 were once flats named Clarence House, while at No.205 an Edwardian Newton Hotel gave way to the interwar HQ of the road hauliers Pickfords.

Opposite the north end of Newton Street, in 1694, a Mr Rathbone built a Watch House for the sum of £8 given for the purpose by the Duke of Bedford. It was moved to Smart's Buildings (p 84) in the early 19th century.

One of the few survivals in High Holborn from that period is Listed **No.207**; unusually in such a commercial area, it retains the typical window panes of the time. For a century from c.1890 it was occupied by Charles Shapland & Co., diamond merchants, silversmiths, goldsmiths and appraisers; Shapland registered a London Maker's Mark in 1896. The firm is remembered for its splendid window displays of specimens of its craft skills. No.207 now houses a card shop.

Next door is the **Princess Louise** pub at Nos.208–209, recalling the popular fourth daughter of Queen Victoria, and worth a visit for its splendid 1891 interior (Listed II★) by Simpson and Sons: the stained glass and mahogany bar fittings are by W H Lascelles & Co. and the polychrome tiles and gold-embossed glass are by Richard Morris & Son. The gents' toilet in the basement has marble urinals and some of the original tiled walls and fittings.

At No.210, the Holborn Cinema was one of eight to open in 1910 in what is now the Borough of Camden, but despite the introduction of a live variety show in 1923 the cinema closed two years later. Later tenants at Nos.210-211 were Crittall's, once a household name as makers of metal window frames. **No.212** was built by Henry Baker in 1854 for the London & Westminster Bank; it is now a branch of NatWest. Pevsner considered it 'surprisingly pure Palladian', except for the rounded ground-floor arches.

On the north side of High Holborn, at the corner with Southampton Place, are **Nos.127-129**, at present a branch of the Royal Bank of Scotland. The building is an early work (1904) of Charles Holden, whose name was later linked to the architecture of London's Underground stations. Here he was partnered by H Percy Adams. Part of the block, No.128, was occupied by 1914 and until WWII by the Blackpool Corporation Information Bureau, to lure Londoners to the Lancashire resort then at the height of its popularity. The building is now Listed.

So, too, is the handsome, 'Franco-Flemish', red-brick block past Southampton Place at **Nos.121-126**, built in 1899-1902, on the site of the first West Central sorting office (p 67), by Ford, Son & Burrows for Parr's Bank. It was later taken over by the London & Westminster Bank, whose name can still be traced above the ground floor on the two corner walls. Early occupants of the offices here included Encyclopædia Britannica and the Central London Railway. In 2009-10 the whole block was completely rebuilt behind the original façade. Opened at Nos.121-123 in 2010 was the first branch of Metro Bank, promising a new kind of banking, open seven days a week, and boasting of its friendliness both to customers and to their dogs.

A house on this site, at No.125, was home in later life to Joseph Grimaldi (1709-1788), a dancer and part-time surgeon-dentist, who claimed in the latter role to have 'had the Honour of attending her MAJESTY, the Prince of Wales, and the Prince and Princess of Brunswic [sic]'. The widowed Grimaldi's latest mistress, a fellow dancer named Ann Perry, adopted his surname and came to live with him at No.125, while Joseph continued to maintain, at her Lambeth home, his earlier mistress Rebecca Brooker, with whom he had fathered several illegitimate children, among them the future famous clown, Joey.

Look across to the buildings that line the south side of High Holborn from Newton Street to the junction with Kingsway, ahead. There may have been scattered houses here from Elizabethan times. In the 17th century it became the proposed site of a market that never was: in 1634, one Henry Darell bought from Trinity College the right to establish two markets and three fairs. His petition to set up them up here in St Giles was strongly opposed by the City of London, and he abandoned his plans. Instead, c.1640, Darell became one of London's earliest property developers, and on the land he built Dayrell's [sic] Buildings, 17 'spacious' 3-storey houses on the Holborn frontage and rounding the corner into Newton Street. Erected east of them was a group of inferior houses called Shenton's Tenements, some facing High Holborn and others in Little Queen Street (p 90, on the line of Kingsway). Twice rebuilt over time, one of Darell's houses, the eventual No.211, survived into the 20th century but was demolished in 1910.

Still standing in the 1840s at No.219, two doors from the corner, was the Sun & Punchbowl pub (later to become the Queen & Prince Albert). Next door at No.218 were the National Baths, described by the journalist Edmund Yates as 'a very dirty and smelly place of recreation'. Finding that it didn't pay its way in the winter, its owners drained the swimming-pool and turned it into a dancing saloon, known at first as the National Assembly Rooms and later as the Holborn Casino. With its 'gaudy gilded vestibule' and marble dance floor, the Casino proved highly popular. Often open until 1 am, it was said to be frequented by a large number of amateur and professional prostitutes, but 'for all its shady reputation, it was a cheerful and bouncy sort of place'.

The venue was rebuilt in 1874, with a new second entrance at No.5 Little Queen Street, and a Holborn frontage extended by removing four houses adjoining the old entrance. It reopened as the

17 Interior of Holborn Restaurant in its heyday

Holborn Restaurant under the 'excellent management of T J Hamp'. Within a short time it had gained an enviable reputation. The building was further extended by Archer and Green in 1883-85 and redecorated by T E Collcutt in 1894. The enlarged site included three Masonic Halls and over a dozen restaurants, and was famous for the fine displays of mosaic and majolica in the public rooms **[17]**. Prices were moderate, being a third of those charged 'further west'. In 1900 *The Freemason's Chronicle* reported that it was 'absolutely the only modern restaurant where a man could order a modest chop and be served with exactly the same courtesy and consideration as when he was dining *en prince*; it is one feature of the place which the Manager – himself one of the most courteous of men – has brought to perfection; and its exists nowhere else'. High praise indeed for a restaurant accustomed to hosting banquets attended by the illustrious.

Only in the early 20th century did the Restaurant extend onto the actual corner site. Previously based there at No.221 had been the National Sunday League, founded in 1855 to encourage the opening of museums, art galleries and libraries on Sunday afternoons, besides excursions and 'bands in the parks', and 'generally to promote Intellectual and Elevating Recreation on that Day'. Sunday *trading*, as nowadays witnessed on this corner, was not on their agenda.

The Holborn Restaurant closed in 1955, to the vociferous regret of its devotees, and in 1957-58 Aviation House was erected on the corner for occupation by the Civil Aviation Authority. This building will be remembered by cognoscenti of the pop world for the De Lane Lea studios in the basement, which recorded such major hits as the Rolling Stones' *I Wanna Be Your Man* (by Lennon and McCartney, 1963) and The Animals' *House of the Rising Sun* (1964); and the first recording together of the Jimi Hendrix Experience in 1966. The reconstructed office block currently houses the Food Standards Agency, while on its ground floor is a branch of Sainsbury's (p 81), which has thus returned to the parish of its birth. Evidently, establishing a market here in the 21st century is not the problem it was in the 17th!

Our walk is at an end. Holborn station is diagonally across Kingsway; or simply cross to Sainsbury's if you wish to embark on Route 4.

Route 4
Tributaries of Drury Lane
Circular walk from Holborn Underground Station (see back cover for map)

Here we explore a quiet backwater, on either side of Drury Lane, ignored by most guidebooks and shunned by most tourists. Figure **[18]** shows its character in the early 19th century.

We begin at **Holborn Underground station**. Opened in 1906 on the Great Northern, Piccadilly & Brompton Railway, this initially served only what became the Piccadilly Line. It was reopened in 1933 equipped with escalators and new Central Line platforms to replace the nearby, inaccurately named, British Museum station of the Central London Railway (see p 71). Leaving the station by its main (Kingsway) exit, walk a few metres to the right, then cross the road to Sainsbury's.

Turn left down the west side of bustling Edwardian Kingsway, then take the first turning on the right into **PARKER STREET**, and into an area with a much longer history. On your right, a restaurant occupies the ground floor of the former Kingsway Corner Buildings. Ahead of us is **No.53**, until recently a public house, known latterly as the Fulmar & Firkin but for decades as the Kingsway Tavern. Though dating only from c.1921, it stands on the site of

an 18th-century tavern named the Crown & Cushion. As an inscription records, the architect was Delissa Joseph, who also designed the original sub-surface concourse at Piccadilly Circus Tube station. A cocktail and table-dancing bar now occupies the ground floor of No.53, while offices above house such unlikely bedfellows as the YMCA and the search-engine providers 'Ask Jeeves'.

Elevated taking-in doors surviving opposite, at **No.62**, once served a printing shop. Continue along Parker Street, whose narrowness at this point reflects its original width throughout its length. First recorded in 1620 as Parker's Lane, it was probably named after Philip Parker, who erected some of its houses. It was built in a meadow known as Rose Field, then owned by Sir Charles Cornwallis, and thought to have provided pasture for a Rose tavern in Broad Street (p 63).

Next on the right, clad in electric-blue glass, is the modern, hexagonal, 13-storey **Parker Tower**, originally the British Institute of Management's Management House. Former Nos.45&47, on this site, long contained premises of the Biblewoman charity, founded in 1857 by Ellen Ranyard (of Hunter Street, Bloomsbury) who, having walked the streets of Soho and St Giles, had been appalled by the squalor she witnessed. Her first project, to sell bibles to poor local women (for a weekly penny subscription), was a success. Her first recruit

18 Part of map by James Wyld (1828) for the Duke of Bedford, showing the tortuous and narrow streets east of Drury Lane before Kingsway was built

75

was a Soho-born woman named Marion B—, whose background gave her readier access to her target buyers than would have been available to a middle-class vendor. Within a month 70 bibles were bought by women of the kind 'who spent most of their waking hours in gin shops'. Here in Parker Street the charity opened a refuge and dormitory for street girls, such as watercress sellers. The superintendent, from 1861, was Agnes Elizabeth Jones, who, however, soon left to become a probationer at St Thomas's Hospital, where she was known as Florence Nightingale's 'best and dearest pupil'. Ranyard's charity went on to pioneer district nursing in London, and by 1900 its Parker Street premises were listed as the 'training home' of the London Biblewomen & Nurses' Mission. At No.43, on the corner now occupied by the Newton Arms (p 88), was the works of Malby & Son, mid-Victorian lithographers and globe makers.

Beyond Newton Street (p 88) is **Nos.39&41**, known as Page House when first refurbished and now occupied by the international law firm, Chambers & Partners. The handsome late-Victorian building once housed a succession of publishers. Built for Eyre & Spottiswoode, it was later taken over by Harrap's and, more recently, Pitman's. Until the 1880s the site was occupied by the printing works of the Hansard family, run by the sons of Luke Hansard, printer to the House of Commons under seven Speakers, who opened his second works here in 1800 when his mushrooming parliamentary work outgrew his premises in Great Turnstile (off High Holborn to the east).

Parker's Lane began as a service area for fashionable Great Queen Street (p 91) to its south; the stables of the Dutch ambassador were located here c.1660. By the 19th century the Parker Street area was a hive of industry and commerce, swarming with warehouses serving the nearby Covent Garden market, and with workshops and small factories producing a wide variety of goods, many connected with the local coachbuilding trade.

For the numerous inhabitants of the neighbourhood's old houses and tenements, living conditions were grim. On Charles Booth's 1889 poverty map, Parker Street was shaded black, meaning 'vicious, semi-criminal'. In his *Life and Labour of the People in London*, he described the people of Parker Street as 'the blackest of the black', treating them very much as a case study of extreme deprivation. Using information gathered by missionaries of the London City Mission, he detailed the occupants of every house in four local streets. Most were Irish Catholics; few of their large families occupied more than one room. In Booth's words, '15 rooms out of 20 were filthy to the last degree . . . Not a room would be free from vermin, and in many life at night was unbearable'. Many residents earned a living 'as market porters, or by selling flowers, fruit, fowls or vegetables in the streets, but as to not a few it is a mystery how they live'. One enterprising family devoted itself to making tiny toy mice; one elderly woman spent her whole time shelling peas. Prostitution was a major industry. 'Drunkenness and dirt and bad language prevailed, and violence was common, reaching at times to murder.' Census returns for 1881 confirm that many single houses were occupied by thirty people or more.

An Act of 1886 empowered the Metropolitan Board of Works (MBW) to sweep all of this away. 108 local houses were purchased for demolition, and much of the land acquired was redeveloped in the next decade by the Board's successor, the newly formed London County Council (LCC). On the north side of a widened Parker Street, red-brick **Parker House**, to which we now proceed, was opened in 1893 as Parker Street House, a lodging-house for 320 single men, sleeping in tiny cubicles. This was a rare early example of LCC involvement in such provision, which was normally left to charitable bodies such as Lord Rowton's. Now run by Camden Council, the hostel still meets a similar need, though the number of beds has exactly halved. Earlier located on the Parker House site were the mid-19th-century Holy Trinity National Schools.

Vanished No.44, opposite, which housed the Bedford Glass Works in the 1880s, later became a basket warehouse. Extant **Nos.40&42** was used initially for basket storage and later, in the interwar years, as a fruit and paper warehouse, with a shopfitter's premises above. The unlabelled 20th-century brick building to the right, formerly called Burwood House, is a rear extension of Puerorum House in Great Queen Street (p 99), on a site occupied in Victorian times by the Masonic Jeweller and Masonic Printing Works. At **No.32** the low 2-storey gabled brick building with a taking-in door, originally a fruit warehouse above stables, more recently housed the China Art Cultural Centre. No.26 was, by 1846, the factory of Corben & Sons, one of London's leading 19th-century coachbuilding firms, with offices adjoining at No.30 Great Queen Street, and still here in the 1920s; maybe it was to this business that the old embossed legend just above the pavement 'est[ablished] 1830' related. Next comes post-modern **Ruspini House**, accommodating some 24 young men and women, and managed by a Masonic trust. It takes its name from Bartholomew Ruspini, who in 1788, with nine others, founded on the New (now Euston) Road a charity to support the daughters of hard-up or deceased Masons. Beyond is **Market House**, social housing built in yellow stock brick to preserve the historic character of the street, as encouraged by its inclusion in the GLC's Covent Garden Action Area; its name presumably recalls the street market which functioned in Parker Street until the 1970s.

Turn your attention once more

to the north side. In 1864, a group of Lincoln's Inn lawyers founded the Central London Dwellings Improvement Co., which acquired slum houses here, and in several courts off Drury Lane, which after renovation together rehoused eighty families. Here today are **Aldwych Buildings**, which originated as a block of one- to two-room artisans' dwellings erected by the LCC in the early 1890s. To the rear, and visible from **PARKER MEWS**, is a row of what look like outhouses, actually the former Aldwych Workshops, built by the LCC at the same time for use by 11 local artisans. These are dwarfed by the huge brick wall of Soho Gyms in Macklin Street (p 86).

North of Parker Street, and parallel to it, ran a once notorious, but now wholly vanished, by-way. An afterthought, shoehorned in between two existing streets, it was built across their gardens, and linked to Parker Street near its east end by a long-lost Brewer Street. At first known as St Thomas's Street, it was renamed King Street in 1765, after local property-owner Joseph King; in 1877 it became Shelton Street, a name now borne by a different street (p 79) on the other side of Drury Lane. By his will of 1672, vestryman William Shelton founded a school in Parker's Lane for 50 poor children, insisting that their uniforms should be green; he also left funds to buy gowns for 20 poor and aged persons. When in 1763 costs were found to exceed income, the parish-run charity was wound down and

the school closed, but what money remained was left to accumulate until 1815, when a new Shelton's School opened in Lloyd's Court (p 20).

Booth described Shelton (late King) Street as so narrow that a cart and a pedestrian could scarcely pass with ease. Though he coded it black, he considered it to be a cut above Parker Street, where rooms were typically let by the night, whereas in Shelton Street lettings were weekly. The MBW clearance all but erased the street from the map, leaving only a short rump at the western end, which was joined to Parker Street by a new roadway, now called Parker Mews and serving only as an entrance to the Drury Lane Car Park.

Continuing west to **DRURY LANE**, cross to its opposite side and turn right. The unsigned footway leading off westward marks the borough boundary, the west side of Drury Lane southwards being in Westminster, and outside the scope of this book; the east side lies in Camden as far south as Great Queen Street.

The Lane is best known to many as the home of the Muffin Man in one version of the eponymous nursery rhyme; and for the historic Theatre Royal, Drury Lane, which *backs* onto its Westminster end. Before Kingsway was built, the Lane was the main thoroughfare from the Strand to High Holborn. Now truncated at the Aldwych, it once continued south-eastward as Wych Street to join the Strand near St

THE NEW MIDDLESEX Theatre of Varieties.

DRURY LANE FRONTAGE

19 The New Middlesex Theatre of Varieties, 1911, which became the Winter Garden Theatre in 1919

Clement Danes. Of ancient origin, the route was described as 'old' when first recorded in 1199. In the following century it was known variously as the Via de Aldewych, as Aldewychstrate, and as Fortescu Lane.

Its present name derives from Drury House, built at the south end in the 16th century by Sir William Drury. The whole length of Drury Lane was built up on both sides well before 1650. For a while very fashionable, it was at first lined by fine houses for the gentry; but as the upper classes migrated westward, many of their gardens were built over with shoddy housing of the worst kind. With two theatres on its doorstep, late-17th-century Drury Lane gained a reputation for rowdiness and bawdiness, and crime and prostitution were rife. Richard Steele referred to the 'ladyships' into which the Lane's courts were divided, presided over by 'matrons of known abilities'. In the words of John Gay:

O may thy virtue guard thee through the roads
Of Drury's mazy courts and dark abodes!

Little changed until the later 19th century, when the notorious slum courts were replaced by model housing or commercial buildings.

Opposite the alleyway where you paused is the modern, hangar-like **New London Centre**. This has engulfed the site of a Victorian pub called the Mogul, behind which stood the Mogul Saloon, a music-hall known affectionately as the 'Old Mo'. Later renamed the 'Middlesex', it was rebuilt by Frank Matcham, reopening in 1911 as the New Middlesex Theatre of Varieties **[19]**. Purchased 8 years later by George Grossmith and Edward Laurillard, it was relaunched as the Winter Garden Theatre, initially specialising in musicals. It was often 'dark' during its chequered existence, and despite some successful long runs, finally closed in 1960. When the site was sold for redevelopment, the planning permission required the inclusion of both housing and a replacement playhouse. The unattractive **New London Theatre**, designed by Sean Kenny and Paul Tvrtkovic, was opened in 1973. Eight years later its seating capacity was increased to accommodate the audiences of the record-breaking musical *Cats*, which ran for 21 years till 2002. In October 2010 Andrew Lloyd Webber's Really Useful Company sold the theatre, and three others, to former television boss Michael Grade.

Leaving Drury Lane for the moment, turn westward now along the footpath. This was called Broker's Alley until 1938, when it was absorbed by former Castle Street (to the west, p 41) to form part of present-day **SHELTON STREET**. The name of the

philanthropic vestryman was borrowed from the old street (p 77) on the opposite side of Drury Lane, of which only a small rump remained at that time. As you pass Arne Street (in Westminster, on your left), Shelton Street widens. Beyond, on the right, **Nos.51&53**, now a sushi bar, housed until 1998 one of the earliest Japanese restaurants in London, the Ajimura, opened in 1972 in Endell Street. The western part of Shelton Street is described in Route 2, but this walk turns right for a brief sojourn in Endell Street (p 48).

Turn right from Endell Street into **BETTERTON STREET**. Here, in 1684, the noted army officer and actor Michael Mohun died. But it was after a fellow thespian that the street, formerly called Brownlow Street (after Sir John Brownlow, p 48), was renamed in 1877. Thomas Betterton (c.1635-1710) was first connected with this district in 1659 when, as an apprentice, he made an amateur appearance at the Cockpit Theatre. He later became the leader of the United Company at Drury Lane, described by Samuel Pepys as the best actor in the world, and because of his fame was buried in Westminster Abbey.

Also buried there was a Brownlow Street shopkeeper. The antiquary and engraver George Vertue, having studied at Kneller's academy in Great Queen Street (p 91), made his reputation in 1715 through his large-scale engraving of Kneller's portrait of the newly crowned George I.

Vertue became a successful independent publisher of prints, and by 1753 had more than 100 of his engravings on sale at his Brownlow Street shop.

Strype (in 1720) described Brownlow Street as 'well inhabited and built'. Early residents included Irishman Bernard Connor, a writer on Polish history and a physician who controversially sought to explain miracles by the principles of medical knowledge. On his deathbed in 1698, he was given communion by William Hayley, the rector of St Giles, and then extreme unction by a visiting Catholic priest. Hayley subsequently buried Connor in the parish churchyard, judging that in his dealings with his Catholic rival Connor was unaware what he was doing.

Also in Brownlow Street, 'over against the Green Ball', was the house of John Lenton, a Holborn-born violinist and composer who was a member of the 'private musick' at the courts of James II and of William and Mary. Among Lenton's published works, available from his house, was his *The Gentleman's Diversion* of 1693, an early violin tutor.

Born in Covent Garden, and resident in Brownlow Street when he died in 1771, was John Lockman, poet and translator (of such authors as Voltaire and La Fontaine), nicknamed 'the Lamb' by his friends because of his gentle manners. Appointed in 1750 as secretary to the council of the Free British Fishery, he wrote prose and

20 Façade of 18th-century Brownlow House, Betterton Street

verse pamphlets in support of the white-herring fishery, and would send gifts of verses and herrings to the future George III.

On the north side and on the site of the recent extension to the Hospital Club (p 50), stood No.36 Brownlow Street, home from 1822 to 1825 of William Henry Hunt, the once famous watercolour painter, who gained the nickname 'Bird's Nest Hunt' from his studies of hedgerows with eggs in mossy nests. He had been born in 1790 round the corner at No.8 Old Belton (now Endell) Street, the son of a tin-plate worker and japanner, whose profession he was regarded as too sickly and lame to follow.

Founded in 1749, at No.28 on the same site, was the British Lying-in Hospital. Its founders, physicians Daniel Layard and Francis Sandys, had been male midwives at the Middlesex Hospital, from which they resigned when its governors rejected their proposal to enlarge the lying-in ward. Their new hospital, the first in the country to specialise wholly in obstetrics, flourished in Brownlow Street for exactly a century, before moving in 1849 to a new building in Endell Street, which later became St Paul's (p 50). No.28 went on to serve as a working men's club, and as a nurses' home after WWII.

On the south side of the street is **Betterton House**, local-authority housing erected by Holborn Borough Council in 1926. The fading red letter *P*, painted to the right of its main door, recalls that the basement was used as a public air-raid shelter during WWII. The block covers the site of Dirty Lane, which once led from old Brownlow House to Long Acre.

By 1877, when the partially commercialised street was renamed and renumbered as Betterton Street, most of its inhabitants were poor. A chimney sweep lived at No.18. At **No.24** is Brownlow House [20], a fine surviving early-18th-century building of four storeys, Listed Grade II★ for its panelled interior and staircase, with a central deal doorframe, and window frames flush with the wall, as permitted until the Building Act of 1709 required that doors and windows be recessed at least four inches, as a fire-prevention measure. The small-paned window to the left of the doorway, now lost in greenery, presumably belonged to the chandler's shop here in Victorian times,

and indeed until the 1930s, when chandler Arthur Puddington traded here. Later, and for a quarter of a century from 1952, Brownlow House was home to the theatrical costumiers Bonn & Mackenzie. Next door, at No.22, is **The Poetry Place**, run by the Poetry Society – their Poetry Café a pleasant stop for refreshment. Continue past the Good Vibes health club on the left, where earlier occupiers Haynes & Co, makers of 'saddle-trees' (or saddle frames), typified the many specialised industries that once thrived locally. Garden Studios, opposite at **Nos.11-15**, cover the site of an old Brownlow Arms pub at No.13. Gabled **No.9** was once another basket warehouse, with a fruit store next door at **No.7**.

Regain **DRURY LANE**. On the right, at No.21, is a historic tavern which, after several years as the Hogshead (the trade name of a large pub chain), reverted in 1999 to its traditional name of the **Sun**. Another pub, the Red Lion & Still, once traded opposite at No.172, fronting a short row of mean dwellings called Back Cottages. Next door, on the corner of Macklin Street (p 86), a shop at No.173 was the cradle of one of Britain's largest supermarket chains. Here John Sainsbury opened his very first outlet in 1869, specialising in dairy produce; his wife was the daughter of a Somers Town dairyman. Noted for its modern methods and attention to hygiene, the business thrived, and soon there were six shops, each managed by one of John's six sons. When, in

1962, his descendant Alan John Sainsbury was created a life peer, the title he chose was Baron Sainsbury of Drury Lane. Four years earlier the original shop had moved across the road to the modern box at **Nos.24&25**, now part of a Majestic wine store (to your right, beyond the Sun). No.25, on this site, served until the 1920s as the Homes for Destitute Women, run by the St Giles Christian Mission (p 103).

Now take in the remainder of Drury Lane's short Camden section. The solid red-brick building on your left, extending north from Betterton Street, was long occupied by a generating station of the Charing Cross Electricity Supply Co., later merged into Central London Electricity Ltd, and later still absorbed by the London Electricity Board.

North of Macklin Street (opposite), modern **Nos.178-179** mark the site of a tunnel entrance to erstwhile slum tenements known originally as Bell Court, and later as The Bells, which survived well into the interwar period. The few older shop buildings remaining beyond typify those which, until post-war years, lined both sides of the Lane, many devoted to ironmongery. At **No.180** is Krantz, established in 1905 as Solomon Krantz & Sons, 'shoe repairers, theatrical, municipal and surgical'. The premises had previously been shared by an ironmonger and a gun-case maker. At small, gable-fronted **No.181**, now selling carpets, an old fascia recalled until recently the business of 'barrow &

21 Painting by J Ogilvy, 1906, of Drury Lane at its junction with Broad Street. The Covent Garden Travelodge now stands on the site of the dairy

trolley maker & hirer' Patrick O'Brien, forced to move here from New Yard (p 99) when that site was needed for the building of the present Freemasons' Hall. Costermongers, as Booth tells us, usually hired their barrows. In 1968-74, **No.182**, with its small gothic-windowed gable, housed the Arts Laboratory, an 'avant-garde space' at which were once exhibited 'impromptu sculptures' by John Lennon. In Edwardian times the premises were a 'metal warehouse', while a tripe dresser traded next door at **No.183**.

Access into Shorts Gardens (p 47), on the left, was once through a narrow covered entrance. Beyond, today, the huge concrete Covent Garden **Travelodge,** previously the Moat House Hotel, stands on the site **[21]** of the pre-WWII wine and spirits store of the caterers Trust House Ltd, which in turn supplanted the large cooperage and barrel-washing plant of Combe's brewery (p 42). Facing Drury Lane here were Victorian flats named Kitchener and Khartoum, themselves on the site of an earlier Ragged Staff Court. Opposite Stukeley Street (see below) and beside a Marquis of Granby pub, ran Ashlin (or Ashlin's) Place, home to some of Combe

& Co.'s stables, and a successor to a 17th-century Paviors Alley. This is said to have been where the Plague of 1665 first broke out, after a group of Flemish weavers opened imported goods from Holland. St Giles was among the worst affected of all London areas, over 1000 people a month dying here at the height of the epidemic. Neighbouring parishes mounted guards to stop people leaving St Giles. William Boghurst, a local apothecary, courageously remained in the district, treating some 40 plague victims every day without ever contracting the disease.

The last building on the east side of Drury Lane is the **White Hart**, a 19th-century rebuild of an old inn, claiming to be London's oldest licensed premises. An inn of this name certainly stood on the nearby corner in 1536-7, featuring in the St Giles' Hospital land deal (p 9) at that time. Two centuries later, highwayman Dick Turpin and his accomplices are said to have planned their nightly raids in that pub.

Backtracking briefly, turn east along very narrow **STUKELEY STREET**, so renamed in 1938 after the antiquarian clergyman William Stukeley, an 18th-century rector of St George the Martyr, Queen Square, the nearest Holborn church. Goldsmith Street, the street's previous name, is recalled in the modern flats of **Goldsmith Court**, on the site of earlier tenements called Goldsmith Buildings, and part of a modern frontage formed by the backs of buildings

in High Holborn, including, at No. 7, 'EC', formerly the Cambridge School of English. Older buildings survive on your right. **No.2**, as late as 1901, housed a Welsh cowkeeper and his family; while **Nos.4&6** were a fruit store; and at **No.10**, on the next corner, was the workshop of David Ap Lloyd, a maker of art chimney-pieces.

Until 1883 the street was known as the Coal Yard, though it is unlikely ever to have been used for storing fuel. It was begun in the 1630s in a field called Bear Close (or Bear Croft), associated with the Bear tavern in High Holborn (p 67). Shown as 'Cole [or Coal] Yard' on early maps, it probably took its name from its builder, presumed to be a Mr Bassitt Cole of Drury Lane. Nor, surprisingly, did the Yard warrant coal-black shading on Charles Booth's poverty map, where it appears only in a 'very poor' dark blue.

According to one tradition, the Coal Yard was the birthplace in 1650 of Nell Gwyn, her father a Drury Lane fruiterer, and her mother an inebriate who drowned in the Thames at Millbank after falling in, allegedly drunk. (However, all accounts of Nell's birth are tenuously founded in tradition rather than fact, and the cities of Hereford and Oxford also claim her as their daughter.) The young Eleanor certainly had lodgings in southern Drury Lane in 1667, outside which Samuel Pepys spotted her 'in her smock-sleeves and bodice, looking upon one; she seemed a mighty pretty creature'.

By then she had progressed from the role of orange-seller in the pit at the Theatre Royal, Drury Lane to that of comedienne on stage, a prelude to her future career as a mistress of Charles II (see also p 117).

A well-attested resident of the Coal Yard was John Thrift. Nicknamed 'Jack Ketch', after a notorious predecessor, he served as public executioner and London's common hangman from c.1735 until his death here in 1752. In his gruesome career, he presided eight times a year at the hanging of felons at Tyburn, performed the hanging, drawing and quartering of convicted traitors, the execution of nine Jacobites on Kennington Common in 1746, and three years later the last public beheading in Britain, of the 80-year-old Lord Lovat. One evening in March 1750, four passing Irishmen encountered Thrift outside his house and allegedly accused him of being a thief escaped from Newgate (he had, in the past, been tried for robbery, though acquitted, and he was, quite probably, a 'fence'). When words turned to blows, Thrift claiming that his accusers attacked him with sticks (which they denied), he went inside and grabbed his scimitar, then chased two of the Irishmen across Drury Lane and into Shorts Gardens, where one of them, David Faris, slipped on some dung. Hacking away at him, Thrift caused five wounds to his head, from which he subsequently died. Thrift handed himself over to a constable, who took him to the magistrate, Henry Fielding. Tried for murder at the Old Bailey, Thrift was sentenced to death, commuted a month later to 14 years' transportation. He was later pardoned and reinstated as hangman, probably as an anti-Jacobite political gesture: his accusers, being Irish, were automatically associated with Papism, and so by extension with Jacobitism.

The cul-de-sac signed as *Stukeley Street*, which shortly leads off the south side, was once called King's Arms Yard after an eponymous pub at No.5. Here the former workshops at **No.12**, now home to graphic designers The Design Conspiracy, boast two preserved taking-in doors. No.14, in the far corner, successively housed a coachbuilder and a wheelwright. Neighbouring late-19th-century artisans included a 'plough-knife maker', a coffee roaster and a manufacturer of coach springs.

Next on the right is a site once occupied by a galleried yard known as The Galleries, its ground floors housing costermongers' donkeys, while their masters slept above. In 1895 the London School Board acquired the site, and opened here the Drury Lane Day Industrial School, an experiment in 'taming the wild ones' – rehabilitating delinquent (but unconvicted) youngsters, by keeping them off the streets and teaching them practical skills. Under a headmaster entitled 'Governor', 100 boys and a dozen girls were securely locked in daily from 8 am, washed and fed, and educated until the bell rang at 6 pm, when they were released to go to

their probably less congenial homes. As a prominent inscription recalls, the present building on the site long housed the City Literary Institute. This was founded in Fetter Lane in 1919 to meet a perceived post-WWI need for non-vocational adult education. With fees set at two shillings (10p) a term, the 'City Lit' thrived, and by 1928 had 5,000 students, taught in 25 different buildings. Offered the redundant industrial school premises in Stukeley Street, T G Williams, the Institute's principal, decided they were suitable, after gaining access to the building by 'unorthodox' means and exploring it by candlelight. By September 1928 it was ready for use. Among those who taught there or gave guest lectures or master classes were Dame Edith Sitwell, T S Eliot, G K Chesterton, C Day Lewis, Dorothy L Sayers and Dylan Thomas. The Institute soon outgrew its new home, which the LCC replaced with the present, plain brick building. Containing a theatre, concert hall and gym, this was opened in 1939 by the poet laureate John Masefield. It remained the City Lit's main centre until its removal in 2005 to Keeley Street (p 102). Now, as **International House, London** it houses a private-sector college offering language tuition and teacher training.

Modern premises opposite, at **No.15**, house Inflight Productions, a specialist media production company supplying audiovisual material to the airline industry. In the window is the (more than) life-size figure of the celebrated aviatrix Amy Johnson, in a heroic pose and holding a model aeroplane, rescued from an airbase by one of the company's directors.

SMART'S PLACE, intersecting from the left, received its earlier name of Smart's Buildings in the early 18th century, when one (or more) of three brothers named Smart built houses on its east side. Charles Booth, having walked local streets in 1898 with Police Constable Tait in order to update his poverty map, described the inhabitants of the 3½-storey houses still standing on the east side to be 'poor but not the lowest, no thieves, road sweepers'. Coding Smart's Buildings a 'poor' light blue, he commented on the broken windows he observed, and the 'cats munching garbage in the street'.

Smart's Place continues to the south of Stukeley Street as a short cul-de-sac which, incredibly, once had an even lesser tributary off its east side. Named Barley Court, it was a haunt of prostitutes, undeterred in their labours by the presence at nearby No.8 Smart's Buildings of what seems to have been the final incarnation of the parish watch house. Still standing in 1861, and then called the 'St Giles Watch and Engine House', this had earlier doubled as a base for the parish watchmen (known disparagingly as 'Charleys') and for the primitive, volunteer-manned, parish fire engine, a successor to the one first introduced in 1639.

An inscription on the left at the south end of the Place, hopefully retained after the building works blocking the Place throughout 2011 have been completed, records the second rebuilding of the St Giles & St George's Almshouses. Their predecessors were relocated from the High Street (p 63) in 1783 to a site between Smart's Place and Lewknor's Lane to the south (p 86), bordering on a Sword-bearer's Alley. They are said to have incorporated an earlier lock-up (or 'Roundhouse'), in which case this will have been the true site of Jack Sheppard's legendary 1720s escape as recounted in Harrison Ainsworth's novel (*cf.* p 23). In 1885 the Almshouses were again rebuilt, with an entrance here at Nos.9&10 Smart's Place, munificently sited in what was described at the time as a 'foul cul-de-sac'.

East of this second impasse, at **No.18**, is Malvern House College, another language school, located in a Victorian factory that in its time housed a printer, 'machine ruler' Thomas Hunt, and (between the wars) a bookbinder. On the corner beyond is a former brass foundry, the 'Victoria Works' of McGlashan & Merryweather (later McGlashan & Sons), coppersmiths of Goldsmith Street. By the 1920s it accommodated the works department of the Savoy Hotel.

On the north side at No.17 is the recently built 4-storey **Dragon Hall (Trust)**, a community centre serving both local residents and the wider public. Facilities include a drop-in for the under-fives, youth clubs, drama workshops, English courses and exercise classes, street-dance sessions, tea dances and jazz evenings. The four rooms for hire include a main hall with a sprung floor.

Previously on this site was a Holborn Borough Council garage, occupying part of a municipal property at the rear of the old Town Hall on High Holborn (p 70). This was Green Dragon Yard (later simply Dragon Yard), accessed through a narrow passageway off the main road. This marked the course of an ancient stream, the boundary between Purse Field (p 88) to the east and Rose Field to the west, a sewer (or 'wydraught') by 1650 when it was covered over 'att great cost' by Thomas Vaughan, owner of the property 'called by the name or signe of the Greene Dragon'. It was replaced by a pathway leading to houses and gardens here at the rear. Jeremy Turpin had built one of these houses in the early 1630s, and this delightful 1640 description of his garden suggests a very fertile soil: "the arbour formed of 8 pine trees, the sessamore *[sycamore?]* tree under the parlour window, 13 cherry trees against the brick wall on the east of the garden, 14 more round the grass plot, rows of gooseberry bushes, rose trees and curran trees, another arbour set round about with sweet brier, more cherry trees, pear, quince, plum and apple trees, a box plot planted with French and English flowers, six rosemary trees, an 'apricock'

tree and a mulberry tree."

By early Victorian times Green Dragon Yard was surrounded by stables and cowsheds. The urban population was unaware of the unhealthiness of the town cow until the outbreak of rinderpest cow disease in 1865, when strict regulations were introduced and the trade – mostly run by Welsh dairymen in London – gradually disappeared. Later in the century the site became the stoneyard of the St Giles District Board of Works (later Holborn Works Department).

Today a metal gateway, imaginatively adorned with red 'scales' suggestive of a dragon's back, gives access to the Soho Housing Association's **Green Dragon House**, the winner in 2000 of a Chartered Institute of Housing award for Best New Development. Occupying a site previously designated as a parking space, this is one of London's first 'car-free' developments, its occupants being ineligible for a resident's parking permit.

Follow L-shaped Stukeley Street as it now turns south, along the line of earlier Goldsmith's Alley, lined on its east side by further new timber-clad flats at **Nos.25-33**, on the site of the old Stoneyard. The offices opposite at **Nos.20-22** occupy the east side of the former brass foundry (see above).

Rounding the corner ahead into **MACKLIN STREET**, the red-brick gothic building on your right, now offices and formerly a Camden Council depot, was opened in 1880 as the St Giles & Bloomsbury Coroner's Court and Mortuary, continuing to serve as Holborn's Mortuary until WWII.

First mentioned in 1633-4, narrow Macklin Street was originally Lewknor's (or Lutenor's) Lane, built in Rose Field (p 74) on land owned by Sir Lewis Lewknor of Drury Lane. It soon gained a reputation for prostitution. In Dryden's *The Wild Gallant*, the old procuress operates at the Cat & Fiddle in 'Lewkner's Lane'; and in Gay's *Beggar's Opera* the lane is one of the places where women are sought for the pleasure of Macheath. Jonathan Wild, the double-dealing underworld supremo, and self-styled 'Thief-taker General', ran a brothel in this lane in 1713 with his lover, Mary Milliner, whom Defoe described as 'a jade of some fame'. The flower painter John Baker (see p 90) is said to have been born in 1725/26 in 'Larkners Lane', the son of a coach painter. Later known as Charles Street, the road assumed its present name in 1878. Charles Macklin was the Irish actor famous for his Shylock who, in 1735, stabbed a fellow actor to death in the Green Room of the Theatre Royal, in an argument over a wig; found guilty of manslaughter, he nevertheless survived, and was still acting at the age of 89.

Walk west along the north side of the street, observing the buildings opposite. Bearing the terracotta legend *Macklin Street Catholic School*, the still flourishing

St Joseph's RC School moved here in 1857 from Dunn's Passage into new premises designed by the church architect J J Scoles, with adjacent accommodation for the school staff, the Brothers of St Joseph, who taught the boys, and the Servite sisters whom we encountered in Route 3 (p 69). In what was termed an 'industrial school' the boys learned bookbinding and carpentry, the girls needlework and artificial flower making. The latter became a revenue-earning industry, and the school had contracts with several 'City warehouses' for the supply of the girls' handiwork. Above the original schoolrooms there had been a dormitory, housing the 30 or so teenage orphaned girls of the St Philip's Home that the Servite sisters had founded. Though much loved, the French nuns were linguistically challenged, and daunted by many of their charges' names: 'O'Shaughnessey' utterly defeated them. They left when, in 1863, the school was presented to the Diocese. During the next half century, the school was staffed successively by two further orders of nuns, the (Holloway) Sisters of Our Lady of Sion, who taught here for 29 years, and then the (Bermondsey) Sisters of Mercy, to whose selflessness the present school owes its existence. When neighbouring Catholic schools lost their premises in the Kingsway development, St Joseph's urgently needed enlargement, which was achievable only by demolishing the nuns' home. This they willingly vacated, seeking no compensation,

and a rebuilt school, absorbing its site, opened in 1908. In 2011 it boasts a shiny new hall, one of various improvements to be made possible by an innovative 'partnership' between the school and the developers of Central St Giles (p 57).

Another of Booth's very black streets, Macklin Street was largely rebuilt in 1889-92. **Powis House,** to the right of the school, was a further block of LCC artisans' dwellings, as were now demolished Lindsey Buildings a little to the west. The two names were borrowed from aristocratic houses (pp 122, 121) in nearby Lincoln's Inn Fields. At **Nos.10-14**, today housing Soho Gyms, was the 19th-century engineering works of Clements, Jeakes & Co., makers of 'household apparatus'. The modern flats of **Winter Garden House** recall, in their name, the theatre (p 79) which once stood around the corner in Drury Lane.

Crossing to the southern pavement, retrace your steps eastward, observing the north side. For some 40 years until the 1970s, red-brick **Macklin House** (Nos.1-7) accommodated youth clubs run by the W H Smith Memorial Institute (*cf.* p 124). The firm founded by the commemorated newsagent and MP (d.1891) had local connections, its stationery division having been among the first businesses in the newly built Kingsway (in Westminster, at No.7). Charities installed here more recently have included the Child Poverty Action Group. Inscribed '1892', Macklin House began as a model lodging house of the Society for Improving the Conditions of the Labouring Classes (SICLC) named Shaftesbury Buildings, after Lord Shaftesbury, a co-founder of the society. SICLC lodgings existing in Macklin Street before the MBW clearance were praised by Booth as being refreshingly well-run and frequented by 'the better class of board or sandwich-men'.

At Nos.11&13 is a group of old warehouses, with tenements above, known once as Staffordshire Buildings and now as **Lupus House**. It long contained the warehouse of the wholesale ironmongers Pfeil, Stedall & Co. With its origins in 18th-century Clerkenwell, and with later offices in St Giles at No.4 Broad Street (p 63), the firm specialised in components for the coachbuilding trade, and here in late-Victorian Macklin Street they stored 'American wheels'. They also marketed many other goods, not made by them but stamped with their own name, ranging from irons and lavatory pans to coal-hole covers and handcuffs. In the 20th century, as Stedall & Co. (the German-sounding 'Pfeil' name having been dropped on the outbreak of WWI), they sold motorcar components, including their outward-opening 'Bloomsbury' van windscreen. Though no longer a family concern, the firm still trades today, near Bristol, as a supplier of commercial vehicle body parts.

Born in a flat at No.13, the son of a hotel chef, was the impresario Eric Morley (1918-2000), the employee and later managing director of the Mecca entertainment group, who in 1949 created the long-running BBC TV series *Come Dancing*, and in 1961 introduced commercial bingo to Britain; but who is most remembered as the organiser of the eventually controversial Miss World beauty contests that he launched in 1952, and for the millions of pounds he raised for charity.

Continue eastwards to a gateway numbered **17a**. Here until quite recently were the offices of the William Shelton Educational Foundation, and of Leverton's Charity, founded by the architect Thomas Leverton (d.1828) to benefit 'six deserving females who have fallen from affluence into distress'. Now based in Gower Street, the several ancient charities of St Giles parish still function today, in a 'consolidated' 21st-century form. Behind the high wall, surmounted by railings, you may glimpse the gabled roofs of the still occupied Almshouses (p 63), today a small community of eight self-contained flats overlooking a secluded courtyard garden. **No.21** is the base of the Covent Garden Community Association. At **No.23**, with its prominent taking-in doors, were the studios of the Grieve family, whose business as theatrical scene-painters flourished for four generations from 1794 to 1887. Thomas Grieve, in the 1850s, was one of a team of artists employed by Charles Kean in his 'archaeologically authentic' revivals of Shakespeare and other historical plays in the London theatre. Much of this scenery was painted in the workshop he opened here, with partners William Telbin and John Absolon, at what were then Nos.34-37 Charles Street. Later taken over by fellow scene painters Bruce Smith and Walter Johnstone, the present No.23 was still in similar use, by Alick Johnstone, in the 1970s.

Beyond Stukeley Street, at the pedestrianised east end of Macklin Street, is **Dragon Court**, a pleasing, low-rise, post-modern office development, its name a further reminder of the once adjacent Green Dragon Yard. It stands partly on the site of the Newton Workshops, home to a variety of industries, whose 20th-century output ranged from scientific instruments to lingerie. Here in Victorian times stood the Casual Wards of the workhouse, where vagrants enjoyed the dubious privilege of a night under cover, possibly in conditions little better than those in the cowsheds which earlier occupied the site. Of its thirty temporary residents in the 1901 census, twenty were men, almost exclusively 'general labourers' from outside London, while the remainder were listed as 'charwomen'. Opposite is **Wimbledon House** (formerly Buildings), LCC dwellings of the early 1890s, more homely than most of those locally, accessible only from behind, and somewhat reminiscent of almshouses.

Emerging into **NEWTON STREET**,

stop to consider its origins. The intrusion of Edwardian Kingsway has obscured the fact that the area to its *west* was long associated with Lincoln's Inn Fields (to its east). Purse Field, on which Newton Street was built, was the westernmost of the three Lincoln's Inn meadows (see also p 106). This Crown-owned land was viewed by c.1600 as ripe for high-class housing development, a move stalled for some years by the lawyers of the Inn. Eventually (c.1635), speculative builder William Newton persuaded a cash-strapped Charles I to grant a licence for the building of 32 houses in Purse Field (see also p 92), some of them here in Newton Street. These, he promised, would increase the value of the property from a meagre £5 6s 8d to £200; in fact, its worth soared within 15 years to £1,700.

The present Newton Street consists of three parts. William's original street is to your left, while the stretch southward to Parker Street was once much narrower, and known as Cross Lane. There, at No.4, was the Rum Puncheon public house. The two sections were initially separated by a small stream (later open sewer), running from the direction of Smart's Place, then south-eastwards to join the Thames. The street's third portion, its southern egress into Great Queen Street, was opened up (p 91) only after WWII. Strype (in 1720) described Newton Street as 'broad', but 'not over well inhabited'. If it was ever fashionable, the

proximity of the neighbouring slums ensured that it did not stay so for long; but at least it can boast of housing, at various times, the Harleian Society, the editorial offices of *The Orchestra*, and those of the radical daily newspaper the *Pall Mall Gazette*.

The **Newton Arms**, on the south-east corner, is a slightly relocated replacement of a pre-WWII pub that itself substituted for a 19th-century 'Archer' public house. The gap to the left marks the site of a once notorious slum named Kennedy Court. To its north, the MBW cleared away the slums of Star Court and Chapel Yard, which had earlier been acquired for renovation by the Central London Dwellings Improvement Company. In their place arose the present stock-brick model tenement blocks named **Holland** and **Thurstan** (Dwellings), which Booth shaded a 'mixed' purple and described as tenanted by market porters and policemen. The blocks were once managed by the South London Dwellings Co., founded in Lambeth in 1879 by Emma Cons, a friend of Octavia Hill who also opened a Working Girls' Home in Drury Lane; Cons was, incidentally, both the founder of the temperance music hall that evolved into the Old Vic, and in 1889 the LCC's first woman alderman (albeit unable to vote). Holland and Thurstan were refurbished in the 1990s by the Shoreditch & Islington Housing Association, preserving some late-Victorian shop fronts facing Newton Street.

Walk north up the street. Further

SICLC dwellings once stood on the west side, now dominated by a 13-storey brick-built block of flats at **No.8**. Beyond this was the warehouse of 'rout furnishers' Simmonds Bros, who hired out furnishings for Victorian social functions. Much of the street's east side was lined in the later 19th century by the Roworth's printing works and the small factories of Woolley & Co., makers of playing-cards. Then a door at No.7, beyond, gave access to the regally-named King's Hall, Crown Room and Throne Room, just three components of the huge, rambling Holborn Restaurant (p 73). Here today are the luxury flats of concrete-colonnaded **Aria House** (1999), presumably so named to suggest its (relative) proximity to the Royal Opera House. We finally pass surviving **No.1** part of building on the corner that includes No.207 High Holborn (p 71), where Whitefield's Coffee Tavern traded in the 1880s, and which in the next century served as offices named Bangalore House.

Turn right at the junction with High Holborn; a few steps eastward will bring you back to Holborn Underground station. Turn right again by Sainsbury's if you wish to proceed to Route 5.

Route 5
Kingsway
& Great Queen Street

Circular walk from Holborn Underground
Station (see back cover for map)

This walk begins, like the last, at Holborn Underground station. From its main exit, walk a few metres north to the traffic lights, then cross the road (left) to Sainsbury's and turn left down the west side of **KINGSWAY**, and view the street from in front of the church façade (Aviation House, see below).

This 100-ft wide, tree-lined avenue was the outcome of London's last great Victorian road-building scheme. Before its construction, the route between Holborn and the Strand had been through 'congeries of tortuous and narrow streets' (see map **[18]**, p 75). Proposals to relieve traffic congestion in narrow Drury Lane (to the west) and Chancery Lane (to the east) by widening or replacing them had been put forward as early as 1836, but came to naught. In 1880, the Strand Improvement Association, in which the architect William M Teulon was a leading light, presented plans to the Metropolitan Board of Works, including a new road from Holborn to the Strand, but these were shelved for lack of funds. In 1892 the newly created London County Council (LCC) entrusted the matter to its Improvements Committee, and work eventually began

eight years later. The £5-million scheme involved clearing a 28 acres of land and, in the process, some of the capital's worst slums. Names suggested for the new road included Queensway (until Victoria died), Empire Avenue, Imperial Avenue and (punningly, perhaps) Connecticut Avenue. Kingsway it eventually became, in honour of Edward VII, who opened the thoroughfare – initially surfaced with wooden block paving – on 18 October 1905. In 1909 Edward Elgar's wife Alice composed a hymn of praise to the new street, to be sung to the tune of her husband's *Pomp & Circumstance March* No. 4. Full of jingoistic fervour it ends thus: *Let ev'ry voice in England say, "God keep the way by night and day, The King of England's Way!" The King's Way, the King's Way!* Despite the grand royal opening, building along both sides was gradual and piecemeal; by the outbreak of WWI several plots still remained vacant, to be developed only around 1920.

At **No.125** today is the preserved façade of Holy Trinity Church. The first place of worship here was a chapel of ease known as the Trinity Church, designed in a neo-Gothic style by Francis Bedford, and opened in 1831 **[22]**. When excavations for the Piccadilly Line undermined its foundations, it was demolished, to be replaced in 1910 by a more classical edifice. Designed by John Belcher, a leading figure in the Baroque Revival, and his assistant John James Joass, it was modelled on Pietro da Cortona's church of Santa Maria della

22   Little Queen Street Chapel (also known as 'the Trinity Church'). Frontispiece to the *Gentleman's Magazine*, vol 102, 1832

Pace in Rome; a planned central tower never materialised. During WWII Latvian and Estonian refugees worshipped here. In 1985 fire destroyed part of the gallery and the church, declared redundant, closed soon after. All but the façade was demolished in 1999 to make way for part of the rebuilt Aviation House (p 74), home to the then new Food Standards Agency. From 2010 the agency lost responsibility for nutrition policy and for food labelling in England but averted its own abolition, which had been threatened under the Coalition Government's purge of quangos.

The original chapel faced onto Little Queen Street, which the northern end of Kingsway supplanted, and whose line it follows. On the church site, at No.7, were the cramped lodgings of the Lamb family. Here in 1796 Mary Lamb stabbed her mother to death with a case-knife, in one of the fits of madness to which she was prone. Judged insane by the court, she was committed to the care of her essayist brother Charles, a responsibility he bore with devotion for the rest of his life. The co-authors of *Tales from Shakespeare* became inseparable, Mary always careful to pack her straitjacket when they holidayed together.

John Strype (in 1720) described Little Queen Street as 'pestered with carriages', and the street long had associations with the coachbuilding trade. The flower-painter John Baker (b.1725/26) was employed here in his youth as a coach-painter at the works of John Sykes.

Among the street's earliest occupants were the bibliographer Myles Davies (b.1662), and Alexander Browne (d.1706), a miniature painter and auctioneer and one of the first publishers of mezzotints. 43 of these, after Lely and Van Dyck, were published from his address here at the Blue Balcony. Describing himself as a 'practitioner in the art of limning', Browne gave drawing lessons to Mrs Samuel Pepys, with whom the diarist suspected he was having an affair. Born in the street in 1826 was the journalist and playwright (William) Blanchard Jerrold, best remembered for his collaboration with Gustave Doré on *London: a Pilgrimage*, though his text scarcely matches up to the power of the artist's images.

James Darling, bibliographer and religious bookseller, opened a shop in Little Queen Street in 1825. In 1840 he established the Clerical Library (later called the Metropolitan Library), aimed at theology students, who for a subscription of one guinea could borrow from his extensive book collection. For some thirty years, the innovative bookbinder James Hayday rented premises at No.31 on the east side of the street. In 1860 George Josiah Palmer moved his Bloomsbury bookselling and printing business to cheaper premises at No.32, later home to *The Church Times*, which he founded in 1863 and edited for 22 years.

South of the former church, and with elaborately decorated pedimented door-cases, are **Craven House** and **Beacon House** (1906), among the earliest of the many stone-faced office buildings lining Kingsway, individually designed in different styles, but of more or less uniform height (typically 7 storeys), each contributing to a harmonious whole. Pevsner remarked only that they had 'no strong personal character'. Craven House borrowed its name from Earl Craven's 17th-century mansion in Drury Lane.

Across the road stands **Africa House**, the last Kingsway block to be completed (in 1922) to designs by Trehearne & Norman. Under way in early 2011 was a £40-million refurbishment of the Grade-II-Listed building. When this is completed you will once again be able to admire the block's decorative features: two African lions sit above the doorway, while high above, along with Britannia, an elephant, camel and crocodile form part of an exuberant assemblage of human, royal and animal figures evoking the southern continent. The block was initially occupied by numerous firms trading in Africa, with such exotic names as the Ashanti & Obuasi Trading Co. Wetherspoon's **Shakespeare's Head** here is of recent origin, like the other pubs in the street. For decades there were no pubs in Kingsway, the LCC having decreed it 'teetotal' in 1900, despite pleas from the Public House Trust Co. (led, ironically, by

Earl Grey) that some of the 50 or so licensed premises lost through demolition should be reinstated. On the expiry of the original leases the opportunity for new pubs and bars was eagerly taken up.

Crossing Parker Street, pass **Kingsway House**, of 1906-07, whose early tenants included such diverse bodies as the Eugenics Education Society and Nobel's Explosives Company. High on the building is a multitude of motifs added by architect Arthur Sykes 'without any discrimination', according to Nikolaus Pevsner. Note the series of projecting balconies held up by alternating pairs of mermaids and mermen. Continue south to the next traffic lights. Here, past a Running Horse alehouse, Little Queen Street ended at a T-junction with its 'greater' neighbour.

We shall return to Kingsway later; for the moment, turn right to walk west along the north side of **GREAT QUEEN STREET**. **No.4**, now the Red Rooms nightclub, was formerly the Blitz Club, a centre of the New Romantic movement of the early 1980s associated with flamboyant, often counter-sexual, dress and with such bands as Culture Club, Ultravox, Duran Duran and Spandau Ballet. Steve Strange, the club's co-proprietor, acted as doorman, enforcing a dress code that excluded those wearing insufficiently outrageous clothes. Mick Jagger was once famously denied admission. A house beyond, on the site of the convenience store at **No.7**, was home,

from 1803, of Henry Fuseli, the Swiss-born painter and art critic.

The rebuilt **George** pub next door occupies a site which before 1878 was the third home of the St Giles & St George's Refuge for Homeless & Destitute Boys, precursor of the Shaftesbury Homes (p 25) and a successor to the boys' refuge at the ragged schools in Broad Street (p 67). Founded in 1858 by William Williams, a disabled solicitor's clerk, the Great Queen Street refuge housed about 100 boys, training them in shoemaking, tailoring, carpentering or wood-chopping, before despatching many of them to Canada or Australia.

The site was later occupied by a theatre which, in its time, staged the English premières of Ibsen's *The Doll's House* (1889) and Synge's *Playboy of the Western World* (1907). Built as a comedy theatre, it opened in 1882 as the Novelty, undergoing seven changes of name in 18 years (including Folies Dramatiques, Jodrell Theatre, New Queen's and Eden Palace of Varieties). Leased in 1900 by actor-manager William Penley, and reopened as the Great Queen Street Theatre, then leased to the German Theatre Co. until finally settling down in 1907 as the Kingsway Theatre, refurbished by one of London's first actress-managers, Lena Ashwell. Bomb-damaged in 1941, the Kingsway closed and was demolished.

Intersecting ahead is Newton Street (p 88), which after WWII was extended

southward to this point across the site of several Blitz-ravaged buildings. It was soon bridged by the offices of Elizabethan House, later Holcroft House, and now newly refurbished by John Robertson Architects as **New Brook Buildings**. The charity Action for Children has occupied part of the eastern portion at **No.10**. On the forecourt are six orange-pink sculpted stones (giant pebbles or small boulders?), installed in late 2010 by the developers Rinkelberg Capital Ltd & Hampstead Capital LLP. The other half of the building, at **No.16** beyond Newton Street, houses that company as well as Fladgate LLP, a major law firm latterly of Lincoln's Inn, first founded in 1760 and taking its name from William Mark Fladgate, who joined the practice in 1835. Winston Churchill and Anthony Eden were among the firm's clients, as, in 1862, was Abraham Lincoln.

Great Queen Street has had a long history. It lay on the line of a private royal road, along which the Stuart kings journeyed towards their hunting park at Theobalds (Herts.), crossing High Holborn just east of Holborn Tube station site, before continuing east via what is now Theobalds Road. Known simply as Queen Street until 1776, the thoroughfare had originally been named, by special permission, after Anne of Denmark, the consort of James I. Before 1612 a petition had been sent to the Earl of Salisbury by 'the inhabitants of the dwellings at the newe gate neere Drewry Lane', asking that the Queen 'gyve a name unto that place'.

Strype called this London's 'first regular street': built progressively between 1604 and 1658, entirely in brick and in a fairly uniform way, it complied with the building regulations newly drawn up by Inigo Jones. The eastern end of Queen Street, running into Lincoln's Inn Fields, was, like Newton Street (p 88), begun c.1635 in the 'Lincoln's Inn' meadow called Purse Field. No buildings survive from this early period, and the sites of some are buried beneath Kingsway. Here stood a Queen's Head public house, and beside it Queen's Head Yard, on the line of Kingsway but unconnected with the maze of courts and narrow streets to the south. Vanished Nos.74-75, likewise on the south side, housed the Victorian printing works of Wyman & Sons (earlier of Messrs Cox & Co.), notable for having taken over the press on which Benjamin Franklin worked in the 1720s (p 101). A copyreader there in 1825 was Douglas Jerrold, playwright and *Punch* journalist (and the father of Blanchard, see above). In his own monthly *Shilling Magazine* (1845-48), he serialised 'St Giles and St James', which melodramatically contrasted the extremes of poverty and wealth in the London of his day. At his funeral at Norwood in 1857, attended by thousands of mourners, Dickens and Thackeray were among the pallbearers.

On the opposite (south) side of the street stands the modern **Kingsway**

Hall Hotel (1999). Middle-Saxon finds unearthed during its construction provided archaeologists with important new evidence of the extent of Saxon Lundenwic. The hotel covers the site of a place of worship which in 1706 was the private chapel of a Mr Baguly. It later became a chapel of ease, presided over by Rev. Thomas Francklin, a royal chaplain who translated Sophocles and wrote four plays. Actor David Garrick is reputed to have been married here in 1746 to the dancer Eva Maria Violetti, though his bride always claimed that the ceremony took place in the parish church. By 1798 the Great Queen Street building was a Wesleyan chapel, to which some of the West Street congregation (p 40) had moved. Rebuilt in 1817, with a fine Ionic portico added 23 years later, this flourished until replaced in 1912 by an entrance to the Kingsway Hall (p 104).

Edward Knight, the comedic actor known as 'Little Knight' because of his short stature, died in a house on the hotel site in 1826. Living there at No.67 in 1750 were the actress-singer Hannah Pritchard and her print-engraving husband William. At the same address a century later was Thomas Sherwin, a maker of backgammon tables. Musician Thomas Augustine Arne, who wrote *Rule Britannia* and composed for the Theatre Royal, Drury Lane, seems to have lived at several addresses in the street, one of them being here at No.66, judging by a garbled ratebook entry of 1748

in the name of 'Augusti... Arne'. In 1814, Lewis Nockells Cottingham, church and domestic architect, and writer on medieval architecture, started his own practice at the same address, which by mid-century housed the coach builders Lambert & Tyrrell. In Carlton House, a later building at No.66, housing the Carlton Publicity advertising agency (his former employers), the celebrated photographer John French first established his own business in 1948, his assistants including such later well-known names as Terence Donovan and David Bailey. In 1779, also on the hotel site, the eminent surgeon John Sheldon, born in Tottenham Court Road, set up a private anatomical theatre, and founded the Great Queen Street Medical Society, which at one time had 150 members and issued diplomas. Sheldon was also among the very first English aeronauts, his balloon ascent from Chelsea in 1784 being caricatured by Paul Sandby.

The south side of the street was once intersected by several narrow yards, each accessed through a square-cut 'tunnel' entrance, and lined in the 19th century by stables and workshops. Some were connected with coach building, a trade especially associated with Long Acre, the street's westward continuation. Immediately to the right of the hotel site was the entry to Middle Yard, westward of which evolved the Masonic complex now monopolising the remainder of the street's south side.

The western part of the street was originally built on land known as Aldwych (or Oldwick) Close. The very slight dip in the modern roadway recalls a small stream that once flowed south-eastwards here, forming the field boundary (cf. p 85). The Close had once belonged to St Giles' Hospital, but by the early 17th century was divided between several owners. An account of 1629 relates that 'John Parker and Richard Brett had divers times attempted to build on a little close called Old Witch, which has always lain open, free to all persons to walk therein, and sweet and wholesome for the King and his servants to pass towards Theobalds'. Now they were tearing down stiles and bridges, and stockpiling bricks. Twice imprisoned for their illicit activity, the hapless pair may have been in the pay of Sir Kenelm Digby, a writer and diplomat noted for his duplicity, and then part-owner of the Close.

In 1635 he sold land to William Newton, with permission to build '14 faire houses' on the south side of Queen Street. Against stiff opposition in the City and locally, Newton obtained a licence to build both here and in Lincoln's Inn Fields, but on the strict condition that he build in the 'Court style', i.e. after the Italian manner being promoted by Inigo Jones. This resulted in one of the very first streets in London built to a regular classical design, with Corinthian pilasters rising from first-floor level to an eaves cornice, and prepared the way for the

disappearance of the then ubiquitous gable front. Designed, then, for aristocrats, the houses were substantial. One early titled resident (exact address unknown) was Lord Herbert of Cherbury, the soldier, statesman and deistic philosopher whom Ben Jonson dubbed the 'all-virtuous Herbert'; he died in Great Queen Street in 1648. There, too, lived the wealthy Paulets; a Paulet House and a Cherbury House (near the west end) were both still standing in 1822. By Georgian times the nobility had moved westward, their mansions being divided to form two or more smaller houses. The street became populated by a host of professionals, artists, writers, and thespians, as well as artisans and tradesmen, while at the same time evolving as the national centre of Freemasonry.

What is now the **Sway Bar** stands on one half of the site of the original Conway House, occupied by the 2nd Viscount Conway in 1639, a year before his defeat by the Scots at Newburn. He was followed at Conway House by two Lord Chancellors. Heneage Finch (1st Earl of Nottingham) lived here in 1676, when the Mace and Purse were stolen, in the small hours, by the notorious thief Thomas Sadler, subsequently hanged at Tyburn for the offence. The Great Seal of England was said to have escaped theft because it was hidden under Finch's pillow. A decade later the house was home to Baron George Jeffreys, the 'infamous' judge who presided over the 'Bloody Assizes'

23 John Opie, engraving from a self-portrait, published 1798

after the Monmouth Rebellion, and later at the trial of Titus Oates (p 103). Demolished in 1743, the large Conway House was replaced by four smaller houses, Nos.62-65. In one of the eastern pair, in 1753-58, lived the MP and poet Isaac Hawkins Browne, whose works included an ode *To a Pipe of Tobacco*, and whom Dr Johnson considered to be the most delightfully witty of 'conversers', complaining that 'when he got into Parliament, he never opened his mouth'. No.63 was the home in 1783-91 of the artist John Opie [23]. There he painted *The Schoolmistress*, and so popular a portraitist was he that his sitters' carriages regularly blocked the street. Nicknamed the 'Cornish Wonder', he had been brought to London in 1780 by the Rev. John Wolcot, better known as the satirist Peter Pindar, who had 'discovered' Opie while a physician in Truro (only later giving up both medicine and the church to write burlesque poetry).

By Victorian times, Nos.64&65 were occupied by (Thomas) Bacon's Hotel, *alias* Freemasons' Hotel, until replaced in 1889 by the Mark Masons' Hall, headquarters of the Grand Lodge of Mark Master Masons, who used it until 1938 (its modern successor is in St James's). (Mark Masonry is the fourth degree of the York rite, and boasts possession of secrets several degrees higher than those of Blue Masonry.) The present Sway Bar premises, on the site, are a rebuild by Ashley & Newman dating only from 1956.

West across Newton Street on the north side of Great Queen Street is the rebuilt **Hercules Pillars** pub, which has been trading on this site since at least 1760. The name was traditionally applied to taverns on the very edge of town, the eponymous entrance to the Mediterranean having been regarded by the ancients as the end of the world. The first meeting in support of Lord George Gordon was held in Great Queen Street in 1780, and in the subsequent rioting on 6 June a mob descended on the street, setting fire

to the residence here of Mr Justice (Robert Kilby) Cox.

Across the road the **Grand Connaught Rooms** (Nos.61–63) cover half of the site of the 17th-century 'statue house', whose façade was graced by a gilded likeness of Queen Henrietta Maria, wife of Charles I, until it was torn down by soldiers in 1651 on the orders of Parliament. It had earlier been home, successively, to the Earl of Northumberland and the Marquess of Normanby. Between 1702 and 1709, it was divided *depthwise* to form Nos.60&61, a passage giving access to the house at the rear. These properties were the original nucleus of the Freemasons' property. The portrait painter Thomas Hudson, who had earlier been the tutor of a young Joshua Reynolds (p 114), lived at No.61 (the 'statue house') for 17 years from 1747; at that time Reynolds is believed to have been romantically attached to one Miss Weston 'of Great Queen Street', possibly related to the Bishop of Exeter, and maybe the Dorothy Weston listed in ratebooks. Hudson was succeeded at No.61 by the portrait painter and etcher Thomas Worlidge and then in 1774 by the recently married actress, Mrs Mary (Perdita) Robinson. Four years later she played opposite Garrick in *The Winter's Tale* at the nearby Theatre Royal, Drury Lane, arousing the interest of an 18-year-old Prince of Wales (later George IV), who wrote to her, signing himself

24 Exterior of the 1774 Freemasons' Hall at Nos.60-61 Great Queen Street. Drawing by J Metcalfe, from *The Builder*, Aug 1866

'Florizel'. Though some 4 years her junior, he took her as his mistress, promising her £20,000 when he came of age; this was never paid. Abandoned by him after two years, she eventually received a pension of £300, but died, sick and poor, in 1800.

Founded in 1717, the Masonic 'Grand Lodge of England (GLE)', also known as the 'Moderns', arrived at No.60&61 Great Queen Street in 1774, having previously met at various venues elsewhere. (In 1813 they would merge with the rival 'Antient Grand Lodge', to form the United Grand Lodge of Ancient Free & Accepted Masons of England.) The GLE occupied the rear house, while lessee Luke Reilly opened the front premises as the first Freemasons' Tavern. The first Freemasons' Hall, designed by Thomas Sandby [24], was constructed at the back in 1774-5, and the Tavern was rebuilt at No.61 in 1788 to the design of William Tyler. Sir John Soane, who became a Mason in 1813, assisted in the purchase of the adjoining houses at Nos.62&63, and in their back gardens built an additional hall (a domed 'Temple') exclusively for Masonic use; enlarged in 1838 by Philip Hardwick, it was never highly regarded. No trace of it remains.

Sandby's Hall was hired out for public concerts and non-Masonic meetings of many kinds. The Anti-Slavery Society was founded at a meeting there in 1807. Here in 1837 Daniel O'Connell extolled Catholic emancipation. In 1846 the hall witnessed the foundation of the College of Preceptors, an examining body for teachers (which immediately proceeded to settle in otherwise residential Queen Square). A few years earlier, in 1840, the Hall hosted a World Anti-Slavery Convention, unfortunately dogged by 'the woman question': females were forbidden to sit in the body of the hall, and forced to occupy the gallery. The fury this provoked among the eminent women attending is said to have encouraged early feminist movements on both sides of the Atlantic.

The old Tavern also had its share of historical events. November 1807 saw the inauguration there of the Geological Society of London, the first such body worldwide, an event commemorated by a plaque erected by the society to mark its bicentenary in 2007. At a public meeting in 1824 in honour of James Watt, the steam-engine pioneer, those attending included Sir Robert Peel, Sir Humphry Davy Bt, William Wilberforce, and William Huskisson – who six years later would famously become the first victim of a fatal passenger railway accident at the opening of the Liverpool & Manchester Railway. On 26 October 1863, the lawyer and amateur footballer sportsman Ebenezer Morley convened a meeting at the Tavern of representatives from a dozen London and suburban football clubs, at which the Football Association of England was formed. Morley himself drafted the FA's first set of playing laws for football, which had thitherto been wholly unstandardised and an often violent affair. And in 1867, Charles Dickens was honoured by a banquet here before his departure on a reading tour of America.

A second Freemasons' Hall and Tavern were built in 1864-69 at Nos.59-63, after a competition in which E M Barry, the architect of St Giles National Schools (p 53), came second, to designs by Frederick Pepys Cockerell. Sandby's Hall was preserved within, surviving until c.1933, when it was declared unstable and demolished. Part of Cockerell's Tavern frontage survives as the main Connaught Rooms entrance, while remaining inside are his 1st-floor 'Grand Hall' and much of his 2nd-floor 'Crown Room'.

Managing the Tavern's dining rooms in the 1870s was the former royal chef Francatelli. Again rebuilt, by Alexander Brown and Ernest Barrow, the Tavern reopened in 1910 as a complex suite of dining, meeting and entertainment rooms, named the Connaught Rooms after the Duke of Connaught, the Masons' Grand Master. Here, on 5 May 1921, at a meeting of film distributors, the film pioneer William Friese-Greene made a speech in which he wondered what a film of his life might be like and whether it would be truthful. A few minutes later he died. Found in his purse was 1s 10d – seemingly all the money he possessed. His patents had been exploited by others, without benefit to him. The film industry gave Friese-Greene a big funeral, and commissioned a monument by Sir Edwin Lutyens for his grave in Highgate cemetery. *The Magic Box*, a film about his life, was eventually produced in 1951 for the Festival of Britain, serving as a further fitting tribute. Now Listed Grade II★, the Grand Connaught Rooms comprise 27 sumptuously decorated rooms for banquets, conferences and exhibitions.

To the right are to be seen the surviving third of Cockerell's Composite-pilastered Hall façade in Portland stone; part of a frieze depicting sun, moon and stars; and two of the four classical female statues, sculpted by William Grinsell Nicholl and representing the four Masonic virtues. While Wisdom and Fidelity are still extant, Charity and Unity were sacrificed in the building of the third, and present, Freemasons' Hall now lining the remainder of the street's south side (see later).

The second Hall covered the site of 17th-century Rivers House. First occupied by the Spanish ambassador, and later by the Countess Rivers, this was demolished in 1739 and replaced with two smaller houses (Nos.58&59). Their frontage was bisected by the covered entrance to Queen's Court (or Place), another of the minor tributaries previously mentioned. There, at No.7, was the final London home, from 1780 till his death in 1784, of Carl Heydinger, a renowned (possibly Silesian) printer and seller of German-language books.

Comic actress Kitty Clive lived at No.59 Great Queen Street in 1743-45. Dr Johnson remarked to Boswell that 'in the spriteliness of humour' he had never seen her equalled. Thomas Vaughan, at the same address in 1768-79, was a mediocre playwright, but notable as the original for Dangle in *The Critics* by Sheridan, his neighbour (see below). Based at No.59 in 1825-29 was the business of William Day, a publisher and printer of lithographs, styled 'Lithographer to the King' in 1833, and later 'Lithographer to the Queen and the Queen Dowager'. The same house was the birthplace in 1848 of the synagogue architect Lewis Solomon.

In 1899, a new west wing was added to Cockerell's Freemasons' Hall, supplanting houses at Nos.57&58, on part of the site of 17th-century Bristol House. The street's largest mansion, this had been home in 1637-8 to the Earl of St Albans (Marquess of Clanricarde), and then to John Digby (1st Earl of Bristol), a descendant of Sir Kenelm Digby (p 93). Later residents included Parliamentary General Lord Thomas Fairfax (presumably; he did sign a military order here), and the Earls of Devonshire and Sunderland. A subsequent occupant was Lord (John) Belasyse, who had served as a royalist army officer during the Civil War. During the Popish Plot crisis (see p 103) he was accused of high treason, of having allegedly procured the murder of Sir Edmund Berry Godfrey (on Primrose Hill), while also hiding the corpse in his coach, while also plotting to poison the King and secretly mustering a Catholic army. Imprisoned in the Tower in 1678, he was released in 1684 when the Duke of York paid £30,000 as bail. Cleared of all charges in 1685, a year later he was appointed to James II's Privy Council. Acquiring Bristol House, he divided it crudely into two (Nos.55&56). Henry Howard (Duke of Norfolk), a staunch Protestant, lived in one half for the next five years. In 1732 the premises ([**25**], p 98) were further divided to form four houses (Nos.55-58).

The Irish dramatist and politician Richard Brinsley Sheridan moved into Nos.57-58 in 1777, having succeeded Garrick as manager of the Theatre Royal two years earlier. With his first wife Elizabeth (née Linley), he spent five years here, already living beyond his means, a failing which eventually led to his pauper's death in 1816 in a sponging-house off Chancery Lane.

The German-born Court painter Sir Godfrey Kneller (d.1723) spent his last twenty years at Nos.55&56, while also owning Nos.57&58. Some writers have wrongly asserted that his next-door neighbour was his intimate friend Dr John Radcliffe, the royal physician. Kneller is said to have allowed the doctor access, through a door, into his back garden, which boasted a fine collection of flowers, until Radcliffe's servants were caught picking them! Kneller informed the doctor that he would shut up the door, whereupon the latter replied that he might 'do anything with it but *paint* it'; to which the artist retorted that he could 'take anything from the doctor but his *physic*'. Radcliffe, in fact, never lived in Great Queen Street: the anecdote actually relates to the duo's earlier residence as neighbours in Covent Garden proper, living respectively in the Piazza and in Bow Street.

In his Great Queen Street property, in 1711, Kneller founded London's first art school, his Academy of Drawing & Painting. Among the twelve Directors of this cosmopolitan establishment were the 'landskip' artist Peter Tillemans, the architect James Gibbs, and the decorative painter Sir James Thornhill, who succeeded Kneller as Governor. The academy was short-lived: factions developed in 1718 and two years later it closed. Among its notable students was the painter and draughtsman John Vanderbank (b.1694), a son of John Vanderbank of Great Queen Street, proprietor of the Soho Tapestry Manufactory and chief arras maker to the Crown. No.55 was the headquarters in 1770-82 of the Commissioners of the

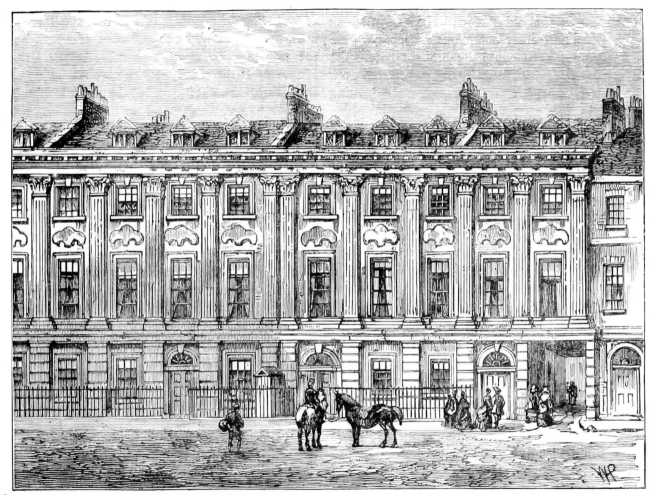

OLD HOUSES IN GREAT QUEEN STREET, SOUTH SIDE, 1850.

25 South side of Great Queen Street
in 1850, with square opening to New Yard
(drawing by 'W.P.')

Coach Office, who since 1694 had regulated London's hackney-carriage trade.

Benjamin Wilson, who lived at No.56 in 1750-61, combined portrait painting with the study of chemistry, and was honoured by the Royal Society for his electrical experiments. He was followed, in 1782-86, by John Hoole, the son of a Moorfields watchmaker, who in his youth had been 'director of the machinery' at Covent Garden Theatre. A clerk in the India House for 42 years, Hoole found time to translate Tasso and Ariosto, and write three plays which were performed at Covent Garden. The Mr Chippendale who lived in the same house from 1791 was not, as has often been asserted, the famous furniture maker Thomas, but an attorney named William. James Boswell had recently lived at No.56, in 1786-88, with his terminally ill, consumptive wife 'Peggie', and there wrote much of his *Life of Johnson*. An LCC blue plaque erected to his memory in 1905 was lost in the building of the present Freemasons' Hall, which also swept away New Yard, a further south-side tributary that once emerged beside No.55.

Nos.57&58, which had housed the Victorian coach-building business of James & William Biddlecombe, had given way in 1899 to a westward extension of Cockerell's second Hall, including a library and museum. Nos.55&56 were pulled down only in 1915, the latter having previously served as a glass mosaic works, and the former as the 'steam black lead pencil factory' of Wolff & Son.

High up on **Nos.19-21** on the north side of the street, a very faint legend recalls the presence until quite recently of the Royal Masonic Benefit Institution. On the ground floor is the unusual shop of Messrs Toye, Kenning & Spencer, suppliers (by royal appointment) of Masonic regalia and ritual equipment, whose bespoke output extends to such equally exclusive items as *Blue Peter* badges. The stated date of establishment (1685) disguises the fact that this was a merger of three businesses, those of William Toye, braid- and lace-maker; Richard Spencer, a Masonic bookseller at No.26 in 1834-74; and George Kenning, a publisher and ribbon-maker, whose printing shop and regalia factory stood at Nos.16&16A. The company is a member of the Tercentenarians, a select group of fifteen surviving family firms with a 300-year pedigree. Two doors away, at **No.23**, is 'Central Regalia', in a similar line of business though installed here only in the late 20th century.

Cross the road and follow the southern pavement westwards, the better to view the buildings opposite. **Puerorum House** (Nos.24,25&26), formerly headquarters of the New Masonic Samaritan Fund, dates from just before WWI, and once housed the offices of the Royal Masonic Institution for Boys, hence the Latin name. Founded in 1798 for 'cloathing and educating the Sons of Indigent Masons', it had earlier been based opposite in the second Freemasons' Hall. Four doors to the left, at **Nos.30&31**, is a classical stone-faced edifice, its façade dignified by four Corinthian columns and a quartet of allegorical statues. Despite appearances, it dates only from 1923-24, when it was designed by E R Barrow as offices for the Royal Masonic Institution for Girls. A frieze recalls its occupation until recently by the Royal Masonic Trust for Girls and Boys, following a merger of the two single-sex charities. The two Masonic blocks, **Nos.27&28**, with broken-pedimented wooden doorcases, and **No.29** date from c.1733 and are the best preserved of the street's older buildings. Edward Blanchard, the playwright son of a comic actor, was born at No.28 in 1820. Using various pseudonyms, among them 'the Brothers Grinn [*sic*]' – much of his output being based on fairy-tales – he wrote countless farces, dramas and comic songs, and for some 35 years the annual Christmas pantomime for the Drury Lane Theatre. First established at No.28 in 1840 was the business of Robert Riviere, a bookbinder of Huguenot descent, who later made bindings for the royal family and exhibited his work at the Great Exhibition. Bookselling, bookbinding and publishing were staple trades of Great Queen Street. A long-demolished house at No.31 was home to the engraver James Basire, with whom the printmaker Alexander Bannerman lodged in 1762, and to whom the artist and poet William Blake was apprenticed for the customary seven years in 1771.

Go past the main entrance to the present Freemasons' Hall (**No.60**, well to the west of the original house with that number**)**, and continue to look at the north side. **Nos.33-35** date from the early 18th century, as does **No.36**, once home to the Women's Protective & Provident League. Founded in 1874 by Emma Paterson, this was a group of trade unions for females employed in such occupations as dressmaking, upholstery, bookbinding and the making of artificial flowers. Its benefits included a library, a swimming club and cheap holidays. The shop front at No.36 is a modern 'Regency-style' pastiche, but some genuine 19th-century specimens survive nearby, recalling a time when the street was lined by shops of many kinds. Late-17th-century **No.37**, now an Indian restaurant, and formerly a coffee house, stands on the site of one of the street's earliest houses, built by 1607 for one Henry Seagood. The drinking-place at Nos.39-40 incorporates a Victorian incarnation of the old Sugar Loaf tavern, which had existed in 1720. London's last surviving example of this once commonplace grocer's sign was, sadly, lost in its late-20th-century renaming as an **O'Neill's**

'Irish theme pub'. It had given its name to a nearby, long-vanished, Sugar Loaf Yard, one of three such offshoots on the street's north side, the others being Bull's Head Yard and Whitcombe Alley (recalling an early Whitcombe's brewery).

We have now reached the end of Great Queen Street. Ahead, at the Drury Lane junction, there once stood a gate, barring public access to the old royal road (see p 91). It was later replaced by an archway, with a tenement above, protecting the privacy of Queen Street residents. So narrow was the aperture, and so difficult to negotiate for a carriage, that it was variously nicknamed 'Hell Gate' and 'Devil's Gap'. The road was widened, and the arch removed, in 1765. The junction with Drury Lane was remodelled in 1927 so that Great Queen Street and Long Acre were better aligned. Cross over to the wide paved area on your right to view the present **Freemasons' Hall**, an ostentatious, Grade-II*-Listed erection. Designed by H V Ashley and F Winton Newman, and built at a cost of £1 million, it was opened in 1933 by the Duke of Connaught, then Grand Master of the United Grand Lodge of England, and was at first known as the Masonic Peace Memorial, in honour of Masons killed in WWI. Urging silence, the Masonic motto *Vide, Aude, Tace* is prominently proclaimed beneath the massive tower. The accompanying gilded clock was installed to celebrate the 250th anniversary

of the Lodge in 1967, witness a stone plaque near the ground some feet to the left of the ceremonial doorway. At the heart of the building is the Grand Temple, and it also houses the various abovementioned Masonic charities that used to be on the north side. There too is today's Library & Museum of Freemasonry. Exhibits include items once owned by such well-known Masons as Sir Winston Churchill and King Edward VII.

On the site of the present Hall, No.52 was home from 1780 to Sir Robert Strange, the Scottish line-engraver remembered for his likenesses of Charles I and his Queen. At No.51, from 1812, were the business premises of brothers Frederick, Alfred and Henry Crace, three members of the celebrated dynasty of interior decorators, whose father John Crace had settled in the street in 1778, successively occupying several different houses. Living at No.51 in 1821-24 was R H Barham, the humorist and minor canon of St Paul's, better known as Thomas Ingoldsby, author of *The Ingoldsby Legends*. Nos.51-52 were, from 1867 to 1893, the headquarters of Kelly & Co., publishers of the annual *Post Office Directory* (see also p 69). Based at No.49, in 1791-1800, was the musician and music publisher William Napier. Piano, violin and cello accompaniments for one volume of his popular collection of *Scots Songs* were provided by Joseph Haydn.

Other Great Queen Street residents (precise addresses unknown) included James

Tyrrell (b.1642), historian and political theorist, and close friend of John Locke; the Hungarian still-life and bird painter Jacob Bogdani (p 38), who died here in 1724 at the sign of the Golden Eagle; portrait painter Charles Philips (after 1737); the artist and print seller Arthur Pond (d.1758), renowned for his collections of Rembrandts and exotic shells; in the 1760s, the portrait painter and coach-painter's son, Tilly Kettle; and the actor John Palmer, who died here in 1768. Living here comfortably in 1782-1808 was the actress Jane Pope, who had created the role of Mrs Candour at the sensational Drury Lane opening of Sheridan's *The School for Scandal*. In her lucrative career she amassed sufficient wealth to be able to bequeath over £5,000 to her sister, together with several properties, including her Great Queen Street house.

Now walk down the east side of **WILD STREET**, the side that is in Camden. On the west side (in Westminster) is the former Lambert & Butler tobacco factory (witness the largely illegible frieze), serving now as the early years care and education centre of the London School of Economics (LSE).

Named Old Weld Street in the early 18th century, and later as Great Wild Street until 1905, the thoroughfare existed as a trackway in 1628, known then only as the 'back side of Drury Lane'. It ran through the field called Aldwych Close (p 93), partly owned at that time by Sir Edward Stradling, who built a large house for himself on the east side of the present street. It had two, separately occupied, wings. From 1640 to 1675 one half was home to the Weld family (of Lulworth Castle, Dorset): 'Wild' is a corruption of their name. In 1651 Sir Humphrey Weld purchased the whole of the building which, as 'Weld House', continued to function as two dwellings. Cecil, 2nd Lord Baltimore and heir to the Maryland patent, died in one part in 1675. The other wing was let successively to the ambassadors of France, Portugal and Spain. In a large garden behind (and east of) Weld House, stood a private chapel, used presumably by the Catholic Welds, and later by Ronquillo, the Spanish ambassador, whose residence was sacked by a mob on the flight of James II in 1688 (p 118).

Among the colourful past residents of Great Wild Street was James Spiller (1692-1730), a comic actor and dancer who spent each summer playing the booth theatres set up at the various London fairs. Separated from his wife, he lived here with his mistress, one Dinah Stratford, who when the 14 pence a week he allowed her proved insufficient, was reduced to the indignity of selling asparagus or hot baked faggots. Spiller shared another of his mistresses with a duke until the latter found him wearing one of the duke's shirts. Charles Dignum (b.1765?), the son of a Catholic master tailor, was brought up in Great Wild Street. As a boy chorister at the nearby Sardinian Chapel (p 118), he came to the attention of the organist Samuel Webbe who, attracted by his fine voice, taught him music. Dignum went on to become a professional singer, hugely popular both with theatre audiences and at Vauxhall. A later occupant of No.55 was the stenographer James Henry Lewis who, considering Samuel Taylor's existing shorthand system to be deficient, devised one of his own. In 1812, at the age of 26, he published *The Ready Writer, or, Ne Plus Ultra of Short Hand*, which he sold in Wild Street at the sign of the Flying Hand and Pen. Here he also taught, composing amusing doggerel verses as a memory aid for students. By the 1860s his book was in its 97th edition.

In 1695 Weld House and its garden were acquired for building by one Isaac Foxcroft and a plasterer called Ralph Lister. Among the resulting streets was **WILD COURT**, a now rather featureless footway which we shall not traverse. On its south side once stood the 18th-century shop of the eminent printer James Watts, a mentor of typographer William Caslon. In 1725-6 the young Benjamin Franklin (**[26]**, p 102) spent 18 months here as a journeyman printer, before returning to Pennsylvania to set up his own successful printing house. His Wild Court workmates nicknamed him the 'Water-American', since he then drank only Adam's ale, while they, in his words, were 'great guzzlers of beer'. In 1768, while on a diplomatic mission to England, Franklin revisited Watts' shop, sending out for a gallon of porter, and drinking a toast with the men to the success of their trade.

18th-century Wild Court residents included Theophilus Cibber (son of the talented actor Colley Cibber), married in 1734 to Susannah Arne, petite singer turned actress, and sister of the composer Thomas Arne (p 92). Described as a 'nasty, ugly, squat little man', the mercenary Theophilus virtually 'sold' his new wife, forcing her to respond to the attentions of William Sloper, a wealthy young admirer, from whose patronage he hoped to benefit. In early 1737 all three were installed at No.12 Wild Court in a bizarre *ménage à trois*, which allowed Cibber to continue milking both his wife's earnings as an actress and his lodger's wealth. Eventually, after several moves of house, Susannah, pregnant with Sloper's child, wisely decided to dump Theophilus in favour of a life-long love affair with William – whom her husband then sued on grounds of adultery and loss of income!

Daniel Fournier, an engraver and printmaker, probably of French Protestant descent, and who died in Wild Court in 1766, wrote a treatise on perspective. While writing it, he had the habit of drawing diagrams with chalk on alehouse tables, for which he became nicknamed 'the Mad Geometer'.

Wild Court was to become a Victorian slum, described c.1900 as a place of 'filthy hovels'. A decade or so earlier Charles Booth's poverty map had placed it only in his second-worst category, coded dark blue for 'very poor'. Perhaps this reflected the efforts of the Society for Improving the Condition of the Labouring Classes, which in 1854 bought houses here for renovation, intending to re-let them to some of their existing inhabitants. Charles Dickens, in *Household Words*, applauded their 'cleansing' of the Court, where 1,000 people were said to have slept each night in appalling squalor.

Continue to the corner of **KEELEY STREET**, so renamed in 1905 after actor-manager Robert Keeley, born in 1793 in nearby Carey Street. Dating from c.1695, and successively named New Weld Street and Little Wild Street, Keeley Street was once shorter. In pre-Kingsway days it formed a T-junction at its east end with narrow Chapel Place (running north to the rear entrance of the Queen Street chapel) and King's Head Yard (trickling south). In the 18th century Little Wild Street contained the headquarters of the Moravian church. James Hutton, a Moravian minister and bookseller, opened a bookshop here in 1736 at the sign of the Bible & Sun. He later became friendly with Charles and Fanny Burney, and also a royal favourite. In 1778, with the King's permission, he visited his 'old friend' Benjamin Franklin in France to request terms for peace with the American colonies.

In 1699 the aforementioned Weld House chapel had been hired by a Calvinist named John Piggot for use as a Baptist place of worship, which was at first very

26 Benjamin Franklin wearing the bifocal glasses he invented in the early 1780s

fashionable, and attended by Daniel Defoe. A special sermon was preached annually to commemorate the Great Storm of 1703, which had destroyed 800 houses in London and 400 windmills nationwide. Andrew Gifford, appointed minister in 1730, was accused by one of his congregation of sodomy in his youth; although the charge was never proved, it led to his ostracism by other London Baptists. A purpose-built Baptist chapel, opened in 1788 on the south side of what was then Little Wild Street, was acquired in 1874 by the St Giles Christian Mission (p 55) for use as its base. Led by missionary George Hatton, this 'huge organisation', as Charles Booth described it, then specialised in work with discharged prisoners, while here in Keeley Street it ran a boys' home. The Kingsway scheme provided the mission with new, larger premises on a triangular site between Keeley and Kemble Streets, occupied until its departure c.1920 for Islington. There is now no trace of either these or of the Victorian model dwellings built in Little Wild Street by the Society for Improving the Condition of the Labouring Classes and named Ashley Buildings after Lord Ashley (later Earl of Shaftesbury), one of the body's founders.

The Great Wild Street Board School on the corner with the north side of Keeley Street survived until the 1930s. Opened by the London School Board in 1885, it succeeded a ragged school which had existed earlier behind an erstwhile Feathers pub on the west side of Wild Street. When the Board School closed because the advent of Kingsway greatly reduced the local child population, its premises served up to WWII as an LCC handicrafts centre, later as the Kingsway Day College, and latterly as the arts and music department of the **City Literary Institute** (then based in Stukeley Street, p 84). On the site today

is the yellow-brick building of the entire 'City Lit' (with entrance in Keeley Street), designed by award-winning architects Allies & Morrison and opened in May 2005. The 'largest adult education centre in Europe' continues to grow, currently serving over 27,000 adult learners.

The west side of **WILD STREET** is lined by one side of **Peabody Buildings**, which would have been in Camden but for a boundary change in 1900. Standing in a large courtyard, these thirteen stock-brick blocks of model housing were built in 1880 for 1,470 of the 'deserving poor'. They were funded by American-born George Peabody, a former Baltimore dry-goods merchant, and are still managed by the Peabody Trust.

In an adjacent Cockpit Alley, the perjurious conspirator Titus Oates had lodgings in c.1678. According to his fabricated testimony, his neighbour the Spanish ambassador at Weld House was among those implicated in the imaginary Jesuit-inspired 'Popish Plot', in which Catholics were supposed to rise in revolt, slaughtering Protestants, setting fire to the capital, assassinating Charles II, and placing his brother James on the throne. Oates's allegations caused great ferment; Catholics were put on trial, and at least 35 judicial murders resulted, in one way or another, from his evidence (some of the victims are buried in St Giles' church, p 18). When he later accused James II of treachery, he was pilloried, whipped

through the streets, and imprisoned for life; yet at the Glorious Revolution he was released and given a pension by William III. A further plot, to assassinate William in 1696, is said to have been hatched by Sir George Barclay and others at the Black Post tavern in Cockpit Alley.

Continue south to **KEMBLE STREET** and turn left along the borough boundary. Kemble Street was built in 1906 just south of old Duke Street (p 118). The Kembles were a remarkable theatrical family active at the nearby Drury Lane and Covent Garden theatres in both the 18th and 19th centuries; Sarah Kemble gained fame as an actress under her married name of Mrs Siddons. On the northern (Camden) side of Kemble Street and supported on splayed stilts, is the towering concrete rotunda of Richard Seifert's Space House, built in 1964-68, later than his Centre Point (p 15), with various structural elements in common. Refurbished in 1996 it is now occupied, as **CAA House** by the Civil Aviation Authority. The tower is tucked politely behind the building's respectfully low-rise Kingsway frontage, in whose construction three earlier blocks were lost, including majestic Magnet House (1915-20) of the General Electric Co.

Bear round the building to the left. We regain Kingsway as it begins its final triumphal march into Westminster to end opposite the BBC's Bush House. This southern stretch we must ignore, other than to observe the emergence nearby of the Strand Underpass, bringing light traffic northward from Waterloo Bridge. Opened in 1964, this incorporates part of the old Kingsway Subway, a tramway tunnel running beneath the road from Theobalds Road to the Victoria Embankment, and providing the only link between the tramway networks north and south of the Thames. A subterranean tram station, known at first as 'Great Queen Street', was later renamed 'Holborn'. Opened progressively in 1905-07, and heightened to take double-deckers in 1929-31, the tram tunnel closed in 1952. Deeper still runs the former Holborn-Aldwych branch of the Piccadilly Tube line, closed to passengers since 1994.

Cross Kingsway to **SARDINIA STREET**, leading east into Lincoln's Inn Fields. The modern street, linking Kingsway with the south-west corner of Lincoln's Inn Fields, dates only from c.1910. It replaced an earlier street which ran a little to the north, crossing the present line of Kingsway diagonally, and entering the Fields through an archway on the west side (p 118). That street took its name from the Sardinian Chapel (p 118) to which it led, but only from 1878, having previously been the eastern end of Duke Street; this in turn was descended from an old trackway called Fortifene Lane. It was in Duke Street, 'opposite the Romish Chapel', that the young Benjamin Franklin lodged in 1725-6 while working in nearby Wild Court (see p 101).

At the junction with Kingsway is the former Stewart House (of 1914-15), designed by the Office of Works. Until recently home to the Public Trustee Office, it has now been refurbished as the **New Academic Building** of LSE (see also p 120). A new addition to the streetscape is the unusual artwork, five storeys high, on the previously chamfered corner. Entitled *Square the Block*, the resin sculpture by Richard Wilson 'both mimics and subtly subverts the existing façade of the building', while at its base it seems to have been 'twisted and compressed as if by a giant hand or greater tectonic forces' – a witty response to the conundrum presented by the angle between the two streets.

Now turn north up the east side of **KINGSWAY** and view the buildings on the west side. Pass classical **Queen's House** at No.28 (see also p 120), and pause in front of boldly pilastered **Victory House**, which long served as offices of the Air Ministry. Designed by Trehearne & Norman and begun in 1919, its name celebrated the conclusion of WWI.

Across Kingsway, north of Keeley Street, is **No.65**, formerly Kodak House (1911, by Sir John Burnet and Thomas Tait), surprisingly modern-looking given its early date. Hailed by some as a precursor of modernism, it is actually an example of Edwardian Classicism stripped of its customary decoration, and adorned only by a series of round bronze plaques and bronze torches by the doorway. The story goes that Kodak's owner George Eastman saw an early draft elevation by Tait before he had added the usual adornments, and liked its modern appearance! The photographic firm remained here until 1982, when the tobacco company Gallaher's moved in. Pevsner, in 1957, considered No.65 to be Kingsway's only building of architectural importance.

Next door are cupola-topped **International Buildings** at Nos.67-71, originally the headquarters of the prestigious International Correspondence Schools (p 44); erected by the Methodist Church, they were leased to provide funds for the extensive social work of the West London Mission. Founded in 1887 in Hinde Street (Marylebone), a second base was established here at the Kingsway Hall in 1912. The pedimented doorway at **No.75** (now a 'Subway' takeaway) was the main entrance to the capacious, galleried hall designed by Josiah Gunton and built behind the Kingsway offices between Great Queen Street and Wild Court. Donald Soper, the first Methodist minister to sit in the House of Lords, was closely associated with the hall in the 1960s. With a fine organ, built in 1912 by J J Binns of Leeds, the church served also as an important concert venue. One Sunday in 1971 the evening service ended at 7.30 pm, 15 minutes earlier than usual. No sooner had the congregation vacated the hall than a large part of the roof collapsed, miraculously injuring no-one. The Kingsway Hall closed the following year, and was used as a recording studio before being sold to developers.

Excluded from the sale was **Wesley House**, the red-brick annexe visible across Kingsway on the north side of Wild Court. This had been home to the Kingsway Crèche, a very early example of such provision for (often single) working mothers. Moralists were scandalised by such an incitement to promiscuity, while xenophobes disliked the French name. Founded in 1888, the crèche moved here from Soho in 1911, and flourished in Wild Court for over 70 years, latterly managed by the GLC. Appropriately, the building later became the London Women's Centre, a base for a whole colony of women's support groups, eventually closed in the wake of the Council's abolition.

Beyond the Subway sandwich shop stand the offices of Regent and Windsor Houses (1913), recently refurbished and renamed **77 Kingsway**. Trehearne & Norman, the architects of these and several other Kingsway/Aldwych blocks, were among the original occupants here. Regent House, by the early 1920s, housed the Metal Airscrew Company and the Aircraft Disposal Company; the street has had aeronautical connections throughout its existence. Windsor House was until the 1980s home to Benson's advertising agency, where Dorothy L Sayers, writer of

detective stories, worked as a copywriter from 1922. Her experience here was doubtless the inspiration for her 1933 novel *Murder Must Advertise*. In 1935, with artist John Gilroy, she designed the toucan used for many years to promote Guinness stout. Just legible is a faded legend over the corner entrance to **Caffè Nero**, recalling Messrs H C Slingsby, makers of trucks before WWII, and later of office trolleys and all manner of office equipment. Such shops serving local offices have wholly vanished from Kingsway in recent years, to be replaced by coffee shops and eateries.

Continue north up the east side of Kingsway, where **Pitcher & Piano**, a bar at No.42, fills the ground floor of former Redland House, a classical building of 1906 by Edwin Lutyens, its doorways surmounted by some exquisitely crisp carvings of still life. Originally named Lincoln's Inn House, the block was built for William Robinson's magazine, *The Gardener*. From 1913 to 1917 it contained the headquarters of the militant Women's Social & Political Union, founded in 1903 by Emmeline and Christabel Pankhurst. The suffragettes' Kingsway base was repeatedly raided by the police, who also tried to have their telephones disconnected, though the General Post Office refused to oblige. Rachel Barrett, on her third release from prison under the notorious Cat and Mouse Act in 1913, was smuggled into Lincoln's Inn House, where she lived secretly for five months, all the

while continuing to publish from here the movement's *Suffragette* magazine.

At **Nos.44-46** are former Kingsway Chambers (1912), in a contrasting Flemish-looking style by Metcalf & Grieg, interwar home to the Cuban consulate. Beyond, at Nos.48-58, are **Imperial Buildings** (1914-15) by the same architects and adorned with some attractive signed sculptures by L F Roslyn. A surprise, among more conventional symbols of empire, trade and industry, is the figure of a bare-breasted woman holding a diminutive ocean liner, above the doorway of No.56.

REMNANT STREET, running eastward into Lincoln's Inn Fields, has been so named since 1935. In pre-Kingsway days this was the eastern end of Great Queen Street, on whose south side stood the large 19th-century book depository of the Society for Promoting Christian Knowledge. A detached remnant of a street this may be, but its present name honours James Farquharson Remnant (1st Baron Remnant), a Lincoln's Inn lawyer, LCC councillor, and MP for Holborn in 1900-28. The Remnants were a long-standing prominent St Giles' family, of whom we are again reminded as, continuing north, we reach **TWYFORD PLACE**. Formerly Stonecutters Alley, the footway was renamed in 1873 (as Twyford Buildings) after the Berkshire location of the Remnants' country home. Facing

KINGSWAY here is the Roman Catholic church of **St Anselm & St Cæcilia**, designed by F A Walters, and opened in 1909 to replace the one in nearby Sardinia Street (p 120). The altar and altarstone, brought from the latter, are said to have come originally from the Lady Chapel of Glastonbury Abbey. The Ionic façade was rebuilt in 1951-54 after damage in WWII.

Beyond is Africa House, which we viewed earlier (p 90). On its site, off pre-Kingsway Little Queen Street, lay George Yard, home to a Catholic infant school and to many 'poor carmen', according to Charles Booth, who was unimpressed by the 'pile of old bread and pea pods' he observed in one corner of the yard.

Cross Gate Street, observing above the doorway at **No.88** the wheel-and-sparks insignia of the British Electric Federation Ltd. Through its numerous subsidiaries, this once ran electric trams and motor buses in towns and cities all over Britain. Though some of the companies' successors still operate buses today, the Gearless Motor Omnibus Co. of 1914 was, unsurprisingly, short-lived!

A few metres beyond is Holborn Underground, where this walk ends. If you wish to embark on Route 6, backtrack to Remnant Street and walk along it to the north-west corner of Lincoln's Inn Fields.

Route 6
Lincoln's Inn Fields
Circular walk from Holborn Tube station. The walk begins on p 110, after a historical introduction. (see back cover for map)

Lincoln's Inn Fields is the largest square in London, covering 7.25 acres. In the 18th century, uniform rows of substantial, grand houses were ranged along three sides of the Square **[27]**. Only a very few of these houses remain; most have been replaced over the centuries by equally large mansions which still give a rather uniform impression on the north and west sides, at least.

Where the square is now was originally, as its name suggests, open fields: Cup Field, plus part of Fickett's Field to the south and Purse Field to the west. For a description and plan of the exact location of the three fields and a detailed description of their early history, the reader is referred to the *Survey of London* Vol. III (see *Sources*, p 126).

As early as 1376 these fields were a common walking and sporting place for the citizens of London, and there is also some tradition of jousting. By the reign of Elizabeth I, Cup Field and Purse Field were pasture grounds in the hands of the Crown. One of the first historical events which can definitely be located in the Fields is the execution on 20 and 21 September 1586 of Anthony Babington and his fellow

conspirators, although the exact spot is not known. One contemporary account tells of Babington being drawn 'from Tower Hill, through the cittie of London, unto a fields at the upper end of Holbourne, hard by the high way side to St Giles: where was erected a scaffolde convenient for the execution', and another describes how 'in the fieldes near Lyncolne's Inne a stage was sett up, and a mighty high gallows was raysed on the same.'

By the beginning of the 17th century the fields were obviously ripe for building development. The first attempts to get permission to build were made in 1613, to vociferous protests from Lincoln's Inn. Nothing came of it, but proposals were put forward to prevent anything of the kind happening in the future, and in 1617 a petition was put to the King that the fields commonly called Lincoln's Inn Fields might be converted into walks in the same manner as Moorfields ten years earlier, to the great pleasure and benefit of the City. As a result, a Commission was appointed in 1618 to survey the fields, raise contributions and lay out the walks. One of the Commissioners was Inigo Jones, and it is often erroneously stated that he was responsible for laying out the Fields. In fact, the Commission came to naught.

In 1638 William Newton acquired the leases of Cup Field and Purse Field. A licence was soon granted for him to build 32 houses, despite protests from Lincoln's Inn, and a number of handsome houses were built over the next two decades (see p 88). In 1657, Cup Field came into the joint possession of Sir William Cowper, Robert Henley and James Cowper. They wanted to complete the three sides of Cup Field by building on the north and south sides. Anticipating objections from Lincoln's Inn, they reached an agreement whereby the Inn controlled the manner in which the building was done. They also agreed to have Cup Field 'levelled, plained and cast into grass plots and gravel walks of convenient breadth, railed along on each side, and set with rows of trees', within two years. Incidentally, in September 1663, Samuel Pepys, who often walked in the fields for recreation, remarks in his diary that he 'took a walk to Lincoln's Inn walks, which they are making very fine'. But to go back to 1657, the three men sold the remainder of Cup Field to Lincoln's Inn, and Lincoln's Inn leased it back to them for 900 years. Building in the Fields was complete by 1659. The north side was known first as Newman's Row, later Holborn Row, the west terrace Arch Row, because of the archway between Nos.54 and 55 Lincoln's Inn Fields (see below), and the south side Portugal Row.

During and after the Great Fire of London in 1666, the Fields became temporary home to a number of refugees, and a Channel 4 *Time Team* dig in 2009 found in a trial trench evidence of their temporary structures and occupation.

Despite the building of the houses and the rudimentary laying out of the Fields, Lincoln's Inn Fields was notorious at the end of the 17th century as an ill-kept and unsafe place. Rubbish was frequently dumped there, many people were hurt by horses being exercised in the fields, various unlawful sports and games were indulged in, and it was a well-known haunt of robbers and vagabonds. The most famous description of all is probably that in Gay's *Trivia* of 1716: 'Where Lincoln's Inn wide space is railed around, cross not with venturous step; there oft is found the lurking thief, who, while the daylight shone, made the walls echo with his begging tone: that crutch, which late compassion moved, shall wound thy bleeding head, and fell thee to the ground…' Cripples apparently congregated here, extorting money and threatening people with their crutches. They were known as 'mumpers'; 'rufflers' were beggars who assumed the character of maimed soldiers and imposed on the sympathy of passers-by.

Clearly, something had to be done, and in 1734 the inhabitants got together and, in a pattern which became common in other London squares from the mid-18th century, applied for an Act of Parliament 'to enable the present and future proprietors and inhabitants of the houses in Lincoln's Inn Fields to make a rate on themselves for raising money sufficient to enclose, clean and adorn the said fields'. This Act provided for the election of Trustees, described their powers, and prescribed penalties for encroaching and committing nuisances. The 21 Trustees, who were all inhabitants of the houses around the square, were elected on 2 June 1735, and they paid compensation of £250 to Anthony Henley and William Cowper, the holders of the 900-year lease of Cup Field from Lincoln's Inn. The Trustees' first acts were to invite tenders for enclosing the central part of the square with iron railings on a stone plinth; to appoint a Scavenger to keep the fields and streets clean and take away household rubbish; to arrange for the laying out of the central garden; to appoint Watchmen to keep the peace and enforce the Act; and to arrange for lighting. To obtain the necessary capital to begin work they raised a mortgage on the rates, which was increased at least once in later years, the first year's rate being set at 2s 6d in the £ (i.e. 12.5%), based on the land tax assessment of each house.

Trustees elected from amongst the inhabitants of the square continued to run the affairs of Lincoln's Inn Fields in similar fashion for almost two centuries, although their powers were gradually eroded in various ways in the 19th century: they lost the power to police the square in 1829 when the Nightly Watch of the Metropolitan Police took over, and in 1856 the Board of Works of St Giles District took on the lighting, cleansing, paving and watering. From the middle of the century a strong public campaign, led latterly by the Metropolitan Public Gardens Association, was waged to open up the central garden to non-residents (it had hitherto been locked, with only ratepayers having keys). Finally, under an Act of 1894 the newly-formed London County Council acquired the central garden, paying £12,000 to the Trustees in compensation. The money was divided among the inhabitants and the Trust was wound up. Management of the garden passed to the Greater London Council on its creation in 1965 and to the London Borough of Camden in 1970.

It is perhaps inevitable that in a crowded metropolis such a large expanse of open ground as Lincoln's Inn Fields should be subject to periodic threats of encroachments; we mention three episodes in particular. At the end of the 17th century there were several proposals to design an impressive building as a focal point. Cavendish Weedon, a barrister of Lincoln's Inn, drew up a scheme that was to include statues of the twelve apostles and fountains using water from Hampstead; at the centre was to be a 'Beautiful Church upon pillars to be called St Maries'. The design of this church has been associated with Sir Christopher Wren, but without any documentary evidence (see Jeffery, Paul, in *Sources*, p 126). In the 19th century the Fields were for several years under threat of being partially submerged under new Law Courts. The first scheme proposed was by Charles Barry in 1842, for a Grecian building 50 ft high and dignified with Doric calumniated façades and porticoes on all four sides. Eventually, the Royal Courts of Justice were erected on their present site from 1868, to designs by George Edmund Street (see Port, M H, in *Sources*, p 126). More recently, in what was hailed as something of a landmark victory, the frontagers of the square successfully petitioned a Select Committee of the House of Lords to overturn a proposed clause in the London Local Authorities Bill of 2005 which would have permitted the London Borough of Camden to set aside the provisions of the 1894 Act governing the square and allowed portions of it to be hired out for large-scale corporate entertainment for a certain number of weeks in the year. This victory led directly to the formation on 31 July 2006 of a body known as the Friends of Lincoln's Inn Fields to work to safeguard the future of this historic public open space and to work with Camden Council and other bodies such as English Heritage to enhance and improve Lincoln's Inn Fields as it moves forward into the third century of its managed existence.

Walk

We begin our walk around the square at the north-west corner (from Holborn Tube take the Kingsway exit, turn left and left again at the traffic lights along Remnant Street). We proceed clockwise round the Square, then walk around the central garden.

As we have seen, the first houses facing the square were built in the mid-17th century. However, they were almost all substantially altered or rebuilt at various points in the 18th century [28].

The prospect in the year 2011 is mainly one of 18th-century houses, with some 19th- and 20th-century insertions. Before the introduction of house numbering to London in the 1760s houses were often known by distinguishing features, and several examples of this are noted below (see Nos.1, 13, 24 and 44). So many are Listed that we merely enumerate them, as follows: Nos.1&2, 5, 6-8, 12-14, 15&16, 18 (incorporating 17), 19, 24-27, 57-60, 64, 65&66; also the Margaret MacDonald memorial seat (p 125), the missing bronze bust to W F D Smith (p 124) and the Philip Twells memorial drinking fountain (p 114).

Lincoln's Inn Fields was a very fashionable address in the mid-17th century, particularly the houses on the west and south sides. Once the smart set moved further west, the square became inhabited mainly by professionals such as doctors and, of course, lawyers, given the proximity of the various Inns of Court. From the mid-19th century legal chambers and offices gradually took over from families, and by the late 20th century there were no privately occupied houses. At the end of the first decade of the 21st century, however, planning permission for a single family dwelling was granted in respect of two properties – Nos.5&6. The same decade has seen a growth in the number of barristers' chambers and occupancy by institutes of higher education with the arrival of the London School of Economics and Queen Mary, University of London (see pp 115, 120). The second decade will witness the first hotel in the square since the late 19th century and the joining of the Royal College of Surgeons, long established in the square, by another medical college (see p 116).

North side

The north side was developed in two blocks: Nos.1-12, and No.13 to Great Turnstile. The terrace was stepped between Nos.12 and 13 (visible in [27], p 107), marking the course of an ancient drainage ditch which once ran across the fields, still reflected in the steeply angled party wall between the present properties.

Nos.1&2 date from the early 18th century. Originally built as two houses, they were united in 1820, with one entrance being made in the centre. The boarded-up windows (2011) suggest an alarming story of neglect, but it was in fact a measure taken to deter squatters, and investigatory work prior to a planning application is proceeding inside. Thomas Macklin, the print seller and picture dealer, began his business at **No.1** in 1779, moving in 1782 to 39 Fleet Street. At **No.2** from 1796 until his death lived Henry Cline, the eminent surgeon. In 1810 he was appointed an examiner at the Royal College of Surgeons, subsequently becoming Master of the College in 1815 and President in 1823, delivering the Hunterian oration in 1816 and 1824. At the first house on the site of **No.1**, known as 'the Red Ball', lived Edmund Ashfield (*fl.*1669-*c.*1680), a pastellist, about whom little is known, although one source describes him as 'a sober Person and suspected to be a Roman Catholick'. The original **No.2** was home in 1675 to Parry Walton, a copyist and still-life painter who studied under Robert Walker and became keeper of pictures to James II. He was also a picture restorer, and worked on the Rubens ceiling at Whitehall. Having left Lincoln's Inn Fields, he returned to live at No.4 where he died in 1702.

Nos.3&4 were again rebuilt in 1972 in neo-Georgian style, replacing a building described by Pevsner as a 'tall Victorian monstrosity'. A stone plaque in the side wall leading up to the steps records that the foundation stone was laid by C J James for Compass Securities Ltd, the architect being T Saunders and Associates. Almost a century earlier No.3 was home between 1896 and 1916 to Ramsay MacDonald, later the first British Labour Prime Minister, and his family (see MacDonald Memorial, p 125). From 1816 to about 1850 No.4 was the headquarters of the Literary Fund Society (now the Royal Literary Fund), founded in 1790 by David Williams 'for the express purpose of affording pecuniary relief to authors in times of distress'.

Nos.5 and 6 have both received planning permission in 2011 for conversion to single family dwellings. **No.5** is an early Georgian house, the façade of which was rebuilt at an unknown date in the 19th century, possibly because the 18th-century wall became unstable. It is believed that nothing remains of the original 17th-century house, although its plan with a central stairwell may have been copied when it was rebuilt between 1715 and 1730. No.5 was occupied by the law firm A F and R W Tweedie (now Vizards Tweedie) from 1865 to c.2008. Their strong-room survives at the rear of the property.

There is a variety of styles of railings and a mixture of red brick and stock brick in successive houses. **No.8** has a fine wrought-iron balcony at first-floor level, and the front door of **No.9** is flanked by Doric columns. **Nos.10&11** is a 1980s building by Westwood, Piet, Poole and Smart. It won a Civic Trust Award, as we are informed by the triangular plaque on

28 View of Lincoln's Inn Fields from the north-west corner (Rudolph Ackermann, 1810)

the front wall. Sir William Randal Cremer, peace campaigner, winner of the Nobel peace prize in 1903 and political radical, lived at his office in **No.11** from 1884, after his wife died. Part of the building later housed the 'Harrisonian' branch of the Church of Humanity or Positivist Church, whose ritualistic worship was of humanity itself. Founded in 1867 by Richard Congreve, in Rugby Street (Bloomsbury), the organisation underwent a schism in 1878, when followers of the lawyer and LCC Alderman Frederic Harrison broke away. In 1909, having latterly been based in Fetter Lane, they took part of No.11 as their headquarters, remaining here until 1916 when they reunited with 'Congrevians' in Rugby Street (see CHR 24 in *Sources*, p 126).

Nos.12-14 were all designed and built by Sir John Soane, architect to the Bank of England, Professor of Architecture at the Royal Academy and a great collector of paintings, sculpture and antique fragments. He moved with his family to Lincoln's Inn Fields in 1794, having purchased No.12 in 1792 and completely rebuilt it. At the back of the site, where the stables and outbuildings had been, he included an office for his growing architectural practice, with a separate entrance in Whetstone Park (see *Streets of Old Holborn*). In 1808 he purchased the freehold of No.13 and extended along the back of the site from No.12, building an extension to his office and a double-height domed space into which he put plaster casts – the beginnings of his museum. Not long afterwards he persuaded his tenant in No.13 to move into No.12 and was able to pull down No.13 and rebuild it. The new house was finished in 1813 and he lived there until his death at the age of 83 on 20 January 1837, gradually filling it with his collections, which he arranged and rearranged almost up to the day of his death. In 1833 he obtained an Act of Parliament to come into effect at his death, vesting his house and collections in Trustees, to be open to the Nation as a museum, and stipulating that it should be left as nearly as possible as it was at his death. No.12 was to be rented out to provide an income for the support of the museum.

Since 1970 Nos.12 and 13 have been run as one building, and visitors to **Sir John Soane's Museum** have had access to both houses (though No.12 will be closed to visitors until the late summer of 2012 for building work). The innovative façade of No.13 incorporates four 14th-century Gothic brackets from the front of Westminster Hall and two Coade stone caryatids modelled on those at the Erechtheion in Athens. No.14 was bought by Soane in 1823 and completely rebuilt in 1824, the front part of the site as a separate property which was rented out to lawyers, and the back part forming an extension to the Museum to the rear of No.13. Since 2008, No.14 has housed the Museum's Education Department and Research Library. The house is usually open to the public for London Open City weekend each autumn.

Between 1760 and 1763 the previous house on the site of No.12 was owned by Frederick Calvert, sixth Baron Baltimore, described by the ODNB as an 'author and libertine'. His debauched lifestyle was the subject of much critical comment, and his trial at Kingston Assizes on 26 March 1768 for the rape of a London milliner was discussed in numerous pamphlets. He sold the house to Edmund Proudfoot, a London merchant, whose occupation of the house is commemorated by a lead cistern bearing the initials and date 'E P 1766' which survives in the courtyard at the back of the house.

The original house on the site of **No.13** was known as 'The Pineapples' from the stone pineapple which decorated both sides of the gateway. From 1666 until 1667 the house was occupied by Lady Fanshawe, widow of Sir Richard Fanshawe (see No.35). Lady Fanshawe then took a 21-year lease on No.26. In 1708 for a short period No.13 was home to Spencer Cowper (1669-1728), lawyer and younger brother of William Cowper, the Chancellor (see Nos.51&52). He rose through the legal ranks and was appointed Justice of the Common Pleas in 1727. From 1746 the house was occupied by Sir Thomas Burnet, Judge of the Court of Common Pleas from 1741, and a Fellow of the Royal Society. He died in the house in 1753 of gout in the stomach. A note in the sewer ratebook for December 1752 reveals that the house was rebuilt after his death.

In the front area of No.13, as in several properties on this side of the square, are decorative metal coal-hole covers through which coal used to be delivered.

Magnificent Ionic columns flank the doorway of **No.15**. The house can be dated to *c*.1742 from the inscription on a lead cistern. Here, between 1757 and his death in 1787, lived Sir William Watson, a physician and scientist renowned in particular for his experiments in electricity. He was physician to the Foundling Hospital from 1762. The next resident was Mr Justice Wilson, a justice of the Court of Common Pleas and Commissioner of the Great Seal, who lived here until 1793. **No.16**, with its semicircular Doric porch, dates from the middle of the 18th century. In the 1930s it was occupied by the London Society for Promoting Christianity Among the Jews. **Nos.17&18** were built in neo-Gothic style in 1871-72 by Alfred Waterhouse for Equity and Law Life Assurance. In January 1774 Lloyd Kenyon, later 1st Baron Kenyon, an up and coming lawyer who was made Master of the Rolls in 1775, got married and moved to No.18. His new bride wrote to her mother with a detailed description of the interior, which must have been typical of many middle-class town houses (see Denvir in *Sources*, p 126). He later moved to No.35. **No.19** was designed by Philip Webb, a leading figure in the Arts and Crafts movement, in 1868-69, and is notable as one of his few non-domestic buildings. **Nos.20-23** are by Wimperis, Simpson & Guthrie and W Curtis Green, and date from 1936-37. A plaque to the left of the front door records in both English and French that this was the HQ of the Royal Canadian Air Force Overseas from December 1941 to July 1946 (see below under *Gardens* for further details).

The house previously on the site of No.22 belonged to Joseph Henry Green, the eminent surgeon and friend and literary executor of the poet Samuel Taylor Coleridge, from 1816 until some time in the 1820s when he moved to No.46 on the south side. Green's mother was Frances Cline, sister of Henry (see No.2). Like his uncle, Green was a surgeon at St Thomas's Hospital and much involved with the Royal College of Surgeons on the south side of Lincoln's Inn Fields, becoming Professor of Anatomy there in 1824 and President from 1860 until his death in 1863. Apart from his work at St Thomas's and the private surgical practice he ran from No.22, Green had a keen interest in philosophy, as did Coleridge. The diarist Henry Crabb Robinson records dining at No.22 in June 1817 to meet the poet and Ludwig Tieck, the German writer and critic. The occasion was the first meeting of 'The Friends of German Literature', a group formed by Coleridge. John Keats (then a medical student) records in April 1819 meeting Coleridge on Hampstead Heath in company with Green, who introduced them. In 1822 Coleridge advertised in the *Courier* a weekly seminar or tutorial for young men between 19 and 25 'for the purpose of assisting them in the formation of their minds, and the regulation of their studies'. The sessions were held between midday and 4 pm at 'Green's fine reception room in Lincoln's Inn Fields' and appear to have run regularly until 1827. Extracts from the notes of one of the participants were published anonymously in *Fraser's Magazine* the year after Coleridge's death.

From 1876 the Inns of Court Hotel (see *Streets of Old Holborn*) had a large and impressive south-facing frontage here. Heckethorn, writing in 1896, described the Lincoln's Inn Fields block as 'of a bold Venetian style, 90 feet in height, built of Bath stone, with columns of red granite in the portico and Aberdeen granite shafts to the mullions of the windows throughout'. He added that the interior of the block 'contains very fine rooms, among which we may specify the Masonic Hall and adjoining dining-room, the reading-room, ladies' drawing-room, and grand dining-hall, the last three on different floors, overlooking the gardens of Lincoln's Inn Fields'.

The present **No.24** was built in 1787 for Meredith Price, a lawyer, whose initials appear with the date on a lead cistern in the house. Decorative metal brackets for oil lamps are on the piers at each end of the front railings. The original house on the site was known as 'the Two Lions'. Here from 1724 to 1762 lived the painter Joseph Highmore and his family – his wife Susanna (née Hillier), a poet, their son

Anthony, a draughtsman who worked with his father until c.1755, and their daughter Susanna (1725-1812), later Duncombe, artist and poet.

Two better-known 18th-century artists lived somewhere along the north side of the square: the portrait painter and writer Jonathan Richardson the elder, resident here, with his wife and eleven children, between at least 1703 and 1724; and Sir Joshua Reynolds, for a short period between the spring of 1740 and the summer of 1743 when he was apprenticed to Thomas Hudson, who had his studios here. All are well represented at the Foundling Museum.

Over the front door of **No.25** is a built-in lamp, which would originally have burned oil, and on it a fine lion door-knocker. The doorcase of **No.26** boasts rich carving of acanthus leaves surrounding a head. **No.27** was home to Robert Smith Surtees, author of *Jorrock's Jaunts and Jollities* among other works, for a brief period from May 1825 when he was articled to a local solicitor.

No.28 was built in 1863 to the design of George Vulliamy. The Renaissance-inspired carved frieze was sculpted by Robert Jackson, who assisted on the sculpture of the Houses of Parliament and was responsible for the monument to Lord Palmerston in Westminster Abbey. The building is of particular interest as a very early purpose-built set of offices for

solicitors, in this case for the firm Frere Cholmely, who practised from this site from 1750 to 1992. An article in *Building News* for 26 June 1863 stresses the amount of thought that was put into the planning of the interior of these solicitors' offices, describing Messrs Frere's chambers as 'probably the most extensive and perfect of their kind'. A three-floor muniment room to the rear of the building came in for special attention for its clarity of storage, its security and its fireproof construction. Sadly, as with several other buildings along this side of the square, radical reconstruction has taken place internally behind the façade.

No.29, formerly the Royal Institute of Chartered Surveyors, was built by F H Greenaway and J E Newberry in 1924 and opened by HRH the Prince of Wales on 28 January 1925. Described by Pevsner as 'a well-mannered building in the Palladian tradition', it won the RIBA London Architectural Medal for 1924. There is a plaque on the side of the building commemorating this, and the names of the architects and builders are also incised into the stone. It occupies the site of former Nos.29 and 29A and of the old buildings in Newman's or Turnstile Row, which forms its return frontage on the east. The houses in Newman's Row included, according to Beresford Chancellor, a well-known curiosity shop and bookshop. Writing in 1932, he remembers 'in past

days…Page's bookshop, as one turned into Great Turnstile'. **Newman's Row** remains the official name of the roadway here, linking the Turnstile with the Fields.

No.30, round the corner on the east side of the square, is called Erskine Chambers, after Lord Erskine, the eminent lawyer (see No.36). Built in dark red brick with Portland stone copings and natural slate, it was designed in 1986 by Casson Conder, whose senior partner was Sir Hugh Casson. The design was influenced by Sir John Soane's No.13, of whose Museum Sir Hugh was a Trustee for several years. The proposed building caused some controversy at the time, since it was built on part of the gardens of Lincoln's Inn.

East side

At the north-east corner, cross to the inner pavement around the central gardens. Here is a modern sculpture in metal entitled *Camdonian*, commissioned by the London Borough of Camden from Barry Flanagan in 1980. Note also the rather fine municipal lavatories.

The whole of the east side of the square is taken up by the wall of Lincoln's Inn, the ancient red bricks gradually merging into the newer 19th-century ones with their blue diamond pattern matching the brickwork of Hardwick's New Hall of the 1840s beyond.

On the south-east corner of the gardens, opposite the main gate of Lincoln's Inn, is a granite **drinking fountain** on an octagonal base erected 'in Memory of Philip Twells, Barrister at Law of Lincoln's Inn, and sometime Member of Parliament for the City of London. 8 May A.D.1880.' Just around the corner from this fountain are a few surviving original kerbstones dating from 1735 when the railings around the garden were first erected.

South side

The buildings on the south side of the square are actually not in Camden: since the formation of the Borough of Holborn in 1900, the boundary with Westminster has run along the middle of the roadway. However, we have elected to treat the square as an integral whole, and continue our clockwise walk along this side.

The south-east corner is dominated by the **Land Registry building** (Nos.32-34) of 1901-07 and 1911-14, built in neo-Jacobean style by the architect Sir Henry Tanner of the Office of Works and loosely based on Blickling Hall, Norfolk. It was erected to accommodate the rapidly increasing business of registration of title to land under various 19th-century Acts of Parliament. The Land Registry moved out of the building in 2010 and it is now owned by the London School of Economics.

No.33 was originally built c.1659. Notable occupants include in 1756-81 William de Grey, 1st Baron Walsingham, Attorney General and Lord Chief Justice of the Common Pleas; and in 1800-21

another eminent lawyer, Sir James Alan Park. The house was extensively altered in 1822-25 by Sir John Soane in his capacity as Attached Architect to the Office of Works. The building was purchased by the Treasury in 1822 to provide improved accommodation for the Insolvent Debtors' Court. The public entrance and offices of the Court, which formed the ground floor, were entered from Portugal Street. Behind rose the upper part of the courtroom, lit on two sides by a clerestory and from above by a lantern, and closely resembling Soane's Five Per Cent Office at the Bank of England. Charles Dickens gives a bleak description of the Court in Chapter 42 of *Pickwick Papers*. No.34 was added to the building in 1847 and converted by Edward I'Anson. Like No.33, No.34 had been home to several distinguished members of the legal profession: 1656-1706 Sir William Montague, Lord Chief Baron of the Exchequer; 1756-57 Sir Robert Henley (afterwards Earl of Northington), grandson of one of the original owners of the Fields (p 108), he also lived at No.33 1749-55 and No.41 1758-68. He was Lord Chancellor until 1766, succeeded by Charles Pratt, 1st Earl Camden, who lived here 1758-1775. His son John Jeffreys Pratt, first Marquess Camden, politician, was born here. From 1779-98 No.34 was home to Sir Francis Buller, said to have been the youngest man ever to have been created an English judge, at the age of 32. The Insolvent

Debtors' Court was abolished in 1861 by the Bankruptcy Act, being replaced by the Bankruptcy Court in nearby Carey Street. The buildings were used to house the Land Transfer Office and demolished in 1911 for the building of the Land Registry.

Next to the Land Registry building is neo-Georgian red brick and stone **Nuffield College of Surgical Sciences** (Nos.35-38). It was built in 1956-58 to designs by A W Hall with Sir Edward Maufe as consultant.

In the original No.35 Sir Richard Fanshawe, diplomat, translator and poet, lived between 1660 and 1662, when he was appointed Ambassador to Portugal. It was home on two separate occasions to Sir James Montagu, afterwards Lord Halifax and Attorney General in 1708-10. Another Attorney General, Robert Raymond, 1st Baron Raymond lived here between 1711 and 1715. From 1728 to 1734 the house was occupied by Nicholas Fazakerley, a prominent lawyer, who was often consulted in Lincoln's Inn by Sarah, Duchess of Marlborough. He moved to No.46 in 1734, where he remained until 1752.

Nos.35&36 were rebuilt as a pair by Sir Robert Taylor in 1754 and destroyed by a bomb in WWII. They had interesting fenestration with a hexagonal theme, repeated in door panels and other internal woodwork. Lord Kenyon, Attorney General and Chief Justice, lived in No.35 from 1784 to 1802, having previously lived at No.18. No.36 was the home of the Lord Chancellor, Lord Erskine (1750-1823). In recognition of this, by 1896 the building had been named Erskine Chambers.

Nuffield College is the residential part of the **Royal College of Surgeons** (Nos.39-43), which occupies a fine Classical building. The College (it acquired its charter from George III in 1803) originally moved to No.41 in 1797 from premises in the Old Bailey. The acquisition of the large collection of anatomical specimens amassed by the famous surgeon John Hunter (1728-93) (now the Hunterian Museum, within) necessitated expansion and in 1803 No.42 was acquired, when George Dance the Younger was commissioned to design a new building. This opened in 1813 and had a portico with six large unfluted Ionic columns surmounted by the coat of arms of the College. In 1834 No.40 was acquired and Nos.41-42 again demolished, leaving only part of the portico, and a large building was erected to the designs of Sir Charles Barry. This building later expanded into the premises behind in Portugal Street which had once been the Lincoln's Inn Fields Theatre (see below). Further expansion came in 1888-91 when Nos.39 and 43 on either side were demolished, the new wings being designed by Stephen Salter, FRIBA. During WWII the College received several direct hits on the night of 10/11 May 1941 and over half the specimens in the Hunterian Museum were destroyed. Between 1952 and 1957 the College was reconstructed through the generosity of a number of benefactors, including Lord Nuffield (1877-1963), who financed the building of residential accommodation (see above). The Hunterian Museum underwent a major refurbishment in 2005 and was short-listed for the prestigious Gulbenkian prize for museums and galleries for 2006.

No.41 was home to Robert Brudenell, 2nd Earl of Cardigan, between 1653 and 1701, and became known as Cardigan House; he was succeeded in the house by his grandson George, 3rd Earl of Cardigan, master of buckhounds to Queen Anne and George I. The 2nd Earl was Prefect of a Society of the Rosary formed to promote devotion to the Virgin Mary among Catholics, probably during the Commonwealth, by a Benedictine monk, Arthur Crowder, and the house was probably the confraternity's (and perhaps Crowder's) base. The house was rebuilt in 1708, only to burn down in 1724, after which it was rebuilt by Henry Hoare, banker and patron of the arts, grandson of the founder of Hoare's Bank. This was for many years his London base; from 1741 he also lived at Stourhead in Wiltshire.

No.42 was the home of Sir Henry Pollexfen, Attorney General and Chief Justice of the Common Pleas, who died there in 1691. He also owned a large house and grounds in Hampstead, which was then sold to Lord Robert Russell, son of the fifth Earl of Bedford. Pollexfen's son Henry sold No.42 in 1702 to Robert Child of the banking family. His father, Sir Francis Child the elder, who had been Lord Mayor of London in 1699, then lived in the house, where he hung his impressive collection of paintings by Rubens, Claude and Van Dyck. Sir Francis acquired the house and estate at Osterley Park a few months before his death in 1713. He was succeeded at No.42 by his son Robert on whose death in 1721 Sir Francis Child the younger, also Lord Mayor of London (in 1731-2), became head of the banking house. He lived here until his death in 1740 and the house remained in the Child family until 1767.

No.43 was home to the painter John Zoffany (p 18) from 1765 to 1769, until he fled abroad, in debt to his landlord.

As noted above, the Royal College of Surgeons building covers the site of the Lincoln's Inn Fields Theatre, which despite the name was in Portugal Street. There were three successive theatres on the site, the first opened in 1660 by Sir William D'Avenant for the Duke's Company in a converted tennis court. It was the first London theatre to have a proscenium arch, and D'Avenant was the first to use moveable scenery on the English professional stage. Samuel Pepys, who became a frequent visitor to this theatre, went to see *Hamlet* here on 28 August 1661 and commented that it was 'done with scenes very well but above all Betterton did the prince's part beyond imagination' (*cf*. Betterton Street, p 79). After 1674 the building reverted to being a tennis court until it was refitted as a theatre by Congreve in 1695. After his company moved to the Queen's Theatre, Haymarket in 1704, the theatre was refitted by John Rich in 1714. It is now particularly remembered for the first production of Gay's *The Beggar's Opera* on 29 January 1728, later immortalised in a painting by William Hogarth. Rich moved to Covent Garden in 1732 and the theatre was closed. It became a barracks and from 1795 to 1848 the London warehouse of Spode and Copeland. Beresford Chancellor relates that when the china warehouse was being demolished for the enlargement of the Royal College of Surgeons a bust of Shakespeare was found enclosed in one of the walls and given to the Garrick Club.

In April 1665, Pepys noticed the actress Nell Gwyn ('pretty witty Nell') among the audience at the Duke's Theatre, as the Lincoln's Inn Fields Theatre was then known. In 1668 or 1669, she famously became the mistress of Charles II. Late in 1669 the pregnant Nell moved to a house somewhere in Lincoln's Inn Fields, where her son,

Charles Beauclerk, later Duke of St Albans, army officer, was born in May 1670 **[29]**. She moved away from Lincoln's Inn Fields later that summer.

No.44, the remaining block on the south side, covers the site of Nos.44-50, which were demolished after WWII, despite having been Listed Grade II in 1947 with this citation: 'houses of interesting design dating from the early 18th century. There have been some alterations, but they remain a picturesque survival of the early appearance of the square, and their loss...would be most regrettable.' Nos.44-46 were demolished in 1959 and replaced by the buildings of the Imperial Cancer Research Fund (now Cancer Research UK), by Young and Hall with John Musgrove as consultant, 1959-62. The laboratories of the charity's London Research Institute are due to move to a new site at Somers Town in 2015. Nos.48-50 were demolished in 1967 and the Cancer Research building was extended in *c*.1972.

The original house at No.44 was known as 'The Two Black Griffins'. Here from 1690 to 1699 lived Sir Robert Southwell, diplomat, Principal Secretary of State for Ireland and President of the Royal Society 1690-95.

No.46 was the town house, 1773-81, of Alexander Wedderburn, Baron Loughborough and later Earl of Rosslyn.

29 Nell Gwyn and her two sons, mezzotint after Henri Gascar, c.1673

He was Lord Chancellor from 1793 to 1801, when he occupied a house with extensive grounds in Hampstead, which after he left was named Rosslyn House (see Wade, Christopher, *Streets of Belsize*). During the Gordon Riots in 1780 he is said to have 'fortified his private house in Lincoln's Inn Fields'. He previously lived at No.64, 1768-72. Joseph Henry Green (p 113) moved to No.46 from No.22 sometime in the 1820s, living here until 1836.

Resident at No.49 from 1809 to 1825 was a Dr John Grove, a cousin of Percy Bysshe Shelley. John's sister Harriet and Shelley were sweethearts and both stayed with him in Lincoln's Inn Fields on at least two occasions in 1809 and 1810. On 26 April 1810 Harriet recorded in her diary: 'Walked in the Fields with dear Bysshe…' But the romance cooled and in August 1811 Shelley eloped with Harriet Westbrook.

West side

We now turn right into the west side of the square. This is where the greatest change has taken place, caused by the building of Kingsway (see p 89). The entrance from the west was not by the present Sardinia Street (which dates from *c*.1910) into the south-west corner of the square, but by Duke Street (confusingly renamed Sardinia Street in 1877) which entered the fields through an archway between Nos.53 &54, hence the old name of Arch Row (see map, p 75) for this side. The archway had three openings [30], a large central one and two side ones.

Each side of the central arch was inscribed *Duke Street, 1648*. The height of the central arch was only 11 ft, and Heckethorn, writing in 1896, comments that it 'ought long ago to have been removed'; in fact it was demolished in 1909.

Nos.51, 52 and 53-54, erected in 1639-40, therefore formed part of a series of houses extending from No.2 Portsmouth Street (which entered at the south-west corner of the Fields, see the sketch map on the back cover) to No.56, of which only No.55 remained after 1912. Nos.51&52 were used between 1705 and 1732 as the official residence of the Lord Chancellor and occupied successively by holders of that office. The first of these was William Cowper, 1st Earl Cowper, great-grandson of Sir William Cowper, one of the original developers of the Fields (see p 108), who took a prominent part in the negotiations for the unification of England and Scotland, becoming the first Lord Chancellor of Great Britain in 1707. The house was extensively altered by Sir John Soane in the 1790s for John Pearce, who lived here from 1795 to 1818. After that date it was occupied by solicitors, among which was a firm with a very long history in the square, Vizards. Set up by William Vizard in 1797, the firm moved to Lincoln's Inn Fields in 1809, settling first at No.3. In 1825 Vizard and Blower moved to No.51 where they stayed until 1832, subsequently moving to No.61 and in 1855 (by now Vizard and Graham) to No.55, where they remained until 1905 when the building was demolished for the building of Kingsway. They moved back to a newly built (and renumbered) No.51 where the firm, by then known as Crowders, Vizard, Oldham and Co., stayed for 80 years until moving to Bedford Row in June 1987 (see also No.5).

Nos.53&54, dating from the mid-17th century, was occupied from the beginning of the 18th century by Don Lewis Da Cunha and functioned as the Portuguese Embassy. About 1720 it became the Sardinian Embassy. Incorporated in the building at the back was a Roman Catholic Chapel, which later became known as the Sardinian Chapel. It is unlikely to have been used for Roman Catholic worship before the reign of James II, when Catholics were once again tolerated. In 1687 the Franciscan Order took a 10-year lease of the house and established a community of ten members. In 1688, however, on news reaching London of the landing of the Prince of Orange, the mob made an effort to destroy monasteries, and the residence of the Franciscans in Lincoln's Inn Fields was besieged for a day and a night. As a result, James II ordered them to break up their fraternity and go overseas. A month after their withdrawal in November 1688, after the flight of James, the London mob

30 Sardinia Street (former Duke Street) c.1890, looking east through the triple archway under No.53 & No.54 Lincoln's Inn Fields. The entrance to the Sardinian Chapel is on the right.

attacked Roman Catholic places of worship as well as embassies of the Roman Catholic powers, and the chapel in Lincoln's Inn Fields was gutted, the furniture and pictures being burned in Lincoln's Inn Fields, a scene commemorated on a silver medallion designed by G Bower, now in the British Museum.

The Chapel was once again attacked by a mob in June 1780 during the Gordon Riots against the proposed repeal of anti-Roman Catholic legislation. It was still known as the Sardinian Chapel, because although it had passed out of the hands of the Sardinian Embassy the previous year under an agreement between the Ambassador and the Vicar Apostolic, it remained under the patronage and protection of the King of Sardinia until 1858. The Riot was graphically described by Charles Dickens in *Barnaby Rudge*, the subtitle of which is *A Tale of the Riots of 'Eighty*. 'It was about six o'clock in the evening, when a vast mob poured into Lincoln's Inn Fields by every avenue, and divided...into several parties'. John Britton, the antiquary, in his *Picture of London* of 1825 describes the scene thus: 'The populace then separated into parties, and proceeded to demolish the Roman Catholic chapels in Duke Street, Lincoln's Inn Fields and [in] Warwick Street, Golden Square, and all the furniture, ornaments and altars of both chapels were committed to the flames.' In Horace Walpole's graphic account he describes how his cousin Thomas, who lived at No.41 from 1772 to 1785, rescued the wife of the Sardinian Minister, Madame Cordon, who was ill at the time and 'dragged her, for she could scarce stand for terror and weakness, to his own house'. The chapel survived, however, and there in 1793 Général Alexandre D'Arblay married novelist Fanny Burney, for the second time, an Anglican wedding having taken place in Surrey two days earlier. Five years later the chapel was bought by a devout Catholic and donated, for continued use as a place of worship, to Bishop John Douglass, vicar-apostolic to the London district.

In 1853 the name of the chapel was changed to St Anselm's, Duke Street and in 1861 to the Church of St Anselm and St Caecilia. It was demolished in 1910, a new building having first been erected in Kingsway (p 106). The rest of Nos.53-54 was demolished in 1912.

The new **Nos.51-54** became the Public Trustee Office, with a main entrance at No.24 Kingsway (see also p 104), until it was purchased by the London School of Economics. The New Academic Building, as it is styled, was opened by HM the Queen and the Duke of Edinburgh on 5 November 2008 and is one of the most environmentally friendly university buildings in the UK. The 8-storey Edwardian block was cleverly converted by Nicholas Grimshaw and Partners, with structural engineering by Alan Baxter and Associates, the internal accommodation being based around a great column-free daylight-flooded atrium.

Queen's House, the present building on the site of Nos.55-56, was built in 1914-15 and has its main frontage on Kingsway (No.28), with a second façade on Lincoln's Inn Fields. Originally the whole row up to No.60 was to have been demolished and rebuilt to front on the new Kingsway. However, after protests to the LCC, including one from the Society for the Protection of Ancient Buildings signed, among others, by Alma-Tadema, Waterhouse, Webb, Sargent and Walter Besant, the last four houses were reprieved. Now owned by the London School of Economics, the building is currently (2011) shrouded in scaffolding while work is carried out to convert the ground floor to a student medical centre.

Henry Arundell, 3rd Baron Arundell of Wardour, one of the chiefs of the Roman Catholic aristocracy in England, lived at No.55 from 1667 to at least 1675. Other notable residents have included, 1768-1779, Sir William Blackstone, author of the *Commentaries on the Laws of England*, and the poet Alfred Tennyson, who in his early life is said to have rented chambers on the fourth floor, visited by his friend Arthur Hallam. At No.56 between 1740 and 1756 lived William Murray (b.1705), later 1st Earl of Mansfield. The poet Alexander Pope was in the habit of spending his winter evenings in the library of Murray's house in Lincoln's Inn Fields, and a few days before his death in 1744 was carried, at his own desire, from Twickenham to the Fields to dine with Murray. In 1756, on being appointed Lord Chief Justice [31], Murray left Lincoln's Inn Fields for Bloomsbury Square, but returned in 1786 to Nos.57&58, which he kept until his death in 1793, although after his resignation as Lord Chief Justice in 1788 he seems to have spent most of his time at Kenwood.

Nos.57&58 were rebuilt in 1730 by Henry Joynes for Charles, Lord Talbot, Solicitor General, and Lord Chancellor from 1733, who lived here until his death in February 1737. The semicircular porch with fluted Doric columns was added by Sir John Soane in 1795 when he subdivided the house. His central party-wall was removed when the two houses were reunited in 1909, but the top-lit staircase and other details survive in No.57. Charles Dickens's friend and biographer John Forster had chambers in No.58 from 1833 to 1856. Dickens often visited him here, and located in this house the residence of Mr Tulkinghorn, the family lawyer of Sir Leicester Deadlock, in *Bleak House* ('a large house, formerly a house of state…let off in sets of chambers now; and in those shrunken fragments of greatness lawyers lie like maggots in nuts'). It was here, too, that on 2 December 1844 Dickens read *The Chimes* to a company of friends, including Carlyle and Clarkson Stanfield.

In 1664 Edward Montagu, 1st Earl of Sandwich, had rented the first house on the site for £250 per annum, a sum that Samuel Pepys (formerly his Secretary) thought was excessive. The Earl commanded a division of the English fleet at the Battle of Lowestoft in 1665 and was appointed commander in chief the same year. On his resignation in 1666 he was appointed ambassador extraordinary to Madrid. He left London on 23 February and Pepys records a visit to him in Lincoln's Inn Fields that morning to pay his respects.

Nos.59&60 (with three decorative oil-lamp brackets on the railings) was built in 1639-41 by Sir David Cunningham, and is the only surviving building of the original pre-Civil War development of the square. Colen Campbell, who illustrated it in *Vitruvius Britannicus*, attributed the design to Inigo Jones, but evidence on this point is not conclusive and others feel that Nicholas Stone is a more likely candidate. Pevsner states that 'whether or not by Jones, this design, with *piano nobile* and pilasters,

is a rare survival of the type of regular, classically detailed street elevations that Jones had promoted at Covent Garden and which was beginning to appear elsewhere in the 1630s'. The house was divided into two in 1752, possibly by Isaac Ware, and reconverted to one house in 1803. After the execution of William, Lord Russell in the Fields on 21 July 1683 (see p 11) the body is said to have been carried back into this house, where his head was sewn back on. The present name, **Lindsey House**, comes from the Earl of Lindsey's occupation at the beginning of the 18th century. Robert, 4th Earl of Lindsey (1715-1809) was later created Duke of Ancaster, and the house was known for a period as Ancaster House. Spencer Perceval, who became Prime Minister in 1809 and was assassinated in the lobby of the House of Commons on 12 May 1812, occupied No.59 from 1791 to 1803, when the two houses were reunited, and remained in Nos.59&60 until 1808. Perceval's occupancy is recorded by an LCC brown plaque, unveiled on 16 February 1914. From 1835 to 1864 James Spedding, literary editor and biographer, occupied chambers at No.60. As one of the Apostles at Cambridge, he became a lifelong friend of Lord Houghton, Edward Fitzgerald, Arthur Hallam, Archbishop Trench, W M Thackeray and Alfred Lord Tennyson, who said of Spedding: 'He was the Pope among us young men – the wisest man I know'. Spedding's main employment

31 William, Earl of Mansfield, engraving from an original picture by J Collyer, c.1775

WILLIAM EARL of MANSFIELD.

Engraved from an Original Picture by J Collyer.

for over 30 years was working on an edition of the works of Francis Bacon.

Now the home of Garden Court Chambers, Nos.57-60 were, until 2005, occupied by Marks and Clerk, Chartered Patent Agents, a firm founded by George Croydon Marks, engineer, patent agent and politician, in Birmingham in 1887. The firm became established in London and in 1908 purchased the lease of Nos.57&58, reuniting the two houses. In March 1918 Marks acquired the adjacent houses, Nos.59&60. He reunited them, making a flat for his own use and establishing his publishing business, the Hertford Record Company, on the ground floor.

The 18th-century houses on the site of **Nos.61-62** were demolished in 1910. The present building, which includes Nos.40-42 Kingsway, was designed by Edwin Lutyens in Edwardian neoclassical style. For a number of years, until 2010, it housed the offices of the Imperial Cancer Research Fund, now Cancer Research UK. The building is currently (2011) being redeveloped for hotel use by the Club Quarters chain, the principal entrance to which will be in Lincoln's Inn Fields. The poet Thomas Campbell lived at No.61 from 1828 to 1841, as did the actor William Charles Macready from 1832 to 1837. Sir Robert Sawyer died in the original house on the site in 1692. As Attorney General in 1683 he had conducted the prosecutions arising out of the Rye House Plot (see p 11). His wife continued to live in the house until 1695, and in 1696 the house was purchased by Sir Thomas Powys, his successor as Attorney General. He lived here until his death in 1719, Lady Powys, his widow, staying on until 1723. More bizarrely, No.62 was the birthplace on 2 February 1778 of Mary Anne Talbot, sailor and soldier. She was purportedly the illegitimate daughter of William Talbot, the first Earl Talbot. Using the alias John Taylor, she became one of the most famous 'Amazons' of the 18th century, and joined the ranks of others such as Hannah Snell and Christian Davies who either chose or were forced to disguise themselves as men to join the military.

No.63 is a Victorian building of 1888 by William Simmons, which stands seven storeys high and has rows of slightly arched windows in concrete, an early use of the material. It is currently (2011) owned by the Royal College of Radiologists who plan to move their headquarters to Lincoln's Inn Fields in 2012. Norton Fletcher, first Baron Grantley, Speaker of the House of Commons from 1770 to 1780, died at his house at No.63 Lincoln's Inn Fields on 1 January 1789.

No.64 dates from the early 19th century. Here for four years from 1862 William Simpson, watercolour painter and journalist, had chambers. A pioneer war artist during the Crimean War, Simpson travelled in India between 1859 and 1862 and whilst at No.64 was working on a large-scale illustrated book of those travels for Day and Son, though the project failed when they went into liquidation. From 1866 he was employed as special artist for the *Illustrated London News*, travelling the world for the paper for the next 25 years. **No.65** was carved out of No.66 by Thomas Leverton in 1772 for Sir Henry Kendall, a Lombard Street banker (see No.66 below). A blue plaque commemorates the occupancy of William Marsden (1796-1867), surgeon and founder of both the Royal Free and the Royal Marsden hospitals.

No.66, formerly Nos.66&67, has a magnificent lantern and decorative iron supports at the top of the steps. The building, known as **Newcastle House**, is occupied by Farrer and Co., solicitors to the Royal Family. The first house on the site was built for the Earl of Carlisle in 1641-2 and known as Carlisle House. The house was purchased in 1653 by Sir George Savile, first Marquess of Halifax, politician and political writer. In 1672 the house was renamed Powis House when it was bought by William Herbert, first Marquess of Powis, peer and leader of the Roman Catholic nobility in the reigns of Charles II and James II. Imprisoned in the Tower in 1678, he was released in 1684. In the same year the house burned down. It was rebuilt by William Winde, but nearly destroyed again by the mob when James II fell in 1688. In 1689, Lord Powis fled to St Germain and was attainted and his property forfeited to the Crown. Between 1692 and 1705 Powis House was appropriated for the Lords Keeper of the Great Seal. In 1694, when Sir John Somers was Keeper, the Great Seal was affixed to the Charter of the Bank of England in what later became the Peacock Room. Somers was a patron of literature, a friend of Addison, Steele and Congreve and universally popular. An attempt at attainting him failed in 1700, but he was nevertheless dismissed.

The Powis family must have had their estates at least partially restored, for in May 1705, the 2nd Earl of Powis sold the house for £7,500 and built a new Powis House at 50 Great Ormond Street. The new owner was John Holles, first Duke of Newcastle, and the house became known as Newcastle House. On his death in 1711, he left his estates to his nephew Thomas Pelham Holles, who was created Duke of Newcastle in 1715. In 1724 he was made Secretary of State by Walpole, an office he held for most of the next 30 years. In 1754 he became Prime Minister for the first of two periods, resigning from office in 1762. For the whole of this period the duke held court at Newcastle House. He enjoyed staging vast entertainments, both here and at Claremont. William Kent carried out substantial interior work for him at Newcastle House in 1725. After his death in 1768, the duke's widow sold the house to Sir Henry Kendall, a banker, for £8,400.

The sale included the site of No.65, which the duke had bought in 1758 to provide an approach to his stables. Kendall built a house for himself on the site of No.65, and divided Newcastle House in two, letting the northern half and selling the southern half to James Wallace (1729-1783), later Attorney General. In 1791, Wallace's son sold his house to James Farrer (1751-1820), and No.66 has been in the occupation of the Farrer family ever since.

No.67 was from 1827 to 1879 the headquarters of the Society for the Propagation of the Gospel. In 1904 the building was acquired by Sir William James Farrer and he reunited Nos.66&67 in 1906 when the back parts were demolished for the building of Kingsway. A survey in 1930 in connection with minor repairs to the roof revealed serious defects in the outside walls, with the brickwork requiring partial rebuilding from the foundations. The restoration, keeping to a late 17th-century appearance, was carried out by Sir Edwin Lutyens and Dendy Watney. A stone tablet supported by cupids with the Farrer crest above elegantly records this restoration and the earlier rebuilding after the fire of 1684: 'Anno 1686/ E Flammis Rediviva/ Anno 1930/ Vetustate Corruens/ Refecta'. The covered passage along the north flank wall facing Remnant Street is an original feature.

No.66 nearly had a very different fate, as it was one of the houses considered in the early 1770s by Josiah Wedgwood and Thomas Bentley when they were looking for new and improved premises for their London showrooms. Part of Wedgwood's success was due to his revolutionary marketing methods, in which he showed various table and dessert services completely set out on a range of tables, with sets of vases decorating the walls, changing the whole display frequently so as to create a spectacle which people, particularly ladies, constantly revisited. In the end No.66 was passed over, and Portland House in Greek Street, Soho, was chosen.

At an unidentified location along the west side of the square between 1809 and 1818 John Thelwall, political reformer and lecturer, ran an 'Institution for the Remedy of Organic Defects and Impediments of Speech'. The author of Old and New London opines that: 'Mr Thelwall…having been in early life a somewhat revolutionary reformer, later turned his attention to philanthropy, and taught elocution with success'. As one of the leaders of the reform movement Thelwall was imprisoned in the Tower in 1794. He was tried on a charge of treason, but like his friends Hardy and Horne Tooke, acquitted. He was friends with both Coleridge (see No.22) and Henry Cline (see No.2), the latter of whom gave evidence at his trial, and for years afterwards held an annual dinner at his house in Lincoln's Inn Fields to commemorate Horne Tooke's acquittal.

Across Remnant Street, on the corner

of Gate Street is the postgraduate **Centre for Commercial Law Studies** of Queen Mary, University of London, a newcomer to the square in 2010 and another indicator of its changing demographic.

Gardens

On the inner pavement at the north-west corner of the gardens stands a drinking fountain in the Gothic style which bears the inscription *The Fear of the Lord is a Fountain of Life. AD 1861.*

Enter the gardens by the gate in the middle of the north side. The aluminium roundels in the pavement record this as part of the Silver Jubilee Walkway of 1977. The present railings around the square date only from the 1990s, the 18th-century ones having been removed in 1941. The decision to replace them and once again to lock the gates at night was taken in an attempt to curb the use of the gardens as a place for homeless people to camp, a situation which reached crisis point in the early 1990s. An exact replica of the railings proved to be too expensive, and they are only an approximation, lacking the stone plinth into which the original railings were set (remains of which can still be seen at intervals).

To the left and right are the remains of decorative iron brackets for oil lamps. Turn left and proceed in a clockwise direction. With the exception of the netball and tennis courts erected by the LCC, and tarmacked instead of gravel walkways, the gardens today look much as they did throughout the 18th and 19th centuries, although the species of trees and shrubs grown have changed somewhat. More detail is in two articles by Susan Palmer in *The London Gardener* (see *Sources*, p 126). Major refurbishment of the garden by the London Borough of Camden working with English Heritage is planned for 2011-12, and portions may be closed at times while this work is carried out.

The granite obelisk bearing a red maple leaf commemorates, in a lengthy inscription, the occupation of No.20 as the headquarters of the Royal Canadian Air Force in Britain during WWII. Opposite is a Canadian maple with a plaque recording its planting by the Right Hon. Jean Chrétien, Prime Minister of Canada. After the war the grateful RCAF presented its ensign to Holborn Borough Council. A maple tree, a gift of the mayor and citizens of Ottawa flown over from Canada in a RCAF bomber, was ceremonially planted. The present obelisk and a new maple tree, inaugurated on 14 May 1998, are replacements, the old plaques having become worn and illegible.

In the north-east corner is a Portland stone plinth designed by Sir Edwin Lutyens originally bearing a bronze bust (*c.*1928) of W F D Smith, 2nd Viscount Hambleden (1868-1928). The bust, by Arthur G Walker, has been missing for some years. As the inscription reveals, Smith was head of the firm of W H Smith and Son, MP for the Strand Division 1891-1910 and Chairman of King's College Hospital, which stood in Portugal Street until 1913. The firm of W H Smith had a long association with the area, having opened offices in the Strand in 1820 (see also p 86). The firm's headquarters and distribution centre was in Portugal Street from 1920 to 1976. The building is now the LSE's Lionel Robbins building. On the corner with Carey Street a plaque on the wall bears the marks of shrapnel from a German bomb dropped during an air raid on the night of 10 October 1940. Several of the trees and seats in the gardens bear memorial plaques, but some of the plaques have lost their trees, victims of the devastating hurricane which hit London on 16 October 1987. The tennis and netball courts erected by the LCC are still being used, the netball games in particular having long been a focus of public attention. Earlier, in 1924, the LCC had introduced an 18-hole putting green.

The octagonal central pavilion was built as a rain shelter in 1879-80 to designs by James William Wild, then Curator of the Soane Museum. Its Moorish style has been obscured by the LCC's replacement of the roof in 1934, and subsequently by the removal of the benches around the edge to deter vagrants. It was later used as a bandstand. Lunchtime band concerts, begun during WWII, continued during the 1950s and '60s and were immensely popular. At one time an LCC brass plaque in the floor commemorated the execution of Lord William Russell (see p 11) more or less on this spot, and there are currently (2011) plans to replace this with a replica.

In the south-west corner stands a bronze bust of John Hunter by N F Boonham on a stone plinth, given (see plaque on the side) by the President and Council of the Royal College of Surgeons to mark the Queen's Silver Jubilee and 'to record their appreciation of the pleasure and satisfaction that the College's long association with Lincoln's Inn Fields... has given to successive generations of fellows, members, students and staff'.

Finally, in the middle of the north side, is the **Margaret MacDonald Memorial**. This monument of 1914 takes the form of an alcove and seat of grey Scottish granite and ship's teak surmounted by a bronze group by Richard Goulden showing Margaret MacDonald kneeling and holding out her arms to nine little children, with the inscription 'She brought joy to those with whom she lived and worked'. A small plaque to one side gives more information about her. The memorial was unveiled on 19 December 1914 by Margaret MacDonald's youngest daughter after a speech by Sir Laurence Gomme, Clerk of the LCC, and the statue was dedicated by Professor Gilbert Murray. Margaret MacDonald was born in 1870, the daughter of John Gladstone; she was a

distinguished scientist, an active social and religious worker and one of the founders of the YMCA. Margaret was attracted to Socialism through her own social work in Hoxton and elsewhere and in 1896 married James Ramsay MacDonald, the Labour leader and future Prime Minister. They lived at No.3 from 1896, where their roomy apartment became a centre for Labour activists at home and from abroad. After her sudden death on 8 September 1911 of blood poisoning, her husband continued to live there until 1916, when he moved to Belsize Park. Of their six children born at No.3, their second child, John Malcolm MacDonald (1901-1981), followed his father into politics and later held a series of high commissionerships in Africa and Asia.

The Terrace restaurant erected by the London Borough of Camden in 2005 has been the source of much local controversy, being considerably larger and more sophisticated than the park café sanctioned by the bye-laws governing the garden. It is currently (2011) empty and awaiting a decision on its future use.

What lies beneath the Fields? Shortly before WWII an underground shelter was built under the Fields and was used by local office workers and particularly by Canadian servicemen stationed nearby. The last of its surface features was removed by the LCC in 1954-55, but the underground shelter is thought to be still there, and the steps down to one of the entrances were uncovered by

the Channel 4 *Time Team* excavation in 2009. Crossing the Fields at greater depth is a Government communications tunnel which linked a huge bunker under High Holborn to a network serving Whitehall and government buildings elsewhere, one of a number of deep shelters in long tunnels under Tube stations built during WWII. The High Holborn tunnel complex was secretly extended after the war to link up with various government buildings in the area and to serve as a nuclear bomb-proof shelter. It had its own artesian well and was planned to be self-sufficient for up to six months. It became a major telecommunications centre, being referred to as Kingsway Telephone Exchange. It is believed to have been decommissioned in the 1970s. Because of the secrecy attached to the underground network, available information is limited, but may be extended when appropriate records are released by The National Archives.

Leave the gardens by the gate in the middle of the north side and retrace your steps to Holborn tube station or to a convenient bus stop on Kingsway or High Holborn.

Sources

Books

Aston, Mark. *The Cinemas of Camden*. LB of Camden, 1997

Bagwell, Philip S. *Outcast London ... : the West London Mission ... 1887-1987*. Epsworth, 1987

Barron, Caroline M. *The Parish of St Andrew Holborn*. Diamond Trading Co., 1979

Bebbington, Gillian. *London Street Names*. Batsford, 1972

Besant, Sir Walter. *London North of the Thames*. A & C Black, 1911

Blackwood, John. *London's Immortals: ... outdoor commemorative statues*. Savoy Press, 1989

Blott, Walter. *A Chronicle of Blemundsbury*. [The author], 1892

Booth, Charles. *Life and Labour of the People in London*. Macmillan, 1892-97

Bowers, Faith. *A Bold Experiment... Bloomsbury Central

Baptist Church, 1999

Britton, John. *Picture of London*. 1825

Britton, John, & A Pugin. *Illustration of the Public Buildings in London*, vol.1. 1825

Bruce, J Graeme, & Desmond F Croome. *The Central Line*, 2nd ed. Capital Transport, 2006

Burnett, John. *Plenty and Want: a social history of food in England from 1815...* 3rd ed. Routledge, 1989

Camden Environment Dept. *St Giles Area: regeneration initiative...* 1998

Chancellor, E Beresford. *The Romance of Lincoln's Inn Fields*. Richards, 1932

Cherry, Bridget, & Nikolaus Pevsner. *London, 4: North*. Penguin, 1999 (The Buildings of England)

Chesney, Kellow. *The Victorian Underworld*. Temple Smith, 1970

Clinch, George. *Bloomsbury and St Giles Past and Present*. Truslove & Shirley, 1890

Clunn, Harold. *The Face of London*. New ed., rev. by E R Wethersett. Spring Books, 1962

Clunn, Harold. *London Rebuilt 1897-1927*.

John Murray, 1927

Colvin, H M. *A Biographical Dictionary of British Architects, 1660-1840*, 4th ed. Yale UP, 2008

Denvir, Bernard. *The Eighteenth Century: art, design and society, 1689-1840*. Longman, 1983

Dobie, Rowland. *The History of the United Parishes of St Giles in the Fields and St George Bloomsbury*. 1829

Edwards, Percy J. *History of London Street Improvements 1855-1897*. LCC, 1898

Evans, Julian. *Semi-Invisible Man: the life of Norman Lewis*. Cape, 2008

Fairfield, S. *The Streets of London: a dictionary of their names and their origins*. Macmillan, 1983

Fletcher, Geoffrey. *London's Pavement Pounders*. Hutchinson, 1967

George, Dorothy. *London Life in the 18th Century*. 2nd ed. Kegan Paul, 1930

Girouard, Mark. *Victorian Pubs*. Studio Vista, 1975

Green, David. *People of the Rookery*. King's College Dept

of Geography, 1986 (Occasional paper 26)

Grey, Edward C W. *St Giles of the Lepers*. Longmans Green, 1905

Hawkins, Desmond. *The Grove Diaries ... 1809-1925*. Dovecote Press, 1995

Hayes, David A. *Victorian Seven Dials: a portrait based on contemporary accounts*. Camden History Society, 2001

Heckethorn, C W. *Lincoln's Inn Fields and the Localities Adjacent...* Elliot Stock, 1896

Hindley, Charles. *The Life of Old Jemmy Catnach, Printer*. Craft Press, 1965

The History of the King's Works, vol.3: *1485-1660 (Part 1)*, HMSO 1975; vol.6: *1782-1851*, HMSO, 1973

Hobhouse, Hermione. *Lost London: a century of demolition and decay*. Macmillan, 1971

Holmes, Richard. *Coleridge: darker reflections*. Harper Collins, 1998

Howard, Alexander, & Ernest Newman. *London Business Cavalcade*. Lincolns-Praeger, 1951

Howard, Diana. *London Theatres and Music

Halls 1850-1950*. Library Association, 1970

Jones, Edward, & Christopher Woodward. *A Guide to the Architecture of London*. 4th ed. Weidenfeld, 2009

Kamlish, Marian. *George Morland, a London artist in eighteenth-century Camden*. Camden History Society, 2008

Kimball, George. *The Pocket Guide to London Theatre*. Rev. ed. Xanadu, 1990

Lane, Michael R. *Baron Marks of Woolwich...* Quiller Press, 1986

Laurie, Peter. *Beneath the City Streets: government preparations for national emergency*. Rev. ed. Granada, 1979

Lees, Lynn Hollen. *Exiles of Erin: Irish migrants in Victorian London*. Manchester UP, 1979

Le Faye, Deirdre. *Medieval Camden*. Camden History Society, 1975

Lehmann, John. *Holborn: an historical portrait of a London borough*. Macmillan, 1970

Lillywhite, Bryant. *London Signs*. Allen & Unwin, 1972

London County Council.

The Housing Question in London. 1900

London County Council. *Opening of Kingsway and Aldwych*, 1905; *Opening of Lincoln's Inn Fields*, 1895

Low, Crail. *Rock and Pop London*. Handbook Publishing, 1997

Mackenzie, D (ed.). *Holborn Old and New*. Princeton Press, for First Avenue Hotel, 1928

Mills, Peter. *The Archaeology of Camden*. Inner London Archaeology Unit, 1982

Moore, Lucy. *The Thieves' Opera: ... lives of Jonathan Wild ... and Jack Sheppard*. Viking, 1997

Morley, Charles. *Studies in Board Schools*. Smith, Elder, 1897

M of L Archaeology Studies *Medieval Settlement in 18th/19th century excavations at Central St. Giles 2006-8*

Museum of London Archaeology Service. *151-165 Shaftesbury Avenue: an archaeological evaluation*. 1996

Museum of London Archaeology Service. *Medieval Settlement in 18th/19th Century

Excavations at Central St Giles, 2006-8*

O'Connell, Sheila. *London 1753*. British Museum Press, 2003.

Paolozzi, Eduardo. *Underground Design*. Architectural Association, 1986

Parton, John. *Some Account of the Hospital & Parish of St Giles-in-the-Fields, Middlesex*. Luke Hansard, 1822

Pearson, David. *London's Mansions: the palatial houses of the nobility*. Batsford, 1986

Pennick, Nigel. *Bunkers under London*. Valknut Productions, 1988 (Tube railways of London, no.2)

Pepys, Samuel. *The Diary of Samuel Pepys*, ed. by Latham & Matthews. Bell & Hyman, 1970-83

Pevsner, Nikolaus. *London, except the Cities of London and Westminster*, 3rd ed. Penguin, 1973 (The Buildings of England)

Philip, A J, & W L Gadd. *A Dickens Dictionary*. Simpkins Marshall, 1928

Phillips, Hugh. *Mid-Georgian London*. Collins, 1964

Reilly, Robin. *Josiah Wedgwood, 1730-1795*. Macmillan, 1992

Richardson, John. *Covent Garden Past*. Historical Publications, 1995

Robertson, Brian. *Roman Camden*. Camden History Society, 1977

Rogers, Eddie. *Tin Pan Alley* (as told to Mike Hennessey). Hale, 1964

Royal Commission on Historical Monuments (England). *An Inventory of the Historical Monuments of London*, vol.2: *West London*. HMSO, 1925

Seven Dials Monument Charity. *The Seven Dials*. 1989

Seven Dials Trust. *Seven Dials Renaissance Studies*. 1998

Shepard, Lesley. *The History of Street Literature*. David & Charles, 1973

Slinn, Judy. *The History of Vizards 1797-1997*. Vizards, 1997

Smith, J T. *Nollekens and his Times*. London, 1829

Strype, John. *A Survey of the Cities of London and Westminster*, 1720

Stubbs, Sir James, & T O Haunch. *Freemasons' Hall: the home and heritage of the craft*. United Grand Lodge, 1983

Survey of London, vol.3: *St Giles-in-the-Fields (part 1), Lincoln's Inn Fields*. LCC, 1912

Survey of London, vol.5: *St Giles-in-the-Fields (part 2)*. LCC, 1914

Survey of London, vols 33 & 34: *St Anne, Soho*. GLC, 1966

Tallis, John. *London Street Views, 1838-40*

Tames, Richard & Sheila. *Covent Garden and Soho: the illustrated a-z historical guide*. Historical Publications, 2009

Taylor, Gordon. *St Giles in the Fields, its part in history*, 7th ed. [The church], 1988

Timbs, John. *Curiosities of London*. J S Virtue, 1877

Wade, Christopher. *Streets of Belsize*. Camden History Society, 2009

Walford, Edward. *Old and New London*, vol.3. Cassell, 1883

Weinreb, Ben [et al.] *The London Encyclopaedia*, 3rd ed. Macmillan, 2008

Wells, Roy A. *Freemasonry in London from 1875*. Lewis Masonic, 1984

Whitley, W T. *The Baptists of London, 1612-1928*. Kingsgate Press, 1928

Maps

'Agas' mid-C16; Hollar 1658-59; Ogilby & Morgan 1682; Strype 1720; Rocque 1746; Horwood 1799; Cassell 1862; parish map 1866; Ordnance Survey 1870 (and later); Booth's poverty maps 1889-98; Goad insurance plans; LCC bomb damage maps

The London Silver Jubilee

Walkway. Rev. ed. Silver Jubilee Walkway Trust, 1993

Periodicals & newspapers

Camden History Review (CHR)
Camden New Journal
Covent Garden Courier/ Covent Garden News
Freemasons' Chronicle, 27 Jan 1900
Holborn & Finsbury Guardian 1893-94
St Giles in the Fields Newsletter

Articles

Adshead, H. 'Seven Dials', *St Martin's Review* (Dec 1951) 359-362

Demos, Mary Ann. 'Benjamin Franklin in Holborn', *CHR* 4 (1976) 25-27

Farmer, Alan. 'Time of Terror' [Gordon Riots], *CHR* 8 (1980) 17-18

Gage, John. 'The Rise and Fall of the St Giles Rookery', *CHR* 12 (1984) 17-24

Geddes, Jennian F. 'The Women's Hospital Corps and the Endell Street Military Hospital', *CHR* 32 (2008) 13-18

Hayes, David A. 'Holborn's Church of Humanity, its roots and offshoots', *CHR* 24 (2000) 6-11

Hayes, Ruth E. 'The Saville Theatre, Shaftesbury Avenue', *CHR* 30 (2006) 30-36

Jeffery, Paul. 'The Church that Never Was: Wren's St Mary, and other projects for Lincoln's Inn Fields', *Architectural History* 31 (1988) 136-144

Palmer, Susan. 'From Fields to Gardens: the management of Lincoln's Inn Fields in the [18th and 19th] Centuries', *The London Gardener* 10 (2004-5) 11-28

Palmer, Susan. 'Lincoln's Inn Fields Part II', *The London Gardener* 12 (2006-7) 54-67

Port, M H. 'The New Law Courts Competition, 1866-67', *Architectural History*.11 (1968) 75-93

Richardson, John. 'The Street of Good Intentions' [Endell St], *CHR* 7 (1979) 28-29

Thomas, James. 'Thomas Neale and the development of Seven Dials', *Journal of Regional and Local Studies* 3 (1982) 28-41

Schofield, John and Graves-Brown, Paul. 'The filth and the fury: 6 Denmark Street (London) and the Sex Pistols', *Antiquity* 85 (2011) 1385-1401

Scholey, Keith. ' Bombs on Holborn in the Second World War', *CHR* 22 (1998) 11-15

Snelling, O F. 'Death of a Bookshop', *Antiquarian Book Monthly Review* 7 (1980) 138-143

Watson, Isobel. 'James Hartnoll 1853-1900', *Housing Happenings* 65 (Christmas 1980)

Exhibition

Palm-Gold, Jane. *The Secret Life of the Rookery* (Coningsby Gallery, 2011)

Websites

Numerous Internet resources, including:
Ancestry (www.ancestry.com)
Charles Booth Online Archive
Old Bailey Online
Oxford Dictionary of National Biography
Times Digital Archive 1785-1985
www.actorscentre.co.uk
www.arthurlloyd.co.uk (music hall & theatre history)
www.camden.gov.uk/ listedbuildings
www.camden.gov.uk/planning
www.phoenixartistclub.com
www.selmer.com
www.stgilesonline.org

Other sources

Camden Environment Dept. *Denmark Street Conservation Area Statement, response to consultation*, 10 July 1998 (Environment Committee agenda item 4C)
Census returns, 1841-1911
Covent Garden Community Association. *Annual Report 1983/84*
Covent Garden Open Spaces Association. *Phoenix Community Gardens Annual Reports*
Crossrail and London Underground publicity
Court Roll of the Manor of Hampstead, 1692
Foster, D. *Alehouses [&c.]* [at Westminster Archives]
Goad Insurance Plans [at CLSAC]
Licensed Victuallers Recognizances, 1723 & 1760 [at LMA]
Lincoln's Inn Fields, Trustees. *Minutes, &c* [at British Library and CLSAC]
London County Council/ GLC street lists
London County Council, Parks Committee. *Minutes* [at LMA]
Post Office London Directories (Kelly & Co.)
St Giles-in-the-Fields & St George Bloomsbury Vestry. Poor Rate [at CLSAC]
Theatre programmes for Ambassadors, Cambridge, Donmar, Phoenix, Saville and St Martin's Theatres

Archive centres

Bishopsgate Institute
British Library Manuscripts Department
Camden Local Studies & Archives Centre
Guildhall Library
London Metropolitan Archives (LMA)
Nationwide Building Society Archive
Sir John Soane's Museum Library & Archive
Westminster Archives

127

Index

Streets included in the
survey are indicated in
boldface, as are the main
entries for these and
other selected subjects;
* = illustration
PH = public house

A

ABC cinema 26
Absolon, John 87
Academy of Painting
 & Drawing 97
Action for Children 91
Actors' Centre 39
Adams, H Percy 72
Addis, William 21
Adrian, Max 40
Africa House **90**, 106
Agate, James 65
Ainsworth, Harrison 23, 85
Air Ministry 104
air pollution
 monitoring station 23
Aircraft Disposal Co. 105
Ajimura restaurant 79
Albery, Donald 44
Albury, Ian 63
Alcazar (flats) 21
Alcazar (music hall) 21
Aldewychstrate 8
Aldwych (area) 8, 46, 77, 79
Aldwych Buildings 77
Aldwych Close 93, 101
Aldwych Cross 8, **67**

Aldwych Workshops 77
All Saints Church 40
Allen, George 28
Allen, Paul 49
Allies & Morrison 103
almshouses 63, 65, 85, 87
Ambassadors Theatre 40
Ancaster, Duke of 121
Ancaster House 121
Anderson, Louisa Garrett 51
Andrew Borde Street 15
Anello & Davide 28
Angel Inn 20
Angels & Bermans 26
Animals, The 74
Anne of Denmark 91
Anthropos Gallery 38
Antient Grand Lodge 94
Anti-Slavery Society 96
Apted's 65, 66*
Arab Press House 69
Arch Row 108, **118**
archæology 25, 46,
 57, 70-71, 92
Archer *PH* 88
Archer & Green 73
Aria House 88
Armitage, Reginald 17
Armstrong, George 54
Arne, Susannah 102
Arne, Thomas 92
Arthur Street 57, 63, 69
Arts Laboratory 82
Arundell, Henry 120
Ashcroft, Peggy 63
Ashfield, Edmund 110
Ashley, F V 100
Ashley & Newman 94
Ashley Buildings 103
Ashley House 62
Ashlin Place 82-83
Ashwell, Lena 91

Astaire, Fred & Adele 63
Astrology Shop 54
Aviation House 74, 90

B
Babington, Anthony 106, 108
Back Cottages 81
Bacon's Hotel 94
Baguly, Mr 92
Bailey, David 92
Bainbridge, Henry 9, 60
Baird, John Logie 40
Baker, Henry 72
Baker, Janet 34
Baker, John 86, 90
ballad printers 36
Balmain, William 19
Baltimore, Lords 19, 101, 112
Bananarama 18
Bangalore House 88
Bankruptcy Court 115
Bannerman, Alexander 100
Baptists 25, 55,
 61-62, 102-103
Barber, Mr 65
Barber, Peter, Architects 54
Barbon, Nicholas 18, 29
Barclay, Sir George 103
Barham, R H 100
Barley Court 84
Barnaby Rudge 119
Barnett, Canon & Mrs 54
Barraud, Francis & Paul 30
Barraud & Lund 30
Barrett, Rachel 105
Barrett, Syd 40
Barrow, Ernest 96, 99
Barry, E M 53-54, 96
Barry, Sir Charles 109, 116
Basire, James 100
Bates, Sir Alan 26, 39
baths & washhouses 54

Baxter, Alan &
 Associates 120
Bayes, Gilbert 25
Bazalgette, Joseph 26
Beacon House 90
Beadworks 39
Beale, Arthur 54
Bear Close/Croft 83
Bear Inn 67, 83
Beatles, The 51
Beatrix, Queen 34
Beatties 30, 71
Beauclerk, Charles 117
Beckham, David 48
Beckwood House 53
Bedford, Earls/Dukes of
 9, 11, 62, 70, 71
Bedford, Francis 89
Bedford Chapel 62
Bedford Estate 61
Bedford Glass Works 76
beggars 54, 108
Belasyse, Lord John 19, 97
Belcher, John 89
Belgo Centraal 44
Bell, Robert Anning 38
Bell Court 81
Bells, The 81
Belton Street 48, 53
Bennett, T P 25
Benson, S H Ltd 105
Bentley, Thomas 123
Berkshire House 54, 66
Bernhardt, Sarah 63
Bessbrook Home 69
Betterton, Thomas 79, 117
Betterton House 81
Betterton Street
 49, 50, **79-81**
Biblewomen 21, 74, 76
Biddlecombe, James 99
Biddlecombe, William 99

Bieda, David 34
Billington, Teresa 70
Binns, J J 104
bird trade 34, 35*
Birkenstock shoes 55
Black, Cilla 30
Black Horse *PH* 60
Black Horse Yard 69
Black Post *PH* 103
Blackman Harvey 44
Blackpool Corporation 72
Blackstone, Sir William 120
Blackwells 28
Blake, William 100
Blanchard, Edward 99
Bleak House 121
Blease, L 70
Blemonde, William 9
Blemundsbury 9
Blitz Club 91
Blomfield, Arthur 19
Bloomsbury 9, 11, 56
Bloomsbury & St
 Giles Baths 54
Bloomsbury Chapel/
 Central Baptist Church
 26, 55, **61-62**, 63
Bloomsbury Court 71
Bloomsbury Distillery 65-66
Bloomsbury *PH* 61
Bloomsbury Street 59, 61,
 62, 63
Blue Balcony, The 90
Board schools 39, 84, 103
Bogdani, Jacob 38, 101
Boghurst, William 83
Bonn & Mackenzie 81
Book Mews 21
Bookseller, The 24, 61
Boon, Charles 42
Boonham, N F 125
Booth, Charles 76, 84,

39-106 *passim*
Borde, Andrew 15
Borders 21, 28
Borough of Holborn Club 60
Boswell, James 97, **99**
boundary marks 41
Bower, G 119
Bowie, David 18
Bowl Inn 48, 53, 65
Bowl Yard 48, **53**, 65
Bramah, Joseph 16
Brett, Richard 93
Brewer Street
 (*later* Hyde Street) 68
 (*off* Parker's Lane) 77
breweries 42, 44, 53, 68, 100
Bristol, Earl of 97
Bristol House 97
Britannia Batteries 62
Britannia House 62
British & Colonial
 Kinematograph Co. 48
British Crafts Centre 44
British Electric Federation 106
British Esperanto Assoc. 71
British Institute of
 Management 74
British Lying-In Hospital
 50, **80-81**
British Museum 26, 34,
 67, 71, 119
British Museum Station
 71, 74
 Station Chambers 71
Broad Place 63, cover*
Broad St Giles,
 see Broad Street
Broad Street 25, 48, 50-51,
 54, 56, **63**, **65**, **66-67**,
 66*, 68, 82*, 87, cover*
 cooperage 51
Broadway, *see* Broad Street

Broker's Alley 79
Brooke, Rev Stopford A 62
Brooker, Rebecca 72
Brown, Alexander 96
Brown Bear *PH* 67
Brown Sugar restaurant 69
Brown's Gardens 21
Browne, Alexander 90
Browne, Isaac Hawkins 93
Brownlow, Sir John 48, 79
Brownlow Arms *PH* 81
Brownlow House 80*, 81
Brownlow Street 79-81
Brudenell, Robert 116
Bryden, Beryl 28
Buckeridge Street 59
Bucknall, Ralph 59
Bucknall Street 59, 61
Buddha on a Bicycle 48
Bude Mansions 28
Buhler, Robert 25
Bull's Head Yard 100
Buller, Sir Francis 115
Bulwer, John 19
Bunch of Grapes *PH* 36, 43
Burnet, Sir John 104
Burnet, Sir Thomas 112
Burnett's Buildings 15
Burney, Fanny 102, **120**
Burton, Mark 17
Burton Lazars 9
Burwood House 77
Bury Place 70
Bussey, George 69
Butchers Arms *PH* 39
Butterfield, William 19

C
CAA House 103
Cadbury-Brown, 'Jim' 45
Caffè Nero (Kingsway) 105
Calvert, Frederick 112

Cambridge, Duke of 26
Cambridge Circus 26, 27
Cambridge School of
  English 83
Cambridge Theatre 36, **43**
Camden Arts & Business
  Consortium 50
Camden Council 22, 63,
  67, 76, 86, 109, 114,
  124, 125
Camden, Lords 115
Camdonian 114
Campaign for Single
  Homeless People 48
Campbell, Duncan 23
Campbell, Thomas 122
Campbell Connelly 18
Canadian Air Force 113,
  124, 125
Cancer Research UK
  117, 122
Canter's Alley 65
Caravan Club 53
Cardigan, Earl of 116
Cardigan House 116
Care, George 67
Carey Street 102, 115, 124
Carlisle, Earl of 122
Carlisle House 122
Carlton House 92
Carlton Publicity 92
Carluccio, Antonio 45
Carlyle, Thomas 121
Carrick's Distillery 68
Carrier Street 59
Carter, Margaret 53
Casson Conder 114
Castle Street 41, 42, 79
Casual Wards 87
Cat & Fiddle *PH* 86
Catholics, *see*
  Roman Catholics

Catnach, James 36
Causeway, The 56
Cave of Harmony 43
Caxton Walk 28
Central London
  Dwellings Improvement
  Company 77, 88
  Electricity Ltd 81
  Railway 13, 71, 72, 74
Central Regalia 99
Central St Giles **57,** 86
Centre for Commercial
  Law Studies 124
Centre Point Tower 12, 13,
  15, 103
Centrepoint (charity) 15
Century House 23
Chamberlain, James 65, 66
Chambers, Helen 52
Chambers & Partners 76
chapbook publishers 36
Chapel Place 102
Chapel Yard 88
Chapman, George 19, 20
Charing Cross Road 12, 13,
  15, 18, 21, 22, **26-28**
Charing Cross, West End
  & City Electricity
  Supply Company 81
Charles I 88
Charles II 11, 19, 29, 62,
  83, 103, 117
Charles Street 86, 87
Charlotte Street 59
Chartists 70
Cherbury, Ld Herbert of 93
Cherbury House 93
Chermayeff, Serge 43
Chesterton, G K 84
Chevalier, Maurice 63
Child family 116
Child Poverty Action Group 86

Children's Theatre 53
China Art Cultural Centre 77
Chinese Church in London 25
Ching Court 41-42
Chippendale, William 99
Chrétien, Jean 124
Christ Church 52, 52*
Christie, Agatha 40, 43
Church Close 56
Church Lane 59
Church of Humanity 111-112
Church Passage 22
Church Street
  (Rookery) 59
  (Seven Dials) 46
Church Times, The 90
Churchill, Sir Winston
  53, 100
Cibber, Susannah 102
Cibber, Theophilus 102
City Literary Institute 84, 103
Civil Aviation Authority
  74, 103
Clairmont, Claire 19
Clanricarde, Marquess of 97
Clare Market 36
Clarence House 71
Clark's Buildings 59-60
Clark's Mews 59
Clarke, Brian 49
Clements, Jeakes & Co. 86
Clements, John 25
Clerical Library 90
Clifford, Sue 45
Clifton Mansions 15
Cline, Francis 113
Cline, Henry **110**, 123
Clive, Kitty 97
Club Quarters 122
Coach Office 99
coachbuilders 77, 84, 90, 92
Coal Yard 83

Cochrane, C B 22, 40
Cock & Pye *PH* 29, 41
Cock & Pye Fields 9, 29, 41
Cock Alley 67
Cockerell, Douglas 18
Cockerell, Fredk Pepys 96
Cockpit Alley 103
Cockpit Place
Cockpit Theatre 79
Cole, Bassitt 83
Cole Yard 83
Coleridge, Samuel T **113**, 123
Collcutt, T E 73
College of Preceptors 96
Collett's (jazz shop) 24
Collins, F & Sons 40
Combe, Harvey C 42, 44
Combe & Co.
  brewery **42**, 43, 44
  cooperage 51, 67, 82, 83
Common Ground 45
Commonwealth House 69
Compass Securities 110
Compasses *PH* 71
Compton, Bp Henry 22
Comyn Ching Company
  34, 38, **41**, 43
Comyn Ching Triangle 41-42
Confederation of
  British Industry 15
Congreve, Richard 111
Congreve, William 117, 123
Connaught, Duke of 96, 100
Connaught Rooms 94, 96
Connection, The 70
Connor, Bernard 80
Conran, Terence 45
Cons, Emma 88
Constantinou, Photini 18
Contemporary Applied
  Arts 44
Continental Garage 19

Conway House 93
Conway, Viscount 93
Cook, S A G 54
Co-op Permanent
  Building Society 70
Cooper, G B 20
Cope, Lady Katherine 65
Corben & Sons 77
Cordon, Madame 120
Cornwallis, Sir Charles 74
coroner's court 86
Cottingham, Lewis N 92
Cotton, Billy 18
Cotton, Rev. Thomas 60
Covent Garden 8, 9
  Action Area 77
  Community Assoc. 44, 87
  Dragon Hall Trust 85
  Hotel 30
  Market 11, 30, 34, 36, 38,
    42, 44, 45, 47, 55, 76
  Open Spaces Assoc. 22
  Travelodge 67, 82
cowkeepers 30, 83, 85
Cowper, James 108
Cowper, Spencer 112
Cowper, Sir William 108, 109
Cowper, William, Earl 118
Cox, Mr Justice 94
Cox & Co. 92
Crace family 100
Craske, Margaret 40
Craven House 90
Cremer, Sir William R 111
Crewe, Bertie 22, 63
Crittall & Co. 72
Croche Hose, Le 55
Crosfield, Michael 47
Cross Keys *PH* 48
Cross Lane 88
Crosse & Blackwell 20,
  21, 22, 27, 28

129

Crossrail 13, 28, 56
Crowder, Arthur 116
Crowders, Vizard,
 Oldham & Co. 118
Crown *PH*
 (High Holborn) 53, 66
 (Seven Dials) **32**, 36
Crown & Anchor *PH* 44
Crown & Cushion *PH* 74
Crown Court 53
Crown Inn 13, 27
Crown Place 15
Crown Street 13, 15, 27
Cuban Consulate 105
Cuban Embassy 66
Cucumber Alley 46
Culture Club 91
Cunningham, Sir David 121
Cup Field 106, 108, 109
Currie, William 65
Curzon Phoenix Cinema 22
Czezowski, Andy 55

D
Da Cunha, Don Lewis 118
Daimler House 62
Dance, George, the
 Younger 116
D'Arblay, Alexandre 120
Darell, Henry 72
Darell's Buildings 72
Darling, James 90
Daughters of Compassion 69
D'Avenant, Sir William 116
Davies, Myles 90
Davy, Sir Humphry 96
Davy, John 46
Day, William 97
Day & Son 122
De Grey, William 115
De Lane Studios 74
Defoe, Daniel 23, 86, 102

Delafield, Joseph 42, 44
Delfont, Bernard 25
Den, The 68
Denmark Place 15,
 16*, 17, 25
Denmark Street 16-18,
 21, 28, 68
Dent, Edward John 45
Design Conspiracy 84
Despard, Charlotte 70
Detroit bar 44
Devereux Partnership 25
'Devil's Gap' 100
Devonshire, Earl of 39, 97
Diaghilev, Sergei 63
Dial House 25
Dickens, Charles 23, 32,
 34, 92, 96, 102, 115,
 119, 120, 121
Digby, John 97
Digby, Sir Kenelm 93
Dignum, Charles 101
Dirty Lane 81
Dobson, Frank 22
Doll, Charles Fitzroy 61
Donmar Warehouse 44
Donovan, Terence 92
Doré, Gustave 23, 24*, 90
Douglass, Bp John 120
Dove, Evelyn 50
D'Oyly Carte Co. 63
Dragon Court 87
Dragon Hall (Trust) 85
Dragon Yard 85
drinking fountains 53,
 63, 110, 114-115
Drury, Sir William 79
Drury Lane 8, 9, 20, 32, 47,
 48, 67, **77-78**, **81-83**, 82*,
 86, 89, 90, 100
 Car Park 77
 Industrial School 84

Dryden, John 86
Dudley, Sir John 9, 21
Dudley, Lady Alicia 15,
 19, 21, 41
Dudley, Robert 19, 21
Dudley Court (C18) 15
 (C20) 50, 51, 52
Dudley House (C17) 21
Dudley House (C19) 50
Dudley Street 23, 24*
Dugdale, William 39
Duke of Newcastle *PH* 40
Duke Street
 (*later* Hyde Street) 68
 (*later* Sardinia St) 103,
 104, 118, 119*, 120
Duke's Company 116
Duke's Court 43
Duke's Theatre 117
Dumb's Alley 69
Duncombe, Susanna 114
Dunn's Passage 69
Duran Duran 91
Duval, Claude 20
Dwight, Reg 17
Dynamite, Ms 50
Dyot, Philip 60
Dyot House 60
Dyot Street Chapel 60
Dyott Street 60-61, 63

E
Eagle & Child Alley 59
Earl Street, *see* Great...;
 Little Earl Street
Earl's Court 43
Earlham Street 26, 36,
 39-40, **43-44**
Early Music Shop 18
Earnshaw Street 57, 63, 69
Eastman, George 104
Eden Palace of Varieties 91

Edexcel 69
Educational Supply Assoc. 68
Edward VII 89, 100
Église Helvétique/Suisse
 26, **53**
Eight Bells *PH* & Yard 21
Eldestrate 27
Elgar, Alice 89
Eliot, T S 84
Elizabethan House 91
Elliott Group 48
Elms Lesters 20
Emery, John 68
EMI Group 26
Emily Davison Club 70
Encyclopædia Britannica 72
Endeavour House 23
Endell Street 45, **48-54**, 65
 Military Hospital 51-52
 Preview Theatre 48
 'Siege' 54
English Heritage 109, 124
Epstein, Brian 25, 30
Epstein, Clive 25
Equity (union) 41
Equity & Law 113
Erskine, Lord 114, 116
Erskine Chambers 114, 116
Esavian House 68
Eugenics Education Socy 91
Evelyn, John 29
Exide House 62
Eyre & Spottiswoode 76

F
Fairfax, Lord Thomas 97
Fanshawe, Lady 112
Fanshawe, Sir Richard 115
Faris, David 83
Farmer, Tom 34
Farmer's Alley/Rents 15
Farrell, Terry 38, 42

Farrer, James 123
Farrer, Sir Wm James 123
Farrer & Co. 122
Fawdrey, Marguerite 38
Fazakerley, Nicholas 115
Feathers *PH* 103
Fenn, Rev. Peter 68
Ferrey, Benjamin 52
Fickett's Field 106
Fielding, Henry 83
Fielding Court 38
Finch, Daniel 47
Finch, Heneage 47, 93
Finney, Albert 43
First Out café-bar 15
Fishmongers' Arms *PH* 40
Fitch Detective Service 62
Five Dials 26
Fladgate LLP 91
Flanagan, Barry 114
Flaxman, John 19
Flegg, B 38
Fletcher, Geoffrey 42
Fletcher, Norton 112
Flitcroft, Henry 19, 20
Flitcroft House 27*, 28
Flitcroft Street 20-21
Flying Hand & Pen, The 101
Folies Dramatiques 91
Fonteyn, Margot 40, 44
Food for Thought 45
Food Standards Agency
 74, 90
Football Association 96
Fopp Ltd 26
Forbidden Planet 24
Ford, Son & Burrows 72
forges 16*, 41, 67
Forster, John 34, **120**
Fortescu Lane 79
Fortifene Lane 104
Fortrey, Samuel 16

Fountain *PH* 54
Fournier, Daniel 102
Fox, Charles 69
Foxcroft, Isaac 101
Francatelli, Alexander 96
France & Sons 32
Franciscans 118
Francklin, Rev. Thomas 92
Franklin, Benjamin 92,
 101, 102, 102*, 104
Freedom Brewing Co. 44
Freemasonry 12, 38, 73, 77,
 93, 94, 96, 97, 99, 100, 113
Freemasons' Hall
 (C18) 94, 95*
 (C19) 96; (C20) 99, **100**
Freemasons' Hotel 94
Freemasons' Tavern 94, 96
French, John 92
French Change 26
French Embassy 101
French Hospital 24-25, 30
French Protestant
 Episcopal Church 62
 School of Westminster 62
Frere, Margaret 39
Frere Cholmely 114
Friends of
 German Literature 113
 Lincoln's Inn Fields 109
Friese-Greene, William 96
Fryer, Walter J 17
Fulmar & Firkin *PH* 74
Fuseli, Henry 91

G
Gallaher Ltd 104
Galleries, The 84
gallows 13, 20, 108
Garden Court Chambers 122
Garden Studios 81
Gardener, The 105

Garnett & Partners 70
Garrick, David 92, 94, 97
gas explosion 68
Gaugain, Thomas 18
Gay, John 32, 79, 86, 108, 117
Gay, Noel 17
General Electric Co. 103
Genesis 18
Geological Society of London 96
George *PH* 91
George I 23, 79, 116
George III 80, 116
George IV 94
George IV *PH* 63
George Street 60
George Yard 106
Georgiou family 61
German Theatre Co. 91
Gibbs, James 97
Gibson, John 61
Gifford, Andrew 102
Giles, Saint 8
Gilliam, Terry 31
Gilman, Harold 25
Gilroy, John 105
Gin Lane 11, 34, 60
Golden Eagle, The 101
Goldsmith Buildings 83
Goldsmith Court 83
Goldsmith Street 83, 85
Goldsmith's Alley 85
Gomme, Sir Laurence 125
Gontarski, Steven 57
Good Earth restaurant 70
Good Vibes 81
Gordon Riots 11, 94, 118, 119
Goslett, Alfred & Co. 21
Gostling, Joseph 41
Goulden, Richard 125
Gower Street Memorial

Chapel 25
Grade, Michael 79
Grand Connaught Rooms 94, 96
Grand Lodge of England 94
Grandage, Michael 44
Grantley, Baron 122
Grape Street 61, **65-66**, 68
Grapes *PH*
  (Earlham Street) 40
  (Seven Dials) 36, 43
Great Earl Street **43-44**, 46
Great Fire (1666) 41, 108
Great Garden 106
Great Plague (1665) 9, 19, 41, **83**
Great Queen Street 9
  12, 76, 77, **91-101**, 98*, 105
  Academy 97
  Chapel **92**, 102
  Medical Society 92
  Theatre 91
  tram station 104
Great St Andrew Street 29, 30, 32, 34, 36
Great Turnstile 76, 110, 114
Great White Lion Street 32
Great Wild Street 101
  Board School 103
Greater London Council 39, 45, 48, 55, 77, 105, 109
Green, Charles 16-17
Green, Joseph Hy 113, 118
Green, W Curtis 113
Green Ball, The 80
Green Dragon House 85
Green Dragon Yard 70, **85**, 87
Green Dragon, The 85
Greenaway, F H 114
Greenland, Alfred 57, 59
Grey, Earl 91
Greyhound *PH* 53, 66

Greyhound Court 53
Grieve family 87
Grimaldi, Joseph 72
Grimshaw, Nicholas 120
Grimstone, William 53, 65
Grock (clown) 28
Grossmith, George 79
Grove, Harriet 118
Grove, John 118
Guild House 41
Guinness, Sir Alec 41, 63
Gunton, Josiah 104
Guy Earl of Warwick *PH* 53
Gwyn, Nell 83, 117, 117*
Gyfford, Wm & Joseph 42

H
Hahn, Daniel 48
Halberstadt Mansions 28
Halifax, Marquess of 115, 122
Hall, A W 115
Hallam, Arthur 120, 121
Hambleden, Viscount 124
Hamp, T J 73
Hampshire Hog *PH* 59
Hampshire Hog Yard 59
Hampstead Capital 91
Hancock, Sheila 39
Hanff, Helene 27
Hardwick, Philip 94, 114
Hare, Doris 25
Harleian Society 88
Harraden, Beatrice 52
Harrap & Co. 69, 76
Harrison, Frederic 111
Harrow Alley 69
Hartnoll, James 24, 27, 28
Harwood, Rev. Edward 68
Hatton, George 47, 55, 103
Hayday, James 90

Hayden, Craig 20
Hayley, Rev. William 80
Haynes & Sons 81
'Hell Gate' 100
Hemingway, Wayne 45-46
Hendrix, Jimi 74
Henley, Anthony 109
Henley, Robert 108
Henley, Sir Robert 115
Henry I 8
Henry III 56
Henry VIII 9
Herbert, William 122
Hercules Pillars *PH* 94
Hertford Record Co. 122
Heydinger, Carl 97
High Holborn 19, 54, 57, **63-65, 66-74**, 83, 88, 125
  Branch Library 70
  Residence 67
High Street, Bloomsbury, *see* St Giles High Street
Highmore family 113-114
Hillier, Susanna 113
Hilton, Jack 63
Hoare, Henry 116
Hog Lane 27, 40
Hogarth, William 11, 34, 60, 117
Hogshead *PH* 81
Holborn (Borough) 12, 18-19, 54, 61, 70, 81, 85, 124
Holborn Artists' Club 69
Holborn Casino 72
Holborn Central Library 70
Holborn Cinema 71
Holborn Hall 69-70
Holborn Poor Law Union 51
Holborn Restaurant **73-74**, 73*, 88
Holborn Row 108
Holborn Station 71, **74**

Holborn Tower 70
Holborn Town Hall **70**, 85
Holborn Works Dept 85
Holcroft House 91
Holden, Charles 72
Holland (Dwellings) 88
Holland & Hannen 68
Hollar, Wenceslaus 19
Holles, John 123
Holloway, Stanley 25
Holme, Daniel 48
Holy Trinity Church 89-90
  National Schools 76
Home for Destitute Women 81
Hoole, John 99
Hopkins, Sir Anthony 39
Horse & Groom *PH* 47
Hospital Club, The **49-50**, 80
How, Edith 70
Howard, Henry 97
Hudson, Thomas 94, 114
Hugh the Smith 67
Huguenot Episcopal Church of the Savoy 62
Huguenots 26, 30, 32, 40, 42, 62, 99
Hund, F & Son 42
Hunkin & Plant 46
Hunt, Thomas 85
Hunt, William Henry 48, 80
Hunter, John 116, 125
Hunterian Museum 116
Huskisson, William 96
Hutton, James 102
Huxley, Aldous 43
Hyde Street 68

I
I'Anson, Edward 115
IKA Project Design 67

Imperial Buildings 105
Imperial Cancer Research Fund 117, 122
Imperial Mansions 14*
Inflight Productions 84
Ingoldsby, Thomas 100
Inns of Court Hotel 113
Insolvent Debtors' Court 115
Institution of Works Managers 54
International Buildings/ Correspondence Schools 44, 104
House, London 84
Irish community 11, 47, 59, 69, 76, 83-84
Islam, Yusuf 61
Italian community 47
Ivy Lane/Street 59

J
Jackson, Robert 114
Jacob, Benjamin 46
Jacobins 60
Jagger, Mick 91
James, C J 110
James I 56, 91
James II 11, 19, 29, 80, 97, 101, 103, 110, 118, 122
Jarrah Properties 25
Jeacocke, Caleb 16
Jeffery, Richard 46
Jeffreys, Baron George 93
Jerrold, Blanchard 90
Jerrold, Douglas 92
Joass, John James 89
Job Centre 18
Jodrell Theatre 91
John, Elton 17
Johnson, Amy 84
Johnson, Samuel 93, 97
Johnstone, Alick 87

Johnstone, Walter 87
Jones, Agnes E 76
Jones, Digby 22
Jones, Inigo 19, 92, 93, 108, 121
Joseph, Delissa 74
Joye, James 30
Joynes, Henry 120
Judd, Rolfe 23

K
Kapoor, Satish C 38
Kaye, Sidney, Firmin & Partners 71
Kean, Charles 87
Keates, James 69
Keats, John 113
Keeley, Ellen 45, **47**
Keeley, James 47
Keeley, Robert 102
Keeley Street 102-103
Keith, Penelope 22
Kelly & Co. 69, 100
Kemble family 19, 103
Kemble Street 103
Kendall, Sir Henry 122, 123
Kendrick's Yard 22-23
Kennedy Court 88
Kenning, George 99
Kenny, Sean 79
Kent, George 71
Kent, William 123
Kenyon, Lloyd (Lord) 113, 115
Kettle, Tilly 101
Key Studios 20
Khartoum flats 82
Kiely, Orla 32
King, Angela 45
King, John 48
King, Joseph 77
King Edward Mansions 61, 65

King Henry VIII *PH* 36
King Street
   (*off* Drury Lane) 77
   (Seven Dials) 45, 54, 55
   Mission Hall 55
Kingman, Tod 20
King's Arms Yard 84
King's Head Court 30
King's Head *PH* 71
King's Head Yard
   (*off* Little Wild St) 102
   (= Matthews Yard) 48
Kingsway 12, 26, 74, 86, **89-91**, 92, 103, 106, **104-105**, 118, 120, 122, 123
Kingsway Chambers 105
Kingsway Corner Buildings 74
Kingsway Crèche 105
Kingsway Day College 103
Kingsway Hall 92, **104-105**
Kingsway Hall Hotel 92
Kingsway House 91
Kingsway Subway 104
Kingsway Tavern 74
Kingsway Telephone Exchange 125
Kingsway Theatre 91
Kinks, The 18
'Kip, The' 34
Kitchener flats 82
Kitten, James 32
Kneller, Sir Godfrey 79, **97**
Knight, Edward 92
Kniveton, Lady Frances 19
Kodak House 104
Krantz, Solomon 81

L
La Giaconda, Café 18
Lamb, Charles & Mary 90
Lamb Alley 67

Lambert & Butler 101
Lambert & Tyrrell 92
Lamé, Amy 15
Lanchester, Elsa 43
Land Registry building 115
Land Transfer Office 115
Lane, K H 25
Langdale, Sir Marmaduke 53
Lascelles, W H & Co. 71
Lascelles Court 67
Lascelles Place 67
Latchfords 51
Laud, Bishop 19
Laurrilard, Edward 79
Lavers & Barraud 49
Lawrence Street 56
Layard, Daniel 80
Laye, Evelyn 63
Leader House 25
Legh, Katherine 9, 20
Lennon, John 30, 82
Lennox, Duke of 48
Lenton, John 80
Lepard & Smith 43
leper hospital, *see* St Giles Hospital
L'Estrange, Sir Roger 19
Leverton, Thomas 87, 122
Leverton's Charity 87
Lewington, Bill 26
Lewis, Cecil Day 84
Lewis, James Henry 101
Lewis, Norman 71
Lewis, R G Ltd 71
Lewknor, Sir Lewis 86
Lewknor's Lane 85, 86
Library & Museum of Freemasonry 100
Lincoln's Inn 11, 77, 88, 91, 105, 108, 109, 114, 115
Lincoln's Inn Fields 11, 12, 88, 92, 93, 104,

106-125, 107*, 111*
   east side 114-115
   north side 110-114
   south side 115-118
   west side 118-124
   Gardens 109, **124-125**
   Theatre 116-117
   Trustees 109
Lincoln's Inn House 105
Lindsay House 24
Lindsey, Earl of 121
Lindsey Buildings 86
Lindsey House 121
Ling, Miss 36
Linley, Elizabeth 97
Linnell, John 61
Lisle, Lord 9, 21
Lister, Ralph 101
Literary Fund Society 111
Little Denmark Street 20
Little
   Earl Street 36, **39-40**
   Queen Street 72, **90**, 106
   St Andrew Street 29, **38**
   White Lion Street 32, **42-43**
   Wild Street 102, 103
Livingstone, Ken 57
Lloyd, David Ap 83
Lloyd Webber, Andrew 39, 79
Lloyd's Court 20, 21
Lock, Matthew 47
Lockman, John 80
Lollards 13
Lombards Court 39
London
   & North Western Rly 68
   & Westminster Bank 72
   Baptist Association 62
   City Mission 51, 63
   County Council 12, 15, 26, 39, 76, 77, 84, 86,

87, 88, 89, 90, 103, 109, 120, 124, 125
Ecology Centre 45
Electricity Board 81
Festival Ballet 44
Medical Mission 51
Nelson Club 57
Residuary Body 48
Savings Bank 70
School of
   Classical Dance 40
   Economics 67, 101, 110, 115, 120, 124
Society for Promoting Christianity Among the Jews 113
Women's Centre 105
Long Acre 42, 46, 92, 100
Loughborough, Lord 117-118
Louise, Princess 47
Lowson, Mrs J 53
Lumber Court 39
Lundenwic 8, 25, 46, 92
Lupus House 87
Lutyens, Edwin 96, 105, 122, 123, 124
Luxton, Joan 53
lying-in hospital 50, 80-81
Lyttelton, Humphrey 28

M
Maan, Gurbachan S 54
McAneary Architects 20
Macari's 28
McAslan, John 68
McBean, Angus 51
M'Cree, George 26
MacDonald,
   James Ramsay **111**, 125
   John Malcolm 125
   Margaret 110, **125**
McGlashan (& Sons;

& Merryweather) 85
Macklin, Charles 86
Macklin, Thomas 110
Macklin House 86-87
Macklin Street 85-87
McLaren, Malcolm 18
Macready, William C 122
Magnet House 103
Maidenhead Close 60
Maidenhead Inn 60
Maidenhead Lane 60
Mail Rail 68
Majestic wine 81
Malby & Sons 76
Malvern House College 85
Management House 74
Mann, Manfred 17
Manos, Granne 54
Mansfield, Earl of 120, 121*
Marceau, Marcel 25
Margaret MacDonald Memorial 110, **125**
Mark Masons' Hall 94
Market House 77
Marks, George Croydon 122
Marks & Clerk 122
Marks & Co. 27
Marlborough, Duchess of 115
Marquis of Granby *PH* (Drury Lane) 82
   (Earlham Street) 82
Marsden, William 122
Marsh, Cummings 23
Marshall, Joshua 19
Marshall, Thomas 20
Marshland, The 9, 29, 30, 41, 45, 47
Martin's Alley 55
Marvell, Andrew 20
Masefield, John 84
Mason, A D ('Red') 34

Masonic Peace Memorial 100
Masonic Printing Works 77
Master's House 9, 15
Matcham, Frank 79
Matilda, Queen 8, 57
Matilda Apartments 57
Matthews Yard 48
Maufe, Sir Edward 115
Maxwell, Robert 45
Mayhew, Henry 36, 60
Medhurst, George 18
Melody Maker 17
Mendes, Sam 44
Mercer, James 50
Mercer Street 32, 41, **42-43**
Mercers' Company 42
Merritt, John 65
Metal Airscrew Co. 105
Metcalf & Grieg 105
Methodists 40, 55, 92, 104
Metro Bank 72
Metropolitan
  Board of Works 12, 26, 68, 76, 77, 88, 89
  Library 90
  Police 60, 109
  Public Gardens Assoc. 109
MGM cinema 26
Micke, Samuel 62
Middle Row 64*, 65, 66*
Middle Yard 92
Middlesex Theatre 78*, 79
'Midtown' 12
Milliner, Mary 86
Mills Music 17
Milton, Mary 19
Minerva Club 20
Minerva Press 70
Ministry of Health 67
Ministry of Works 51

Moat House Hotel 82
Model Zone 71
Mogul *PH*, Mogul Saloon 79
Mohun, Michael 79
Mole & Mole 61
Molteni & C Dada 23
Mon Plaisir restaurant 30
Monmouth, Duke of 11, 29
Monmouth Coffee Co. 32
Monmouth Court 36
Monmouth Street 29-30, **32**, **38**, 41, 42, 43, 55, 63
Monmouth Street (C18) 11, **23**, 24*, 29
Montagu, Edward 121
Montagu, Sir James 115
Montagu, Lady Wortley 23
Montague, Sir William 115
Montand, Yves 25
Monty Python 31
Moor Street 26
Moorfields Eye Hospital 67
Moorse, Henry 69
Moravians 102
Morley, Ebenezer 96
Morley, Eric 87
Morrell, W T 47
Morris, Richard & Son 71
Morris, Victor 17
mortuary 86
Moss Empires 17
Motograph House 41
Mountbatten Hotel **32**, 36
Mountjoy, Lord 9
Mousetrap, The 40, 41
Murray, Flora 51
Murray, Gilbert 125
Murray, William 120, 121*
Museum House 62
Museum of Freemasonry 100
Museum of London 25, 57
Museum Stn Buildings 71

Museum Street 68
Musgrove, John 117
Music Copyright Assoc. 28
Music Room, The 17
Musical Bouquet Office 69
Mysteries (shop) 30

N
Napier, William 100
'Narrows, The' 68
National
  Assembly Rooms 72
  Baths 72
  Farmers' Union 25
  Land Company 70
  schools 19, 20, 53-54
  Sunday League 73
  Theatre 43
Nationwide Building Socy 70, 71
Natural Shoe Store 55
NatWest Bank 72
Neal Street 44, **45-46**, 47, **54-55**
  Restaurant 45
Neale, Thomas 11, **29-30**, 45
Neal's Passage 46
Neal's Yard 30-31, 31*, 46, 48
  Dairy 32, **46**
  Remedies 31
  Salad Bar 31
  'Negroes' 32, 55
netball courts 124
Neurath, Eva & Thomas 68
New Academic Building 104, **120**
New Belton Street 48, 51, 53
New Brook Buildings 91
New Compton Street 22-23, 28
New London Centre 79

New London Theatre 79
New Masonic Samaritan Fund 99
New Middlesex Theatre of Varieties 78*, 79
New Oxford House 70
New Oxford Street 12, 13, 15, 26, 48, 57, 59, 61, 62, 68, 69, 70, 71
New Princes Theatre 63
New Queen's Theatre 91
New Romantics 91
New Weld Street 102
New World (shop) 48
New Yard 82, 98*, 99
Newberry, J E 114
Newcastle, Duke of 123
Newcastle House 122-123
Newland 47
Newman, F Winton 100
Newman, John Henry 69
Newman's Row 108, **114**
Newton, William 88, 93, 108
Newton Arms *PH* 76, 88
Newton Hotel 71
Newton Street 72, **87-88**, 91
Newton Workshops 87
Nicholl, William Grinsell 96
Nicholls, Horatio 17
Nisbets London 26
Noah's Ark *PH* 60
Nobel's Explosives Co. 91
Noel Gay Organisation 17
Norfolk, Duke of 97
Norman, Samuel 32
Normanby, Marquess of 94
Northcote, Anna Stafford 40
Northington, Earl of 115
Northumberland, Earl of 94
Nottingham, Earl of 47, 93
Nottingham Court 47, 48

Nottingham House 47, 51
Novelty Theatre 91
Nuffield, Lord 116
Nuffield College of Surgical Sciences 115

O
Oasis Sports Centre 54, 66
Oates, Titus 20, 93, **103**
O'Brien, Patrick 82
O'Connell, Daniel 96
O'Connor, Feargus 70
Odeon Covent Garden 25-26
Odger, George 19, 56
Odhams Press 45, 69
Odhams Walk 45
Office of Works 104, 115
Old Belton Street 48, 53, 80
Old Weld Street 101
Oldcastle, Sir John 13
Oldstrate 27
Oldwick Close 93
Oliver, Jamie 61
Olivier, Laurence 43
O'Neill's *PH* 100
Opie, John 93-94, 93*
Oporto Stores *PH* 66
Oratorian Fathers 69
Orchestra, The 88
organ grinders 47
Our Mutual Friend 32
Oxford Street Station 13

P
Page House 76
Page's bookshop 114
Pages (tableware) 26
Paget, Dame Rosalind 50
Paine, James 34
Painted Glass Works 49
Palin, Michael 31
Pall Mall Gazette 88

Palmer, George Josiah 90
Palmer, John 101
Palmer, Samuel 67
Palmer's Charity, Mrs 39
Pankhurst family 70, **105**
Panormo, Louis 15
Paolozzi, Eduardo 13
Paramount Group 15
Park, Sir James Alan 115
Parker, John 93
Parker, Philip 74
Parker House 76
Parker Mews 77
Parker Street 74, 76-77
Parker Tower 74
Parker's Lane 74
Particular Baptists 25
Paterson, Emma 100
Paulet House 93
Paviors Alley 83
Peabody Buildings/Trust 103
Pearce, John 118
Pearson Education 69
Peel, Sir Robert 96
Pelham, Henry 19
Pell, John 19
Penderell, Richard 19, 20
Pendrell House 22
Penley, William 91
Pennethorne, Sir James 48
Pepys, Samuel 79, 83, 90, 108, 116, 117, 121
Perceval, Spencer 121
Perry, Ann 72
Peto, Sir Samuel M 61, 62
Pfeil, Stedall & Co. 87
Philips, Charles 101
Philips UK 23
Phoenix *PH* 21
Phoenix Artist Club 22
Phoenix Cinema 22
Phoenix Garden 22

Phoenix Street 22
  (= Bucknall Street) 61
Phoenix Theatre **22**, 28
Piano, Renzo 57
Piccadilly Line 74, 89, 104
Pickfords 71
Pickwick Papers 115
Pierce, Edward 34
Piggott, John 102
Pindar, Peter 94
Pineapples, The 112
Pitaunce Croft 9, 11,
  56, 59, 60
Pitcher & Piano *PH* 105
Pite, William & Arthur
  Beresford 50
Pitman & Co. 76
Pitt's Toy Warehouse 32
Pitts, Johnny 36
Pizzey, Mr 36
PKO bank 25
Place, The 67
Plague (1665) 9, 19, 41, **83**
Plumtree, Henry 61
Plumtree Street 61
Plunket, Oliver 20
Pneumatic Dispatch Co.
  67-68
Poetic Films Ltd 48
Poetry Place/Society 81
police barracks 60
Pollexfen, Sir Henry 116
Pollock's Toy Museum 38
Pond, Arthur 101
Poole, Henry 62
Pooley, F B 45
Pope, Alexander 120
Pope, Jane 101
Popish Plot 97, 103
Portsmouth Street 118
Portugal Row 108
Portugal Street 115, 116, 124

Portuguese Embassy
  101, 118
Portwine, A S & Son 39
Positivist Church 111-112
Post Office 67, 68
Post Office Railway 68
pound (& cage) 13, 65
Powell & Moya 50
Powis, Lords 122-123
Powis House (Lincoln's
  Inn Fields) 122-123
  (Macklin Street) 86
Powys, Sir Thomas 122
Poynter, Ambrose 62
Pratt, Charles 115
Pratt, John Jeffreys 115
Presbyterians 60, 68
Price, Meredith 113
Princes Circus 63
Princes Theatre **63**, 68
Princess Louise *PH* 71
Pritchard, Hannah 92
prostitution 32, 39,
  40, 76, 84
Proudfoot, Edmund 112
Prudence & Peter,
  Lodge of 38
Psychic Press 70
Public Health Laboratory
  Service 11
Public House Trust Co. 90
Public Trust Office
  104, 120
Puddington, Arthur 81
Puerorum House 77, **99**
Pulse Films 21
Punjab restaurant 54
Purcell, John 18
Purse Field 85, 88,
  92, 106, 108
Pyramide de la Tremblade 40
Q

Queen Alexandra
  Mansions 61, 65
Queen & Prince Albert *PH* 72
Queen Anne's Bath
  48, 49*, 65
Queen Mary, University
  of London 100, 124
Queen Street (Great),
  see Great Queen
  (Seven Dials) 46
Queen's Court 97
Queen's Head *PH* 92
Queen's Head Yard 92
Queen's House 104, **120**
Queen's Place 97

R

Radcliffe, John 97
ragged schools 25,
  30, **63**, 103
Ragged Staff Court 82
Ramsden, Jesse 16-17
Ranyard, Ellen 74
Rathbone, Mr 71
'Rat's Castle' 59
Rawlinson, J A 70
Raycol British 44
Raymond, Robert 115
Ray's Jazz Shop 24
Read, Rev. Joseph 60
Really Useful Co. 39, 79
Red Ball, The 110
Red Lion & Still *PH* 81
Red or Dead 45-46, 55
Red Rooms, The 91
Redemere, Herbert de 55
Redgrave, Michael 63
Redland House 105
Regent House 105
Regent Sounds Studios 18
Regent's Place 15
Reilly, Luke 94

Reinhardt, Max 40
Remnant, James F 105
Remnant, Samuel 19
Remnant Street 105, 123
Resurrection Gate 19, **20**
Reynolds, Sir Joshua 94, 114
RHWL, architects 46, 53
Rich, John 117
Richardson, Jonathan 114
Rigg, Diana 22
Rights of Man Society 60
Rimbault, Stephen 32
Rinkelberg Capital 91
Rippon, Richard 45
Rivers, Countess 96
Rivers House 96
Riviere, Robert 99
Robertson, John 91
Robin Hood *PH* 60
Robinson, Henry Crabb 113
Robinson, Mary ('Perdita') 94
Robinson, William 105
Rock & Sole Plaice 51
Rock Stop Music 28
Rodney, Lord 19
Rolling Stones, The 18, 74
Roman Catholics 11, 20, 59,
  69, 97, 101, 103, 106, 110,
  116, 122, 118-120
Roman road 8, 9, 56, 68
Roman tombstone 70-71
Ronquillo 101
'Rookery', *see*
  St Giles 'Rookery'
Rose *PH* 74
Rose & Crown *PH* 67
Rose & Crown Yard 15
Rose & Three Tuns *PH* 40
Rose Field 74, 85, 86
Rose-Morris 17
Roslyn, L F 105
Rossiter, Leonard 26

Rosslyn, Earl of 117-118
Roubini Global Economics 67
Rough Trade records 46
Roumieu & Aitchison 28
Roworth & Co. 88
Roxy Club 55
Royal
  Bank of Scotland 72
  Canadian Air Force 113,
  124, 125
  College of
  Radiologists 122
  Surgeons 110, 113, **116**,
  117, 125
  Court Upstairs 40
  Courts of Justice 109
  Institute of Chartered
  Surveyors 114
  Mail 67, 72
  Masonic Institution
  for Boys/for Girls 99
  Masonic Trust 77
  Opera House 63
  Shakespeare Company 44
Rum Puncheon *PH* 88
Running Horse *PH* 91
Rushworth, W 70
Ruspini House 77
Russell,
  Lord Robert 116
  Lord William 11, 121, 125
Rye House Plot 11, 122
Ryle, Ann 36

S

Sadler, Thomas 93
Sainsbury, John 81
Sainsbury's 74, 81
St Albans, Duke of 117
St Albans, Earl of 97
St Andrew Street,

  see Great...;
  Little St Andrew Street
St Anselm & St
  Cæcilia Church 106, 120
St George's, Bloomsbury
  (church) 60
  (parish) 11, 12
St Giles (parish) 8, 9, 12
St Giles 'Blackbirds' 55
St Giles 'Bowl' 11, 20, 65
St Giles Buildings 47
St Giles Christian Mission
  36, 55, 81, **103**
St Giles Church **18-19**,
  23, 56, 63, 80
St Giles Church House 60
St Giles Churchyard
  19-20, 103
St Giles Circus 13, 14*
St Giles Coroner's Court 86
St Giles Court 57, 60
St Giles District Board
  of Works 63, 70, 85, 109
St Giles Engine House 84
St Giles Evening Institute
  for Women 53
St Giles Field 9, 29
St Giles Free Library 70
St Giles High Street 8, 9,
  13, 14*, **15**, 17, **18-20**, 23,
  56-57, 64*, 66*
St Giles Hospital **8-9**, 15,
  19, 22, 25, 55, 57, 65,
  67, 83, 93; seal 8*
St Giles Mission House 60
St Giles National School
  19, 20, **53-54**
St Giles Passage 22, 25
St Giles Pound 13, 65
St Giles 'Rookery' 11, 12,
  25, 56, 58*, **59-60**, 60*
St Giles Roundhouse 23, 85

134

St Giles Watch House 84
St Giles' & St George's
   Almshouses 63, 65, 85, 87
   Baths & Washhouses 54
   Coroner's Court 86
   Mortuary 86
   Ragged School 25
   Refuge for Homeless
      & Destitute Boys 63, **91**
   Vestry 45, 50, 60, 67
   Vestry House 20
   Workhouse **50-51**, 87
St Joseph's School 61, 69, **86**
St Martin's Theatre 40-41
'St Mary's Church' 109
St Mungo's hostel 54
St Paul's Hospital 24, **50**
St Philip's Home 86
St Thomas's Street 77
St Vincent de Paul,
   Socy of 69
Salisbury, Earl of 91
Salter, Stephen 116
Salutation Court 66
Samett, Lucien 21
Sandby, Thomas 94
Sandwich, Earl of 121
Sandys, Francis 80
Sardinia Street 104, 118
Sardinia Street (C19) 119*
Sardinian Chapel 101, 104,
   118-120, 119*
Sardinian Embassy 118, 119
Sassoon, Vidal 38
Saunders, Nicholas
   30, 31, 32, 46
Saunders, T &
   Associates 110
Savile, Sir George 122
Saville Theatre 25-26
Savoy Hotel 85
Sawyer, Sir Robert 122

Saxon period, *see* Lundenwic
Sayers, Dorothy L 84, 105
School Board for London,
   see Board schools
Scofield, Paul 63
Scoles, Joseph John 86
Scott, Harold 43
Scott, Sir Giles Gilbert 22
Scott Brownrigg 53
Scumoween Squat 67
Seagood, Henry 100
Seaholme, Catharine 19
Seifert, Richard 15, 103
Selmer Co. of London 28
Serjent, E T 67
Servite Sisters 69, 86
Seven Dials 32-38, 33*
   (area) 9, 11, 12, 23, **29-46**
   (column) 32, **34**
   Club 44
   Gallery 44
   House **36**, 46
   Housing Action Area 36
   Mission 40
   Monument Charity 34
   Ragged School 30, 63
   Trust 30, 34
   Warehouse 43
Seven Dials Mystery, The 43
Severenska 40
Sex Pistols, The 18
Shackly, John 42
Shaftesbury, Earl of 25,
   26, 87, 103
Shaftesbury Avenue
   12, 17, **23-26**, 32, **54**, 55,
   60, **61-63**, 69; Chapel 25
Shaftesbury Buildings 87
'Shaftesbury Circus' 26, 63
Shaftesbury Homes **25**, 91
Shaftesbury Hospital 24
Shaftesbury Hotel 32

Shaftesbury House 25
Shaftesbury PLC 43
Shaftesbury Theatre
   62-63, 65
Shaftesbury Young People 25
Shakespeare's Head *PH* 90
Shaldon Mansions 17, 28
Shanghai Blues 70
Shapland, Charles & Co. 71
Sheard, Charles 69
Sheldon, John 92
Shelley, Mary 19
Shelley, Norman 53
Shelley, Percy Bysshe
   19, 118
Shelton Street 29, **41-42**,
   43, **44-45**, 48, **79**
Shelton Street (C19) 77
Shelton, William 41, 77, 87
Shelton's School 20, 41, 77
Shenton's Tenements 72
Sheppard, Jack 11, 20, **23**, 85
Sheridan, Richard B **97**, 101
Sherwin, Thomas 92
Shoe Black Society 69
Shoreditch & Islington
   Housing Association 88
Short, Dudley 53
Short, Thomas 47
Short, William 47, 48
Shorts Gardens 34, **46**, **47**,
   50, 51, 53
Siddons, Sarah 19, 103
Siebe, Augustus 18
Silberman, Leon 28
Silver Jubilee Walkway 124
Simmonds Bros 88
Simmons, William 122
Simpson, William 122
Simpson & Sons 71
Sir John Soane Museum
   112, 114, 124

Sisters of Mercy 86
   of Our Lady of Sion 86
Sitwell, Dame Edith 84
Sketches by Boz 23, 32,
   34, 59
Slam City Skates 46
Slingsby, H C 105
Sloper, William 102
Small, William R 70
Small Faces, The 18
Smart's Buildings 84
Smart's Place 69, **84-85**, 88
Smith, Bruce 87
Smith, Christina 44, 45
Smith, Ray 24
Smith, Robert 30
Smith, W F D 110, 124
Smith, W H 86, 124
Smith, Zepherina 50
Soames, Michael 40
Soane, Sir John 19, 94,
   112, 114, 115, 118, 120
Society for Improving the
   Conditions of the
   Labouring Classes
   47, 60, 87, 102, 103
   for Promoting Christian
   Knowledge 105
   for the Propagation of
   the Gospel 123
   for the Protection of
   Ancient Buildings 120
   of the Rosary 116
Soho Baptist Chapel 25
Soho Gyms 77, 86
Soho Housing Assoc.
   21, 22, 85
Soho Outreach Centre 25
Solomon, Lewis 57, 97
Somers, Sir John 123
Soper, Donald 104
Souk Medina 31-32

South London Dwellings
   Company 88
Southampton, Earl of 56
Southampton Place 72
Southwell, Sir Robert 117
Sovereign House 61
Space House 103
Spandau Ballet 91
Spanish & South
   American Clubs 15
Spanish Embassy 101, 103
Spedding, James 121
Spencer, Richard 99
Spiller, Eliza Ann 21
Spiller, James 101
Spittle Houses 9, 20
Spode & Copeland 117
Sprague, W G R 40
Spread Eagle *PH* 67
Square the Block 104
Stacey, James 21
Stacey Street 21, 22
Staffordshire Buildings 87
Standard Life 23
Stanfield, Clarkson 121
Star Court 88
'statue house' 94
Stedall & Co. 87
Steele, Richard 79
Stevens, Cat 61
Stevenson family 55
Stewart, Dave 38, 50
Stewart House 104
Stiddolph, Sir Richard 22
Stiddulph/Stidwell Street 22
Stone, Nicholas 121
Stonecutters Alley 105
Stoneyard 85
Stradling, Sir Edward 101
Strand Improvement
   Association 89
Strand Underpass 104

Strange, Sir Robert 100
Strange, Steve 91
Strangeway, John 39
Stratford, Dinah 101
Street, George Edmund 109
Stuart, Esmé 48
Stukeley Street 83-84
Sudbury Dairy 82*
suffragettes 51, **105**
suffragists 70
Sugar Loaf *PH* 100
Sugar Loaf Yard 100
Sullivan, Leo Sylvester 62
Summerson, Sir John 34
Sun *PH* 81
Sun & Punchbowl *PH* 72
Sunderland, Earl of 97
Surtees, Robert Smith 114
Swan Electrical
   Engraving Co. 27*
Swan Inn 67
Sway Bar 93, 94
Swedenborgians 15
Sweep's Alley 44
Swift, Clive 39
Swiss Protestant
   Church 26, **53**
Sword-bearer's Alley 85
Sykes, Arthur 91
Sykes, John 90

T
Tait, Thomas 104
Talbot, Lord 120, 122
Talbot, Mary Anne 122
Tallis, John 56, 66*
Tanner, Sir Henry 115
Tanqueray, Charles 65-66
Taylor, Sir Robert 115
Telbin, William 87
Temple Arms *PH* 36
tennis courts 116, 117, 124

Tennyson, Alfred 120, 121
Terrace, The 125
Teulon, William M 89
Thames & Hudson 68
Thaw, John 22
Thelwall, John 123
Therapy Rooms 31
Thomas, Dylan 84
Thomas, Marshall 20
Thomas Neals 44, **46**
Thorney Street 61
Thornhill, Sir James 97
Three Compasses *PH* 69
Thrift, John 83-84
Thurstan (Dwellings) 88
Tieck, Ludwig 113
Tillemans, Peter 97
Tiller Girls 40
Time Team 108, 125
'Tin Pan Alley', *see*
  Denmark Street
Tin Pan Alley Studio 17
Tin Pan Alley Traders'
  Association 18
TK-Maxx 28
Toms, Carl 43
Tooke, Horne 123
Torday, Emil 25
Tottenham Court Road
  Station 12, **13**, 14*
Tower Court 39
Tower Street 38-39, 53
Toye, Kenning & Spencer 99
tram tunnel 104
Travelodge 67, 82
Trehearne, W J 71
Trehearne & Norman
  90, 104, 105
Trentishoe Mansions 27
Trinity Church 89, 89*
Tristan Bates Theatre 39
Trust House Ltd 82

TSQ health spa 43
Turk's Head *PH* 60
Turmeau, John 43
Turnstile Row 114
Turpin, Dick 83
Turpin, Jeremy 85, 79
Tweedie, A F & R W 111
Twells, Philip 110, 115
Two Black Griffins, The 117
Two Brewers *PH* 38
Two Lions, The 113
Two Spies *PH* 46
Twyford Buildings 105
Twyford Place 105
Tyler, James Endell 48
Tyler, William 94
Tyrrell, James 100-101

U
Ultravox 91
Unitarians 62
United Free Methodists 55
United Grand Lodge 100
Ustinov, Peter 26, 40

V
Vanderbank, John 97
Vaughan, Thomas
  (fl.1650) 85
  (fl.1768) 97
Veitch, Zepherina 50
Ventana Court 51
Vertue, George 79-80
Via de Aldewych 67, 79
Victoria Works 85
Victory House 104
Vincent, Henry 70
Vine Street 65, 66
Vinegar Lane 53
Vinegar Yard 50, 53, 67
Vintage Showroom 40
Violetti, Eva Maria 92

Vizard, William 118
Vizards (Tweedie) 111, 118
Vulliamy, George 26, 53, 114
Vyne, The 65

W
Walker, Arthur G 124
Wallace, James 123
Waller, John 34
Walpole, Horace 120
Walsingham, Baron 115
Walters, F A 106
Walton, Parry 110
War Office 51, 52
Ware, Isaac 121
Warren, Rebecca 58
Warwick & Hall 70
watch-houses 71, 84
water clock 46
Waterhouse, Alfred 113
Waterman, Dennis 26
Watney, Dendy 123
Watney & Reid 42
Watson, Sir William 113
Watt, James 96
Watts, G F 19, 54
Watts, James 101
Waugh, Evelyn 43
Webb, Philip 113
Webbe, Samuel 101
Wedderburn, Alexander
  117-118
Wedgwood, Josiah 123
Weedon, Cavendish 109
Weld family 101
Weld House **101**, 102, 103
Wells, H G 43
Wesley, Emily 40
Wesley, John 19, **40**
Wesley House 105
Wesleyans, *see* Methodists
West Central

Iron Works 20
  Post Office 68
  Sorting Offices 67, 72
West Central Street 68
West London Mission 104
West Street 40-41
  Chapel 19, **40**, 92
Westlake, Nathaniel 49
Westminster Ophthalmic
  Hospital 67
Weston, Dorothy 94
Westwood, Piet, Poole
  & Smart 111
Wettech, Adrien 28
WH Smith Memorial
  Institute 67
Wharton, Duke of 21
Whetstone Park 112
Whitakers 61
Whitcombe Alley 100
White Hart Inn 83
White House 15
White Lion Street, *see*
  Great...; Little...
White Swan *PH* 38
Whitefield, George 40
Whitefield's Coffee
  Tavern 88
Whitfield Partners 34
Whittle, James 32
Wholefood Warehouse
  31, 46
Wilberforce, William 96
Wild, James William 124
Wild, Jonathan 11, 20, 86
Wild Boar Alley 69
Wild Court 101-102, 105
Wild Street 101, **103**
William III & Mary 29,
  34, 80, 103
Williams, David 111
Williams, Monica 18

Williams, T G 84
Williams, William 91
Wilson, Mr Justice 113
Wilson, Benjamin 99
Wilson, Richard (b.1953) 104
Wimbledon House 87
Wimperis, Simpson &
  Guthrie 43, 113
Wincott, Geoffrey 53
Winde, William 122
Windsor Castle *PH* 69
Windsor House 105
Winter Garden House 86
Winter Garden Theatre
  78*, 79
Wiseman, Jacques 16
Withers, Robert Jewell 49
Wolcot, Rev. John 94
Wolff & Son 99
Women's
  Freedom League 70
  Hospital Corps 51
  Protective & Provident
    League 100
  Social & Political
    Union 70, **105**
Woodyard Brewery **42**,
  44, 51
Woolley & Co. 88
workhouse **50-51**, 87
Working Girls' Home 88
World
  Anti-Slavery Convention 96
  Assoc. of Detectives 62
World Food Café 31
World War One 51-52, 100
World War Two 12, 19, 20,
  21, 22, 48, 51, 55, 56, 59,
  60, 81, 90, 91, 106, 115,
  116, 124, 125; bunker 125
Worlidge, Thomas 94
Worrall & Co. 53

Wray, Christopher 23
Wren, Sir Christopher
  32, 109
Wright, Lawrence 17
Wright House 17
Wylson & Long 40
Wyman & Sons 92
Wynyard, Diana 50

Y
Yardley of London 66
Yates, Edmund 72
YMCA 54, 74, 125
York Mansions 15
Young & Hall 117
Young Men's Society 55

Z
Zaehnsdorf, Joseph 26
Zeno's Greek Bookshop 18
Zoffany, John 18, 32, 116